Not Tonight, Dear

Not Tonight, Dear

How to Reawaken
Your Sexual Desire

**Anthony Pietropinto, M.D.,
and Jacqueline Simenauer**

DOUBLEDAY   New York London Toronto Sydney Auckland

PUBLISHED BY DOUBLEDAY
a division of Bantam Doubleday Dell Publishing Group, Inc.
666 Fifth Avenue, New York, New York 10103

DOUBLEDAY and the portrayal of an anchor
with a dolphin are trademarks of Doubleday,
a division of Bantam Doubleday Dell
Publishing Group, Inc.

Library of Congress Cataloging-in-Publication Data

Pietropinto, Anthony.
  Not tonight, dear : how to reawaken your sexual desire / by Anthony
Pietropinto and Jacqueline Simenauer.—1st ed.
    p. cm.
  1. Sex   in   marriage. 2. Sexual   excitement. I. Simenauer,
Jacqueline. II. Title.
HQ21.P534   1990
616.85′83—dc20   89-25807
                                                                    CIP

ISBN 0-385-23775-8

DESIGNED BY ANNE LING

PRINTED IN THE UNITED STATES OF AMERICA

JULY 1990

FIRST EDITION
BVG

To my wife,
Joy Ann,
and our daughters,
Rita Diana and Laura Joy,
who are everything a husband and father could desire
A.P.

To my husband, Peter,
who is always there for me
To my daughter, Tara,
who is my joy
To Latchmi Sawh,
for her support, and
To my mother, Tillie Himelstein,
who lives on in my heart
J.S.

Contents

I Defining Desire Disorder

    1 What Is Wanting?   1
        Sexual Desire and the Lack of It

    2 How Long and How Far   17
        Types of Desire Disorder

II Why Desire Diminishes

    3 What Did You Expect?   35
        The Effect of False Expectations

    4 On a Role   53
        New Identities in a New World

    5 Two to Tangle   79
        Problems in Relationships

    6 Personal Problems   107
        Individual Conflicts and Desire Loss

    7 Any Body Can Fail—But Most Don't   131
        Physical Factors Affecting Sexual Desire

III   Self-evaluation

      8   Check It Out   147
          Evaluating Your Desire

IV   Therapy and Self-help

      9   The Full Treatment   193
          Types of Therapy for Desire Disorder

     10   Depending on You   196
          Experiential Therapies

     11   Fantasyland   208
          Taking a Fantasy Break

     12   The Best-Case Scenario   242
          A Cognitive Approach

     13   A Different Focus   256
          Sensate Focus Exercises

     14   Tandem Treatment   266
          Overcoming Desire Discrepancy

     15   Infuriating Obstacles   290
          Fair-Fight Techniques

     16   Out of Your System   305
          Family Systems Therapy

     17   The Paradox of Desire   317
          A Postscript

❧ *I* ❧

DEFINING DESIRE DISORDER

❧ 1 ❧

What Is Wanting?

Sexual Desire and the Lack of It

"So, did you talk with Paul at dinner last night—about the way you've been feeling?" the therapist asks. "About how you always seem to be too tired to get interested in having sex?"

"Well, not really," Marilyn confesses, looking a bit embarrassed. Marilyn, a twenty-five-year-old junior executive in a bank, has been married for two years to Paul, a stockbroker of the same age. "You really can't hear yourself talking in that restaurant, the way they blast hard rock all night. And the place is so cavernous that when everybody talks, the place is one big wall of sound."

"Maybe I'm showing my age," the therapist says, "but why don't the two of you eat at a small, cozy place, with dim lights and soft music? With the sort of ambience we used to call 'intimate.'"

"That would be a disaster for us," Marilyn scoffs. "We'd both doze off before the first course and my bangs would probably catch fire in the candle. By the time we get to a restaurant, it's at least ten o'clock. Sometimes Paul comes there directly from the office and I've got my finance classes after work most nights. Paul is always bringing work home and I've got assignments to prepare for the next day.

"A sedate little bistro might be fine if you want to unwind, but Paul and I would just run down completely. That's why we go to madhouses like Mighty Nation—certainly it's not for the cuisine. At that hour, we need an atmosphere that keeps our adrenaline flowing—the noise, the ear-splitting music, the walls literally plastered with machine parts and gadgets, the latest fad foods, and all the 'beautiful people,' young, upscale, on-the-go. Mighty Nation is . . . us!" Marilyn shrugs. "It may sound ridiculous to you, but if we lived next door to Mighty Nation, we might be able to get to our bedroom before the adrenaline wore off. I don't know, maybe this feeling of being tired is a cop-out, but I still enjoy sex on the rare occasions when we get around to it and I still love Paul. I suppose I could give up those mornings at the health club, but then I'm so sedentary the rest of the day, and besides, Paul isn't much of a morning person."

"So, how does Paul feel about the way your sex life has been going?"

"He's not happy about it, but not as upset as you might think. He knows that we're both heavily involved in developing our careers at this point in time, and where there are a lot of demands in one area, it usually means sacrificing something in another. It's a competitive world and I'm going to have to put in some long hours and strong effort if I want to get somewhere. At least, I feel I'm finally on the right track.

"I wish there were more time for other things, sex among them," Marilyn continues. "I mean, is it that much different from going weeks without a date in college when you were catching up on term papers and cramming for exams?" She pauses before answering her own question. "Yeah, I guess it is, because in college you didn't get to make up your own schedules and assignments. Here, I get to set the priorities.

"For a while, I told myself that as long as Paul and I were enjoying sex whenever we got around to it, there was really no problem. But not really having the desire to get around to it might be an even bigger problem than wanting to have sex and not being able to function. At least, from what I've heard, impotence and frigidity are easy to treat now. Maybe the knowledge that there are a hell of a lot of women out there who feel the way I do kept me from coming in here sooner."

"There *is* a lot of it going around," the therapist concedes.

"Maybe Paul is as much to blame for this as I am," she continues. "Sure, he's pretty understanding and always ready to accommodate, but he's a perfectionist and a superachiever, and not the easiest person to live with and love. Or is it just me, after all? Where do you attack a desire problem? Is it me? Is it us? Is it them, the crazy world around us? Frankly, Doctor, is this a problem that should be treated? More important, *can* it be treated? Is it some sort of new epidemic?"

Marilyn has addressed many important questions. It's a problem that's always been with us, but years ago we didn't tend to think of desire as a separate component of sexual activity. Even though it's an old problem, it's definitely increasing. Most sex therapists say that lack of desire is the problem they see most commonly. The changing world we live in undoubtedly has played some role in the increase. There are many causes for loss of desire and different treatment approaches, but on the positive side, all you really need is the motivation to change, a little time and effort, and your own imagination.

"Not tonight, dear."

It is a rare person, married or otherwise involved in an intimate relationship, who has never heard or uttered a variation of that phrase. For many, the words are accepted as casually as a partner's turning down a second cup of coffee. There's always tomorrow night or next Saturday. And love does inevitably involve some compromise.

Yet, there is an undeniable element of rejection in those three little words at a time when the need for closeness and intimacy is strongest. Rejection is painful, and in many relationships, the couple either sets up an elaborate set of nonverbal signals and maneuvers to avoid direct requests for sexual intimacy and the risk of refusal, or they settle into a predictable routine of scheduled sex on certain nights, sacrificing the excitement of spontaneity for the security of acceptance.

For the single person, desire is just as problematic. The unmarried person who demurs is apt to hear comments such as "You say you care about me, but you don't seem really interested. . . . Is something the matter with you?"

Romances are nipped in the bud before they can blossom into love affairs. Marriages founder, not in tempestuous storms, but in the doldrums of lifeless matrimonial seas. Relationships that may be able to withstand situational hardships, goal conflicts, incompatibility, or infidelity sometimes crumble when a partner feels constantly undesired.

As Robert Frost noted:

> *For destruction ice*
> *Is also great*
> *And would suffice.*

WHEN A LOVELY FLAME DIES
The Problem and the Search for Remedies

This is a book about sexual desire and, in particular, the lack or deficiency of it. Many experts contend that there has been a dramatic increase in the number of couples with this complaint. Dr. Patricia Schreiner-Engel of Mount Sinai Medical Center in New York notes, "Lack of desire is like a fever. Something is going on." She has joined Dr. Raul Schiavi in a comprehensive research project to add to our rapidly expanding knowledge of this troublesome malady.

Some therapists say that more cases are now being treated simply because people are more willing to seek out therapists, or that in the past, desire problems were frequently treated under a different label, such as sexual dysfunction or marital conflict. While we will be exploring the issue of whether or not problems with sexual desire are truly on the rise, that particular question should not overly concern us. The important fact is that the concerted efforts of sex therapists throughout the country have given us a new understanding of this phenomenon and new methods of dealing with it. Help is available for those who want it, whether the problem is a recent one or merely a long-neglected one.

A scant decade ago, a therapist dealing with a couple like Marilyn and Paul might have assumed that Marilyn had some unconscious personal aversion to sex, rooted in some repressed emotional trauma or conflict, treatable only by frequent individual psychoanalytic sessions. Or he might have concluded that Marilyn's sexual disinterest reflected displeasure with some aspect of the marriage, and he may have encouraged the couple to explore the nonsexual elements of their relationship. Or if the therapist was trained in the then-new methods developed by Masters and Johnson, he might have prescribed a specific program of sensual exercises for the couple, hoping that sexual activity in a nondemanding, pressure-free atmosphere would make the bedroom a more desirable place for Marilyn. And, just maybe, one of these approaches might have worked, assuming that Marilyn's lack of sexual desire stemmed from some personal or marital conflict.

In many cases, however, the difficulty is not a reaction to some other primary problem. Therapists have come to acknowledge that sexual desire can and should be regarded as an entity in its own right, a natural human need that can be affected by, but is not totally dependent on, a variety of psychological factors. When desire diminishes or was never strong to begin with, therapists no longer immediately shift their focus to other aspects of the sexual act, such as arousal or orgasm, nor do they ignore the physical realm and delve into the psyche, assuming that desire will return when the mental conflicts are resolved.

We have interviewed twenty-two of the top sex therapists in the country, most of whom direct or have directed sex therapy clinics. Some have written revolutionary books advocating techniques they have found effective during their years of treating patients. We have drawn on their expertise, as well as the writings of other pioneers and on our own extensive psychiatric, clinical, and research experience to bring our readers the most recent innovations in dealing with sexual desire problems. We have adapted these techniques so that readers, without the assistance of a therapist, can raise their own or their partner's level of desire.

WHO NEEDS IT?
How This Book Can Help

People who suffer from low desire often have to be told that they're suffering. The low-desire person does not give much thought to his or her lack of libido until a partner begins to complain about their frustratingly low frequency of sexual activity. Single people may come to the slow realization that an empty social calendar and failure to maintain relationships beyond a few months might be related to an underheated interest in sexual matters— especially when hearing "Is something wrong?" from several different prospective love interests forces them to conclude that something *is.*

We traditionally think of women begging off with complaints of fatigue or headache, but low sexual desire affects both sexes and several of the therapists whom we interviewed are treating at least as many men as women. Perhaps a significant number of women escape the therapist's office by taking refuge in disinterested sexual compliance, but suffice it to say, there are plenty of representatives from both genders in the growing ranks of people with diminishing desire.

A deficit doesn't mean a complete absence of interest in sex; rather, that there are too many times when you wish you could get more interested and can't, or there is too great a difference between your level of desire and your partner's to bridge the gap comfortably with compromise. If you believe you have a desire deficit, this book can help. It will not replace a skilled therapist, but it has advantages that even the best therapist cannot offer. Desire resides entirely in the mind, it is subject to a wide range of influences, and it is highly personal. By reading about the full spectrum of possible influences, you can select those that most affect you, among them many that you never really previously thought about.

This book will help you to get in touch with your desire, identify what helps or hinders it, and show you how to improve it in the privacy of your own psyche—and bedroom. As you read, your mind will absorb and process the wealth of theories and techniques that have been developed and used by the most successful therapists, and you may accomplish more in the privacy of your head than in the time-bound confines of a therapist's office. The mental nature of desire makes it particularly amenable to improvement through reading. Since *you* are the only one who can tell when you feel desire and can identify the times and circumstances when it occurs, you can accomplish significant improvement on your own, without the assistance of an outside person.

You may be one of the many who would desperately like to improve your partner's interest in sex, rather than your own. How the partner of a person with low sexual desire reacts can strongly affect the course of future lovemaking, and a negative overreaction can turn sporadic indifference into a permanent aversion. By understanding the factors that decrease desire, you will feel less rejected and frustrated, so that you can focus on improving the relationship. Even when the problem begins as a result of low desire in just one partner, a two-party system of response and counter-response soon develops, invariably one that reinforces sexual avoidance. Nothing will kill any chance of a partner's improvement more quickly than saying, "It's *your* problem, so you'd better fix it." When someone is making efforts on your behalf, it's hard to stand around without joining the effort.

People say they "feel" desire. Designating sexual desire as a "feeling" acknowledges the powerful emotions involved, but tends to disregard the role of conscious thought. We often regard "feelings" as the opposite of "thought," as something that lies beyond logic and rational control. Many people regard sexual desire as something beyond their control. They view desire as something that they either experience or they don't; if they don't, there is no way they can bring it about. It may be very exciting to feel totally swept away by a raging flood of sexual desire, but it's devastating to feel that when desire fails, there is nothing you can do to restore it.

Actually, thought has profound influences, both positive and negative, on desire. Many therapists rely primarily on cognitive therapy, which centers on ideas and intellectual responses to potential sexual situations. When one is dealing with a thinking being, it's just about impossible to dispense with cognitive elements. As soon as you say, "How do you feel?" the thinking apparatus in the respondent starts formulating some intelligent reply.

You *can* think your way into sexual desire. You can't think your way directly into an erection or an orgasm, but desire, although initially elusive and unpredictable, can be developed and enriched through mental exercise as surely as a program of calisthenics at your local health club can build up your chest and abdominal muscles.

The first step down the path to improved desire is a thorough understanding of what it is and the broad area it covers.

THE EPIDEMIC
Desire Disorder on the Rise

"Inhibited sexual desire has emerged . . . as the leading sexual disorder and a major underlying factor, if not a direct cause of many marital breakups," reported science writer Jane E. Brody in the New York *Times*. "The problem affects single people as well as married couples and those committed to long-term relationships."

Dr. Shirley Zussman, a past president of the American Association of Sex Educators, Counselors and Sex Therapists, wrote in the journal *Sexual Medicine Today:* "Lack of sexual interest is the most common problem people bring to sex therapists today. Over 50 percent of the patients referred to us describe a lack of desire as their chief complaint."

How widespread is the problem of desire disorder? If it affects you or your partner, does it really matter how many others are distressed by it?

The answer to the second question is yes. The more people that are affected by it, the less likely we are to see desire disorder as a severe deviation from the norm and the more comfortable we will be in confronting it and trying to improve the situation. A person who masturbates and feels guilty about it is better able to assess his behavior and decide what, if anything, to do about it if he knows that his sexual practices are engaged in by a large percentage of others, rather than if he thinks he has a unique proclivity. Where sexual behavior is not harmful to or exploitative of others, any change in preferences or practices should be motivated not by a sense of guilt or shame but by the belief that a change will ultimately be more satisfactory to a person and his partner.

In actuality, no two people are exactly the same in their sexual desire. Ask a thousand people to describe their favorite sexual fantasy or their concept of the ideal sexual encounter in detail and you wouldn't get two identical answers. Because our sex lives—and particularly desire, the most brain-centered component—are influenced by such a vast array of prior life experiences, including what we have heard, read, and fantasized about, sex is a highly individualized matter. Since, except for autoerotic activities, sex is a partnership endeavor, there must be cooperation and compromise. Generally, our capacity for enjoyment of sex embraces a wide enough range of variations with respect to activities, time, and frequency, that we can have satisfactory sex lives even if we don't always have our "druthers."

But just how many people have a desire disorder troublesome enough to have a serious impact on their sexual enjoyment or to cause severe conflict in their relationships? The American Psychiatric Association estimates that 20 percent of the population, both male and female, have low or absent desire for sexual activity. This is slightly less than the 30 percent of men estimated to have premature ejaculation and the 30 percent of women with inhibited orgasm. Since these statistics refer to how many people are experiencing difficulty at any given time and do not include those who develop the problem later, when others are improving, it is apparent that an effortless, problem-free sex life is *not* experienced by a sizable majority.

In interviewing leading sex therapists, we learned that most of them believe the incidence of desire disorder is definitely increasing. While a few said that desire problems constituted as little as 15 percent of their caseload, most said that the percentage was approaching or even exceeding 50 percent.

The American Psychiatric Association says that there are more women than men with low sexual desire, but virtually all of the therapists whom we interviewed said that the number of males coming in for treatment was definitely on the rise and, in some clinics, outnumbering women. The increase in men with this complaint might be attributed to one or more recent developments: (1) Something has happened in the course of modern sexual relations to cause a drop in desire among men, possibly because they feel insecure or threatened; (2) men have become more willing to request help through therapy and the statistics reflect a willingness to be treated, not an increase in the problem; (3) in past decades, men so totally controlled the frequency of sexual relations that a low level of male desire was never challenged by a dissatisfied female partner. Now, women are more apt to complain and press their mates into seeking treatment when the frequency of intercourse drops to unsatisfactory levels.

The Sexual Revolution enabled people to recognize and speak openly about their sexual needs and problems. They no longer have to suffer in modest silence, their unhappiness aggravated by the false belief that everyone else is enjoying a sex life in which everything proceeds smoothly along nature's course. This new freedom and sophistication might have brought into the open the cases of desire disorder that were as numerous three decades ago, but went unrecognized and untreated.

When the more mechanical components of the sex act—erection, lubrication, ejaculation, orgasm—are intact, it is easy to gloss over the serious problem of lack of desire. People will say, "Our sex life is fine. We just don't seem to have the time or the energy at the end of the day to get around to it. Anytime we do, it's great!" Many women fall into a pattern of sex-on-demand with their mates, so that an apparently normal sex life goes on, with no acknowledgment of the woman's problem. Some men may use the excuse of work pressures to mask a lack of desire; others may form an uneasy truce with their spouses whereby a minimal amount of sexual activity is routinely scheduled. So, while erectile dysfunction, premature ejaculation, and lack of orgasm are difficult to deny, desire disorder lends itself to a wide variety of evasions and subterfuges.

Is it overdramatic or realistic to say that America is experiencing an *epidemic* of desire disorder? If the American Psychiatric Association's estimate of 20 percent is anywhere near accurate, that's an epidemic. Of course, epidemics usually refer to diseases and desire disorder is not a disease in the medical sense. Its ubiquity should comfort us, by reminding us that sexual desire is not always effortless and is not something that can be taken for granted.

People who lack sexual desire should not feel there is something very strange or pathological about them. The fact that a drive which is basic, unconscious, and virtually unerring in animals has evolved into a complex, interpersonal inclination, modified by a wide array of situational and interpersonal influences, is testimony to the depth and sensitivity of the human psyche. Those people whose desire seems to be always high and never affected by conflict or stress are often egocentric and emotionally detached from their partners. The more sensitive and introspective an individual is, the less likely he or she is to be always ready and eager to engage in sexual activity.

So, if you or your partner has a deficit in sexual desire, whether consistent or episodic, remember that the problem is shared by many and does not necessarily indicate some deep, unresolved psychological problem. More important, it is a situation that can be helped, even without consulting a therapist.

Do not think of the situation in terms of whether or not there is a "real" problem, one that warrants a diagnosis or formal treatment. That's like asking whether losing weight, drinking less alcohol, or getting more exercise is something you *have* to do or something you choose to do because it will improve the quality of your being and your life. Regular sexual activity is not very fulfilling unless it is accompanied by true desire. Desire, as much as the more physical components of sexual activity, can be improved by knowledge and practice.

Improvement of desire, for self or partner, should be not so much a question of what one needs but of what one wants. We have learned much about human sexual desire in the last ten years. The first step in the acquisition of this knowledge and the enrichment it offers is to *want* it.

A MISSED STEP
Defining the Problem

In the seventies, the hot topic was the "Big O." Better Orgasms were the goal of every self-help book and popular magazine back in the days when the Sexual Revolution was at its peak and everybody was concerned with "getting it on" (and "getting off") as frequently as possible.

In the nineties, with casual sex out and safe sex in, concern has shifted from the Big O to the "Little D," the desire deficit. Since Masters and Johnson emerged from their sex lab in 1966 to write *The Human Sexual Response,* we've learned just about all there is to know about sexual anatomy and physiology. Sex therapists were able to guide their clients through the four stages of sexual response so carefully documented by M&J: arousal, plateau, orgasm, and resolution. For the majority of those clients, problems of premature ejaculation, erectile dysfunction, and inhibited orgasm responded to courses of treatment that were brief, simple, and involved a minimum of delving into past experiences and psychological traumas.

This meticulous, objective study of human sexual behavior ultimately called attention to sexual desire, a vital component of the human sex act that simply did not fit into the Masters and Johnson model. Of course, the eminent researchers were aware that desire existed, but they apparently assumed it could be safely included under the phenomenon of arousal. Many therapists fell back on their old psychotherapeutic experience when the new sex therapy failed to help patients with desire problems; those therapists who tried to stick to the Masters and Johnson book did not fare as well. The experts took a long, hard look at human sexual response and concluded that desire could *not* be lumped in with arousal, but must be dealt with as an independent entity.

People will generally agree that "desire" is a wish or craving of some sort, but "sexual desire" can be interpreted in a variety of ways, depending on how you define its goal. Some might define it as the wish to have sexual intercourse with a specific person, while others might accept a more general definition, an awareness of an urge to engage in activity leading to erotic stimulation, even if it does not proceed to intercourse or orgasm. But according to any definition, desire is a *mental* process: a thought, wish, or fantasy with a sexual content. It usually precedes sexual arousal, which is manifested by erections in men and vaginal lubrication in women, but is independent of these physical processes. Thus, an impotent man can have very strong desire.

Desire does not always culminate in sexual activity, even if suitable objects are readily available. A single woman, for example, could feel genuine sexual desire for a man, yet elect not to get intimately involved unless she has a commitment from him. A man might feel desire for his wife but, because he is angry at her, decide to boycott the bedroom for a while.

Although some experts insist that human desire is strictly an interpersonal response, directed toward a specific person, we include urges for some type of sexual stimulation or release that can arise without thinking of a specific partner. For people who use masturbation as their main sexual activity, partners exist only in fantasy and may be anonymous images; some may even masturbate without thinking of anything outside their own bodies.

Just thinking about sex might not be enough to constitute *desire*. We might imagine or recall detailed sexual acts without experiencing pleasurable erotic feelings, emotions toward another person, or the wish to engage in such activities. Just as one could participate in sex for nonerotic reasons, one can certainly think about it without feeling desire. Desire, then, is a "gut reaction" to a potential sexual activity, not merely a decision to engage in it.

Desire is *not* a bodily response. Penile erections, vaginal lubrication and engorgement, increased heart rate, and rapid breathing are manifestations of arousal, the next step in the sexual response cycle. Desire persists throughout arousal and reinforces the physical reactions that make sex possible and pleasurable, but desire should not be confused with the first *physical* stages of response. Yet, women might falsely interpret a lack of erection in their mates as indicating "he doesn't want me," or men might equate women's failure to achieve orgasm as a lack of genuine desire for sexual relations.

Many men might protest at this point that their erections are predictably proportional to the amount of desire they feel. Women might likewise point out that a good fantasy is the only thing that will guarantee them a strong orgasm, regardless of clitoral stimulation or other foreplay. This doesn't contradict the status of desire as an entity separate from arousal and orgasm, but merely underscores its importance as one of the stages leading to arousal and orgasm. The woman who, through fantasy, uses her desire for a certain soap-opera heart-throb to facilitate her orgasm is actually, while engaged in the arousal stage of the sex act, backstepping to stage one—desire—to increase her arousal and allow her to progress to the heights of stage three.

Can you be aroused without desire? Unequivocally, yes. In men, erections may occur as a reflex response to being touched or while they are asleep, even without an erotic dream. Women have shown in laboratory studies the vaginal changes we associate with female arousal without reporting any subjective desire. Yet, the two stages of sexual response are so closely related under most circumstances that we cannot avoid discussing arousal. Not all cases of erectile failure or lack of orgasm are due to desire problems, but some are. It's important to know the difference.

Desire is where it all begins. Desire may be compared to an automobile's starter mechanism. When the machine works flawlessly, the turn-on is instantaneous and the engine hums into action. When there is a malfunction, we say, "It won't start." Sometimes the starting mechanism is, indeed, at fault, but in many cases the starter is secondarily affected by a problem elsewhere in the system. We're writing a book about stage one, but sometimes you have to be aware of what's happening farther down the line.

A PROBLEM IN SEARCH OF A NAME
Recognizing Desire Disorder

Although many sex therapists report that lack of desire is the problem they are treating most frequently, ten years ago nobody spoke about it. It was a condition without a name.

How is such a thing possible? Did desire disorder, as it is now most frequently termed, spring up like a new disease, the way

Legionnaires' disease or Lyme's disease came into being? Not likely, but where were the diagnosticians when historians recorded Napoleon's apocryphal declination, "Not tonight, Josephine," or when ancient apothecaries were rummaging among oyster shells and unicorn horns for an effective aphrodisiac to meet the demands of their clamoring clientele?

Dr. Domeena C. Renshaw, director of the sexual dysfunction clinic at Loyola University Medical School in Maywood, Illinois, assured us that when her clinic opened in 1972 there were many cases of people with low desire and no "mechanical problems." Since Masters and Johnson didn't cover such cases in their landmark work on sexual disorders, *Human Sexual Inadequacy,* published in 1970, Dr. Renshaw resourcefully marked the charts "D.D." for "desire disorder." Dr. Constance Avery-Clark, a research and clinical associate at the Masters and Johnson Institute in St. Louis, confirmed, "Ten years ago the diagnosis didn't really even exist."

The diagnosis didn't exist, but the problem certainly did. Dr. David M. Schnarch, director of the sex and marital health clinic of Louisiana State University in New Orleans, helped put the situation into perspective by pointing out that when he was trained as a psychotherapist, clients with low desire were viewed as lacking motivation and, therefore, unsuitable candidates for any type of treatment.

Once therapists had acknowledged desire's existence as a distinct phase of the sexual response cycle, it was, for the first time, possible to regard problems in this area as distinct from sexual dysfunctions—the performance problems—such as impotence or frigidity.

The condition may be further divided into the rarer cases of aversion, (where a person considers sex unpleasant, repugnant, or anxiety-provoking) and the far more common state of having a low (hypoactive) or absent level of sexual fantasizing and wish for sexual activity, although sex is regarded as enjoyable or neutral.

But how do you define a "problem" level of desire versus the lower end of the "normal" range? Perhaps the best way to illustrate this bugbear is with an anecdote related by psychologist Bernie Zilbergeld, author of *Male Sexuality,* a story that he has heard repeatedly, with minimal variation, from sex therapists at conferences throughout the country. A couple goes to a therapist because the husband wants to have sex at least five times a week and preferably every night, but the wife wants to have sex only twice a week. The therapist strives to help this woman overcome her problem of low sexual desire, but the treatment fails. Ultimately, the couple divorces and the woman remarries. Her second husband wants to have sex only two or three times a month. When the couple appears for therapy, the husband is diagnosed as having low desire and the woman is considered "normal."

Many couples consult sex therapists because, while both partners enjoy sexual relationships, one partner wants sex considerably more often than the other. In such cases, instead of labeling the reluctant partner as having low desire or the other as sexually demanding, therapists will say the couple has a *desire discrepancy.* If you were to ask most couples, "Which of you is more interested in sex?" you would probably find at least as many who would single out one partner as those who would say, "We're about the same." Over the course of a relationship, the equilibrium might shift so that the partner who was originally less interested becomes the one with the higher level of desire. Men may become more preoccupied with business as they age, or women may lose desire with several small children to care for. A capable therapist will not necessarily try to increase the desire level of the less interested partner, but will help the couple find a better means of compromising between the discrepant interests, even if it means helping the high-desire person become satisfied with the quality of sex rather than the quantity or to become more content with nonsexual forms of intimacy.

It would be wonderful if we could turn desire on and increase its intensity whenever we wished, but nature did not provide us with a volume control knob. Nearly everyone has the potential to increase desire. It makes little sense to worry about whether improvement is sought to correct an actual disorder or simply to close the discrepancy gap and bring more love and pleasure to a relationship.

Who, after all, would *not* want to feel an increase in sexual desire? Many experts will argue that if a couple is perfectly content with sex once a month or no sex at all, then there is no desire problem. We would agree that there is no problem in *need* of improvement, but it is nevertheless probable that one or both partners have a desire disorder. If a couple is incapable of having children and does not want children, there would nevertheless be an infertility condition even if there were no wish or reason to have it treated.

Whether or not a person is involved in a relationship, an increase in sexual desire is invariably beneficial. Desire attracts us to other people, arouses our interest in them, and makes them special to us. For the person in a marriage or a love relationship, desire not only improves sexual relations but communication and cooperation between the pair, since a highly desired partner is bound to be more prized and the relationship more highly valued. In the case of the unattached person, desire will motivate him or her to try to meet prospective partners and help overcome the natural shyness and reticence that characterize new relationships.

Desire can have important influences on us outside of the sexual realm. People with a high level of sexual desire are more aware of themselves as men or women. They are more conscious of their bodies and are more likely to exercise and control their weight. They dress with more flair and groom themselves carefully. Unconsciously, they want to attract others and, therefore, they make themselves more attractive. Healthy sexual desire is as important for people without partners as it is for those in a relationship.

Even those who, by choice or circumstances, will never become involved with a sexual partner can benefit from sexual desire. The indulgence in exciting fantasies and daydreams, whether or not accompanied by physical self-gratification, can provide pleasurable stimulation and a heightened sense of enjoyment of one's body and mind.

While fantasy can be a powerful source of gratification, we do not underestimate the importance of love nor the power of sex to draw and bind people together so that love can develop and flourish. The pleasures and benefits of caring relationships are richer than impersonal desire and satisfaction; however, it is not because love relationships transcend sexual desire but rather because they add to it the qualities of concern, empathy, self-sacrifice, esteem, and affection. Love, such as that extended to friends, parents, or children, can be nonsexual; for sexual love, desire is an indispensable ingredient and the beginning of sex in a context of caring.

❧ 2 ❧

How Long and How Far

Types of Desire Disorder

All cases of desire disorder have a common denominator: deficient or absent sexual fantasies and desire for sexual activity. Beyond this core problem, cases show considerable variations, depending on the duration of the problem, its persistence, and its scope.

These factors often provide clues about the origins of low desire and the best way to correct it. We have already mentioned one way to subdivide desire disorder: into cases where there is a strongly negative attitude toward sex (aversion) and those where there is a positive or neutral feeling (hypoactive desire).

If desire remains unvaryingly low for longer periods of time, we speak of the disorder as *persistent*. If there is a series of periods of low desire alternating with an average interest, the condition is *recurrent*. Recurrent lows are more likely due to situational influences, such as work demands or family conflicts, while persistently low desire suggests a chronic problem in the person or the relationship that needs to be confronted.

Has the person *never* experienced desire at an average level or was the desire level once considerably higher only to drop sharply at some point in life? A *primary* disorder means that desire has always been low, while *secondary* means that a decline occurred somewhere in time after a promising start.

How pervasive is the lack of interest in sex? In *global* disorders, the person has no interest in sex whatsoever; not only does the person lack interest in intercourse, but also there is no fantasizing, romanticizing, masturbation, or erotic physical contact. Such a person is totally turned off. In the far more common *selective* disorders, the person has lost interest in a certain partner or activity, yet remains sexually desirous with respect to other actual or potential partners or activities. For example, a man may have no interest in sex with his wife, but will masturbate, be stimulated by nude photographs in magazines, or want to have sex with prostitutes.

These subdivisions constitute four pairs of characteristics that can be used to define any individual case, according to onset (primary or secondary), duration (persistent or recurrent), limitations (global or selective), and feelings (hypoactive or aversive). If a woman had a high level of sexual desire at the start of her marriage but loses interest in having sex with her husband for weeks at a time, even though she doesn't find it unpleasant and still fantasizes about having an affair with William Hurt, we could categorize her desire problem as secondary, recurrent, selective, and hypoactive.

We will illustrate some of these types of desire disorder as they might appear in the therapist's office, beginning with a case of primary desire disorder.

AS YOU (NOT I) LIKE IT
Primary Desire Disorder

Cathy is twenty-three. She has been married and divorced already, and has been living with David, twelve years her senior, for over a year. She could not be described as inexperienced. Even though both David and she are working, finances are strained because David is paying close to $1,000 a month to his ex-wife for the support of their six-year-old son. Still, David has decided that the cost of therapy for Cathy, the designated patient in the relationship, must be paid if they are ever going to get married as they originally planned.

"Sex is a large part of the problem," Cathy explains. "Maybe the biggest part. We *do* have sex, usually as often as Dave wants it, which comes to at least three times a week, sometimes a lot more. I never say no to him. Well, maybe if I'm really pissed off about something, but Dave has been with me long enough to know that I don't stay mad long, so by now he knows enough not to approach me till I've cooled down. But Dave says I'm not really into it, that I just have sex to make him happy and that I should want it, too.

"I've tried making advances, so that he wasn't always the one to make the first move. It doesn't work, because he says, 'Do you *really* want to, or are you just trying to make me happy?' Well, to be honest, I don't care either way. He takes it personally, as if there's something wrong with him in my eyes, but I've *always* been this way.

"Dave says it's my Catholic upbringing, that the nuns and priests ruined me by making me feel guilty. Hell, I don't think that's true; the nuns never talked about sex at all. They may have been against it, just as they were against robbery and murder, but we never got a lecture about not killing people and we never got lectures about sex either.

"As for my home life, my parents weren't swingers, but they obviously had nothing against sex either, since they had seven children in eleven years of marriage. My mother finally went on the pill after the last baby was born, and she died of a blood clot in her lungs six months later. David, the amateur psychiatrist, says maybe that's the problem. I'm afraid God is going to strike me dead, like my mother, if I enjoy sex. I just don't think he's right. My mother's going on the pill was because she didn't want more children, not because she wanted or didn't want sex. She wasn't even thirty-three and she had seven of them. The place was a nuthouse! And naturally, me being the oldest, I got to do all the diapering and feeding, especially after Mom died.

"My father finally remarried and even had another kid, but his second wife lived in a separate apartment. She told my father that she had nothing against us, but there was just too much chaos for her. Maybe that's why I never thought much about sex when I was a kid. I never had any privacy and never had any time. I did think about marriage, though, especially about having a home all my own. And I definitely did not think about having any kids to share it with.

"So, when Eric, my first husband, started paying attention to me, I was glad. I was seventeen when we first started going out together. We never went all the way till we were married two years later, but we got into some pretty heavy stuff. Eric never seemed at all concerned about what I wanted to do, as long as I let him do what he wanted or did what he wanted. Even after we were married, neither one of us complained about sex. What made me split up with him was that I wasn't getting *anything* out of the relationship, except a little privacy. He had nothing to say to me, we had nothing in common. I wasn't just bored with sex, I was bored with everything. Maybe he was just too young. I still talk to him occasionally on the phone and he seems a lot deeper and more interesting now. We were both just too young.

"I dated a few guys after I split with Eric. If I went out a couple of times with one, I would usually let him go to bed with me. Nobody ever said, 'But do *you* really want to?' Do you think they cared? Not that I acted as if I was doing them a favor or didn't want to do it . . . well, I mean, it just never seemed to be a problem.

"David was special. He spent a lot of time with me at work and taught me a lot about the business. When he changed companies and got a supervisory position, he arranged for me to be hired so we could keep working together. Nobody ever spent time with me before; nobody ever seemed to have any. That's why I love him so much, even though he's older and has all the hassle of an ex-wife and a kid that he spoils rotten every other weekend. And he talks about *me* having guilt! I know that sex is important to him and that's why I tried to keep him happy any way he wanted.

"But he's got this hang-up about my having to want sex the way he does. 'Doesn't it feel good to you?' he asks. So, I rub my earlobe and say, 'Yeah, and this feels good, too, but I never think about rubbing my earlobe and if I do I don't say, "Wow, I can't wait to do it again." ' I like Chinese food, but if I had to go a year without any, I wouldn't be miserable. He says I'm inhibited and don't know it and that I need therapy. When he gets angry, he calls me an uptight, frigid bitch and says I'm sick."

What Cathy has is a primary desire disorder, demonstrated by the fact that she has never had a desire for sex at any point in her life. She does not have a sexual aversion disorder, because she makes no attempt to avoid sex when her partner initiates it and she does not find it unpleasant. David sometimes accuses her of being "frigid," so the therapist will find out whether or not she ever has orgasms during sexual activity with a partner or through masturbation. Even if Cathy does have problems with attaining orgasm, her lack of sexual desire is an independent concern.

On the positive side, with regard to improving desire through therapy, Cathy is not opposed to engaging in sexual activity and does find it enjoyable to a degree. She has strong affectionate feelings for David. Her early life was traumatic and she may have experienced a deeper depression during her adolescence than she consciously perceived. David, "the amateur psychiatrist," may have been correct in assuming a connection between her mother's death and Cathy's disinterest in sex, although the existence and influence of such a link cannot be assessed without a lot more exploration. Her experiences with partners who were satisfied with mere compliance prevented Cathy from questioning her own attitudes and level of emotional satisfaction.

What factors play a role in primary desire disorder? Innate low level of desire, early childhood and adolescent experiences, lack of positive relationships with the opposite sex, chronic depression, or taboos instilled by authority figures—any of these can be instrumental in fostering and maintaining primary desire disorder, but all can respond to treatment.

USE IT OR LOSE IT
Secondary Desire Disorder

Alex is paunchy, balding, and looks older than his fifty-nine years. His voice is stern, almost authoritarian, and yet he looks like a beaten man. Monica is thirty-eight, attractive, neatly but conservatively dressed. Her mouth assumes the same stiff, pouting expression that Alex has and her folded arms mirror his sullen posture. Monica could pass for his daughter. But she's his wife.

"Can you believe he actually had me arrested?" Monica complains. "His own wife!"

"She stole a *hearse,*" Alex emphasizes.

"Well, what choice do you have when you're married to a funeral director?" Monica snaps. "My car had broken down. I desperately needed one, and I didn't have a dime because we were in the middle of one of our separations where he punishes me by cutting off my money."

"Money is apparently what she wants from the marriage at this stage," Alex says glumly.

"And what do *you* want?" Monica counters. "You don't seem to want *anything.* That's why we're here, isn't it?"

Alex shrugs, beaten again. "Sex is the end of a relationship, not the beginning. In my generation, a man and a woman didn't go to bed together until everything else was going right. I guess that holds later, too. When things aren't going right, they're not going to go right in bed either, and you don't even want to try.

"Not that things were ever super for us in that area. Monica was a virgin until she was twenty-one, then got involved with a guy who promised to marry her but only strung her along for three years. Her next boyfriend got her pregnant, then split. I took a beating from my first marriage; three kids and twenty years, then she started cheating toward the end.

"I want the old Monica back. She was fun-loving and happy, in spite of all she'd been through. She had gone back to college when I met her years ago. She was really special and she made me feel special, too. We had our sexual problems and we were in therapy a couple of times. I'm a premature ejaculator and she's slow to warm up and slow to come down. Sometimes it would take an hour and a half of foreplay to get her anywhere near climax. And, of course, I had to be careful not to get physically stimulated, so I'd be able to last five minutes during intercourse. The last time we had sex, I guess it was about like always—not traumatic, not terrific. There were plenty of traumatic times in the past, when we both got more frustrated than satisfied, and I sure as hell don't want to go back to that.

"An older man with a young wife has some inspiration. But I never felt she was really mine. I was jealous, I admit it. Monica was insecure herself and I suppose I didn't help things any. So, she got involved with women's consciousness-raising groups and she'd be the only married woman in the group and I felt threatened. She was going to college, meeting men closer to her own age. We'd go to therapy sessions and she'd find herself attracted to the male therapists. One time, I started going to a female associate of the marriage counselor for a few sessions, and that drove Monica nuts.

"She says she's been faithful to me and maybe she has; still, she openly admires other men and I've never heard her praise one who wasn't slim and handsome. So, I'm insecure and sometimes I drink and occasionally I've pushed her around when I was drunk. That leads to her joining battered women's groups and separating for a while. I hate being alone! I've tried therapy, alone and with her, and here we are again.

"I am not a tall, blond, slim man like Monica prefers. I am not a Greek god. When she's angry at me, she calls me a 'fat, old, Latvian grandfather.' Her therapist told her she's got to release anger, and boy, she does that!

"What does a fat, old, Latvian grandfather do in bed with a hostile young wife? I don't seem to have the desire to find out."

Monica breaks into his monologue with genuine concern. "If I'm as horrible as you make me sound, why would you *want* to go to bed with me?"

Although Monica incisively seemed to capture the essence of Alex's loss of desire in one short question, his bland expression gives no indication that he realized it. The session and the work of therapy must go on.

Alex has a case of secondary desire disorder, because it developed after a period of average sexual desire. While some cases of secondary desire disorder might seem to occur as spontaneously and independent of life experiences as hair loss, Alex seems to have plenty of psychological conflicts going on, relating to both his own insecurity and poor self-image and to the hostility that has developed between him and his wife. Alex's loss of desire cannot be blamed simply on aging, but if the situation is not corrected, it will be harder for him to recapture his former level of desire even if he divorces Monica and finds another partner.

Sexual abstinence can also contribute to secondary desire disorder. "Use it or lose it" is a favorite saying of many therapists.

Where desire is concerned—and this is particularly true in women—many people can go for long periods, especially in the absence of a suitable partner, with little or no sexual cravings and yet experience a full-power desire surge when someone worthy of interest becomes available. In a significant number of others, however, the longer that desire is not part of the psyche, the harder it is to feel a renewal. Even when the former level of desire was average or higher than average, there is difficulty reactivating it. Like many who have a primary disorder, people with secondary lapses might feel totally apathetic or even negative about resuming sexual activity, despite their former interest.

Often people with secondary desire disorder that develops after a period of abstinence have strong psychological reasons for being unable to reawaken desire. They may have been deeply hurt by rejection or might feel they are unattractive or inept lovers. Or they may be mourning the loss of their last lover. If so, these conflicts must be resolved before desire can return. Whatever the circumstances, if desire can be maintained even in the absence of an active sex life through fantasy, introspection, and self-stimulation, the abstinent person will not worry about a future relationship being jeopardized by secondary desire disorder.

THE SLEEPING BEAUTY
Global Desire Disorder

"I mean, is it possible you just *outgrow* it?" Glenda exclaims, with a little groan of exasperation. She extends her long legs and crosses them at the ankle, so that her body is as close to horizontal as it can get while maintaining a sitting position. She tosses her long blond hair over the back of her chair and stares at the ceiling, as though she were on the proverbial psychoanalyst's couch.

"I don't know how else to explain it. I'm not angry at Victor and there's nothing about him that I find repulsive or even unattractive. I have nothing against sex. I don't hate men, I'm in good physical health, I have a great kid, and I enjoy my job. So *what* happened? Somewhere along the line, I just plain lost interest."

Glenda uncrosses her ankles and pulls herself erect in the chair, her wide blue eyes now focusing on the therapist's questioning face. "It's almost like the way it was with my dollhouse. I don't know just when I lost interest in it; it wasn't anything as definite as deciding I was too old or discovering boys or finding a new activity. I can't even say when was the last time I played with it." Then she smiles sheepishly. "But I know you're not supposed to *outgrow* your desire for sex—not at thirty-two, anyway.

"If I can't explain it to myself, how can I explain it to a seven-year-old who wants to know why her mother and father are living apart and talking about divorce when she's never seen them fight or even disagree. And I *like* Vic. If he weren't so damn sensitive, he might have been able to accept my having sex with him even though I wasn't interested. But that's not his way! He kept trying to come up with different ways to turn me on, holding himself responsible, and that only made things worse, of course. He kept me up for hours, reading everything from Henry Miller to Kahlil Gibran, along with some sleazy anonymous writers in magazines that make *Penthouse* look like *Muppet Magazine.* He tried everything from X-rated video cassettes to writing his own love sonnets.

"So, here I am. Maybe you can figure out where my desire went. I've looked everywhere!"

"When you're going over familiar territory," the therapist answers, "you may overlook a nook or cranny that a less confident person wouldn't be so quick to pass over. But more likely, you might be looking for something that still exists, but in a different form. Glenda, do you have any other video cassettes at home, besides the ones your husband brought in to turn you on?"

She nods, puzzled. "Sure. Jane Fonda's workout, *Casablanca,* son of Jane Fonda's workout—"

"Walt Disney's *Sleeping Beauty?*" he interrupts.

"Mind reading!" she exclaims, visibly impressed. "Do you do card tricks, too?"

"Just playing percentages," the therapist admits. "You've got a seven-year-old girl and that was a bestseller."

"Darn!" she pouts. "I *was* hoping for magic. So, now you're going to tell me that I'm the Sleeping Beauty who just needs to be reawakened. . . ."

"No," he says. "I was wondering if you remember the scene where the wicked fairy's henchmen explain how they've been looking for the missing princess in every nursery and cradle for the past sixteen years."

Glenda smiles wistfully and nods. "Oh, yeah. Poor Maleficent! It was so hard to get good help, even in those days." She pauses. "Hmmm, I think I'm still lost in the woods somewhere. Are you saying the desire is there, only it's changed? If I'm not interested in *anything* sexual—not my husband, not any other man, not even fantasies about TV hunks or older Brat Pack members . . ."

"Are there any other men in your life who might attract you?"

"Well, I deal with male customers all the time," Glenda answers. "They're bright, successful, and attractive enough, but I haven't been tempted to get into an affair with one. And it's not because of Vic or the messes you get into mixing business with pleasure—the desire just isn't there! It's *gone."*

"Changed, certainly, but not gone," the therapist disagrees. "You can't repeal the law of conservation of energy. Glenda, could you run better at age nine or at thirteen?"

"Nine. I was a total klutz at thirteen."

"But by sixteen, you had developed your body into a lean, mean running machine, right?"

Glenda lowers her eyes self-consciously. "Now, come on, Doctor, I *did* change out of my Nikes before coming here."

"Any woman who would buy Fonda I *and* II must use her legs for more than something to hang her Hanes on. Your new body was a liability at thirteen until you got to know it better and coordinate it. Then, it was infinitely better than the one you used to play tag in the school yard.

"Well, your psyche has been in the throes of a growth spurt lately. You told me you've been taking on new responsibilities at the office, you've moved from routine clerical tasks to some really creative advertising campaigns, and maybe more important, you've been doing a lot of reading about women's issues and developing your personal philosophy. Why shouldn't your desire change along with the rest of your psyche, even if it means going into a cocoon for a while before the metamorphosis is complete. It can't just disappear. You wouldn't deliberately kill off sexual desire and it's too hardy to die accidentally. It's dormant, but it's there."

Glenda has a case of *global* desire disorder. The problem that brings her into therapy is her lack of interest in marital relations, but her disinterest extends to *all* sexual activities. Hers is a secondary desire disorder, since she previously had an active interest in sex, both in terms of marital sex and attraction to men in general.

In selective desire disorder, it's as if you can't get reception for a particular TV channel. In global desire disorder, it's as if somebody pulled the plug. In a situation like Glenda's, however, the experienced therapist realizes that the problem may be originating in one area, such as the marriage, and spreading secondarily to others, even though it appears that everything blacked out at once. Did Glenda get so preoccupied with her new career and intellectual interests that she simply had no time for sex, even on a fantasy level? Did Vic's obsessive efforts to rekindle her desire force her to retreat even further from sexual interest as a defense against what she felt were unreasonable expectations? Did she perceive her husband, perhaps unconsciously, as unsympathetic to the time demands of her new interests, so that she was more angry at him than she realized? And having turned off to Vic, was she so guilty about those aspects of sexual desire directed toward potential extramarital partners, even on a fantasy level, that she felt compelled to shut off *all* desire?

People who have been raised in repressive homes, where sex was considered taboo or sinful, or those subjected to early sexual trauma, may grow up with a primary global desire disorder. As our society has become more liberal concerning sexual activity, we are seeing fewer of the primary global desire disorders—the maiden aunt, the spinster schoolmarm, or the sheltered mama's boy. Global disorders, because they extend even to enjoyable thoughts about sex, are so pervasive that we might expect few people to develop them once they have experienced normal desire. Yet, a significant degree of emotional depression or stress can quickly lead to a total loss of desire.

Since sexual activity, although essential for species preservation, is not needed for individual survival, Nature often conserves physical and psychic energy during high stress periods by "blowing the fuse" where sex is concerned. When the individual has been able to cope with the situations that are causing stress, the sexual desire may return spontaneously.

In other individuals, widespread loss of interest may have originated because of marital conflict or guilt over an extramarital affair, but the interruption of desire is enough to cause an interference with all desire.

The global versus selective losses might be compared with strings of Christmas tree lights. In some strings, one bulb goes out and the others stay lit. In others, loss of one bulb results in the whole string going out. Individuals, like Christmas tree lights, are wired differently.

CAPTAIN'S PARADISE LOST
Selective Desire Disorder

"I like women. I think I do. Maybe I hate them," Mario says. "I have a set of standards that are unrealistic in this day and age: I want women to be virtuous, virginal, and faithful. So far, the only woman who's been all of that is my wife, Tina. And now I have absolutely no interest in her sexually."

Mario is a forty-year-old lawyer with three children. He's been married fifteen years and his wife says he's had two affairs during that time. His wife only counts the ones she can't deny, because Mario moved out for several months during the course of them. The most recent affair was with Betty, with whom he lived for five months until his wife told him she would "see a lawyer." That brought Mario home, toting several sacks of dirty laundry for Tina to wash.

"Betty has long, silky blond hair," Mario reminisces. "She looks thirteen, even though she's twenty-seven. I never have relationships for only one or two nights. I always build up this fantasy world, but I'm disappointed. I never get a virgin. I want exclusivity, even though I can't offer it in return.

"I didn't have sex until I was eighteen, but I was interested in it when I was nine. A friend told me about it, and about this girl in the building who liked to fool around. So, I started doing some heavy petting with her, and then with her cousin. It seems like I was always interested in sex. Even at seven or eight, I had fantasies of dressing little girls I liked."

"Did you say 'undressing'?" the therapist interrupts.

"No—dressing. Even now, I buy clothes for my girlfriends. I like them to look sexy, but conservative."

"How many girlfriends have you had?" the therapist asks.

Mario shrugs. "Maybe about six serious ones, but a lot of others, too. It's like a lineup. I don't ever want to be without one. There were times I felt like it was a juggling act. One day, I made love to Sylvia in the morning, Betty at noon, Vicki after dinner, and my wife, Tina, at bedtime. It was like a lousy *job*. I felt like a plumber or something."

"How do you manage to find the time?" the therapist wonders.

"I'm a lawyer. I can make my own hours," he replies. "I've taken some of them to Mexico or Europe. My wife doesn't ski and I do, so I tell her I'm going to Europe to ski. There are office accounts I can draw on for funds. You know, when I was a kid, I saw this movie, *The Captain's Paradise*, about a guy who had two different women in different places. It made a tremendous impression on me, even back then. I always thought that would be the ideal situation."

"Where does Tina fit into things now?"

"I don't want to lose her," Mario says. "I realize I'm in a Never-Never Land of fantasy. I take crazy risks, like inviting Betty to the office Christmas party, when I know my wife will be there, or flaunting these young girls in places I'm likely to run into friends. The highs are terrific, the lows are miserable. Tina is my anchor to reality. I don't want to lose that anchor. I tell her that.''

"And what does she say?''

"That she doesn't need a fourth child,'' Mario says, a bit crestfallen.

"The sexual desire for Tina was always there before?''

"To be honest, I find nothing attractive about her below the waist,'' Mario says. "She has a fat rear, heavy legs. Well, she's thirty-six now, and I never go after a girl over thirty, unless they're exceptionally young-looking. Still, I never had a potency problem with Tina before, even if I'd been out screwing all day. Since I broke up with Betty, I have no feelings at all for Tina.

"It's not that I feel negatively about her. She's a wonderful woman, better than I deserve, and she was absolutely right about refusing to put up with my living with Betty. But I saw Betty this week, happened to catch her when she was parking her car, and we talked for about half an hour. She refused to take me back under any circumstances, and you know, if she'd asked me to, I would have moved back in with her in a minute.

"And my sex drive is there. I've been seeing two hookers. I feel a little bad about that, but they're young, high-class girls. I don't see how I could ever limit myself to one woman. When I was eleven, I lived in a big apartment complex, and there were a lot of young women there. I would fantasize that I was living with all these women in some remote locale, maybe an island, and I would be the only man there. . . .''

Nobody would say that Mario has lost interest in sex, but in his marriage, which he wants to keep, there is a definite problem with sexual desire. The lack of desire is *selective,* since it is limited to his wife. Nearly all cases of selective desire disorder involve a loss of interest in the spouse or steady partner. Theoretically, if a person had sexual desire toward the spouse but couldn't feel it toward others, this, too, might be called a selective desire disorder—but who would complain?

Someone who has no desire for sex with a partner but practices masturbation regularly would qualify for the designation of selective desire disorder. Similarly, someone who enjoys oral sex but has no desire for intercourse could merit that diagnosis. How about a person who thinks intercourse is fine, but is turned off by sexual variations or masturbation? Most likely, such a limitation of desired sexual activity would be rooted in feelings of guilt about practices believed to be "abnormal," but could pose problems if one partner were more adventuresome than the other.

Mario's desire was becoming progressively focused on young women. If a man of twenty-five refuses to consider a partner over thirty, no one would question his taste. But if a man of fifty-five found any woman over thirty sexually undesirable and shunned all activity with his middle-aged wife, we would consider this a selective desire disorder deserving of treatment.

Rare is the person who would find *any* member of the opposite sex desirable, regardless of appearance or behavior, and we would characterize such a person as having excessive desire. We all have our particular turn-ons and turn-offs where prospective partners are concerned. Often, however, we lose desire for someone we once found attractive, and if we continue to find others desirable, we are faced with a selective desire disorder.

If a person loses sexual desire, does it matter whether the deficit is global or selective? While either type can be devastating to a person and a relationship, we can find clues to the causes of the loss, according to the pattern. A selective type virtually eliminates the possibility of a physical origin, such as hypothyroidism or low testosterone. Psychological depressions are more likely to cause a global desire loss. It is interpersonal conflicts, therefore, that tend to limit the loss of desire to the partner involved.

The prognosis is better for selective desire disorders, since the person does feel *some* desire. Just as in a system of electrical circuits, it is easier to shunt power from an active line into a dead one than to regenerate power in a system that has shut down completely. A person may be able to redirect desire from remote fantasy objects to a satisfactory partner more easily than reawakening desire from zero level.

Cases of all types of desire disorder—hypoactive or aversive, primary or secondary, global or selective—can be helped. While the pathway to increased desire may be smoother in the cases where desire was once present (secondary desire disorder) or where desire is retained toward some potential partners or activities (selective desire disorder), even people who have never experienced desire or who have lost it totally can achieve a satisfying level of desire.

The most important factor in ensuring a favorable outcome is motivation: the *desire to desire*. It is a mistake to regard desire as something that is entirely spontaneous and not attainable through effort. Some people, perhaps only at certain ages or under certain circumstances, may be able to experience a full measure of desire without giving it a moment's thought. But desire, like love, usually requires a degree of effort and monitoring to keep it flourishing.

Perhaps it is because desire, for most of us, is first experienced in adolescence, when it grips us unawares, that we tend to regard it as a natural force, spontaneous and beyond our control. We are swept into our first feelings of love without a lot of forethought and conscious commitment. Yet, we soon learn that the warm, exhilarating feelings that accompany love do not remain constantly at that level, and that love, although it can be enduring and can grow with time, needs care and attention or it can quickly deteriorate into apathy or even animosity.

Why then, if even the most incurable romantic will concede that the course of true love does not always run smoothly, do people expect desire to be ever-present and never-wavering? Probably it's because love is thought of as a "higher" human emotion, while desire is regarded as a "carnal" drive, something more of the body than the mind, which does not warrant much thought and which will take care of itself, much as the heart, lungs, and intestines go on about their business without our conscious direction. Or if it does involve the mind, we think of desire as belonging to the baser, primitive areas, maybe occasionally restrained by higher intellectual functions, but not as an integral part of the dispassionate, rational mind.

But since *human* desire is ultimately directed toward another person, the process is infinitely more complex than a simple reflex action; it involves the coordination of higher and lower brain centers, emotion and logic, body and spirit. True, when desire is operating smoothly, it seems as uncomplicated as turning on a television set. When desire fails, we often feel dumbfounded and helpless, since it never occurred to us that something so consistent and natural would ever be absent.

Once we understand the many influences that can activate or inhibit desire, we are able to work on what is interfering with its genesis and expression. As in repairing an automobile, we have to understand all the parts of its operation and the normal sequence of their interaction; the key to restoration of sexual desire lies in identifying potential sources of the problem. We cannot acquire an understanding of desire if we regard it as some mysterious force that occurs spontaneously, unmodified by external or psychological influences, or does not occur at all.

In the pages that follow, we will discuss the factors that influence desire. We will be reporting on the current treatment used by prominent therapists and adding our own suggestions on how to modify these methods to improve your own sexual desire and that of your partners. While it's easier to work on your own problem than someone else's, if you can figure out what may be interfering with a partner's flow of desire, you often will be in a position to help even if he or she lacks the insight that you've acquired.

The path to improved sexual desire is relatively clear once you have the main prerequisite: the desire to desire.

❧ *II* ❧

WHY DESIRE DIMINISHES

🌺 3 🌺

What Did You Expect?

The Effect of False Expectations

"It's just a different world," says Julia R. Heiman, Ph.D., director of the University of Washington Medical School's Interpersonal Psychotherapy Clinic. "Our society is built around finding something better and there's a lack of satisfaction in sex.

"Money is made on people not being sexually satisfied, in the sense that the ever-better sexual partner is sold in advertising, in commercial films, in just about every economic aspect. The philosophy that runs throughout Western culture is that there is something better and you can find it. And so, when people have a sex life that is not all that exciting and kind of routine, they label it as something *wrong.* Sex does decrease in frequency for *everyone* and it shouldn't automatically be considered bad."

Dr. Heiman says she doesn't have a single answer to explain the increasing prevalence of lack of desire, but she has certainly touched on some of the answers. Whether the negative influences come primarily from the environment, a conflicted relationship with a partner, or from purely personal factors, such as fears or past traumas, people usually will not seek a why for their sexual interest, since reasoning is so intellectual and desire seems so emotional and removed from logic.

You *can* fight back, regardless of the cause, but you've got to know where the opposition is coming from.

In this section, we will be exploring the causes of desire loss. Understanding these sources of trouble will help you to identify what might be impeding your own sexual desire or that of your partner. These factors have the potential to lower anyone's desire, intermittently or constantly. Even if there's no problem now, knowing about them may help you recognize the difficulty if a drop in desire should occur in the future. Simply *expecting* some problems with desire can do much to avoid problems. Time, stress, and circumstances are never completely avoidable, but overreaction to their effects on sexual desire can be circumvented. The person who expects desire to be constant and carefree is ultimately more vulnerable to desire loss than one who does not take it for granted.

"Is it natural, I ask you, for a man to be less interested sexually in his wife just because they've been married four years?" demands Maureen, a twenty-five-year-old redheaded homemaker. "Should you expect less interest in sex just because a couple has children in the house?" Her pale skin begins to flush as her oratory heats up. Her husband, Stewart, a tall twenty-nine-year-old, scrunches his six-foot frame down into his chair as though trying to burrow into the cushion. "Can a normal husband go *weeks* without making a sexual overture to his wife? Can a man be more interested in watching football than having sex?"

"Yes," the therapist says quietly.

Maureen emits a gasp, as if she's just been punched in the stomach. "Did you say *yes?*" she squeals. Stewart cringes, even though the flak is now being aimed at the therapist. The therapist nods, unintimidated. "I was asking rhetorical questions," Maureen protests. "I didn't even expect you to answer, much less answer yes. I didn't expect you to say *that.*"

" 'Expect' is a good word to explore," the therapist says. "Tell me, Maureen, what did you expect me to say, if I did say anything?"

"Well, the sort of thing everybody says," Maureen replies, calming down a little. "That sex is a vital, loving part of any marriage, and that if a couple really cares about one another, they'll want to be close physically as well as emotionally. Sex is a natural thing, after all. It's pleasurable. If a husband or wife doesn't care about it, there's something definitely wrong with the relationship!"

"So, you think your marriage is in big trouble?" the therapist says.

Maureen hesitates for a long moment, as if fearing a trap.

"Yeah! I don't know exactly what the trouble is, but that's what we're here to find out. Maybe Stewart is tired of being married, maybe he's got problems at work he's not telling me about, maybe he's found a woman who's more attractive than me." Stewart groans, but Maureen presses on. "Whatever it is, I want to get to the bottom of it, and I hope *you*, Doctor, aren't going to say, 'You're a perfectly normal married couple, go home and watch television together.' "

"Stewart, do you have anything to say?" the therapist asks.

"It's not like it was when we first got married," Stewart hastens to admit, "but it's not because something terrible is going on, the way Maureen thinks. In a way, I wish there were some deep problem I've been hiding, so we could deal with it and get back to the way things were. It's pretty much my fault, since I was the one who would usually make the suggestion; not that Maureen didn't want it, too, but it was usually me that took the first step. Lately, sex has been something I keep postponing, like paying a bill; it's become a chore, like mowing the lawn.

"Now that I think back, it's been going on for a while, but since I made it a point to have sex at least once on the weekend and usually once during the week, Maureen probably didn't notice any difference."

"I noticed!" Maureen grumbles.

"But the sex *was* good," Stewart emphasizes. "That's why I didn't worry much about what was happening. It's kind of like the dinner routine. You sit down around six-thirty each night and the food tastes good and you must be hungry, because you clean your plate, but how often do you think, 'Boy, am I hungry! I can't *wait* to have dinner!'?"

"Sure, but if there was no dinner waiting for you, you'd soon think about being hungry, wouldn't you?" Maureen interrupts.

"Exactly," Stewart agrees. "Maybe the problem is that we expect our appetite for sex to be the same way: if we're not hungry now, we'll get hungry later. And it just doesn't work that way."

"Speak for yourself," Maureen says heatedly. "I got to the point where I was *starving* for some physical closeness. I guess I have a *normal* sexual appetite."

"So, why didn't *you* speak up," Stewart asks her. "Am I the only one who can get things started?"

"I *did*, remember?" Maureen argues. "But I knew you just weren't that interested and that killed interest for me, too."

"Okay, then, that's my point exactly," Stewart replies. "At the dinner table, you don't lose your appetite just because the person you're with isn't hungry. You know, that's where I think we both went wrong, taking it for granted. I kept expecting my sexual desire to come back spontaneously, figuring it would be just a matter of time. And you got so worried that something was terribly wrong because you expected everything to work out 'naturally.' I underreacted and you overreacted, but both of us expected too much; namely, that unless something is seriously wrong, sexual desire will stay by itself at a steady level without our doing anything to help it along."

"Do you really think it's all that simple?" Maureen asks. It's not a challenge, just an honest question. "That you get bored with routine, that you have other pressures, that the kids are underfoot?"

"I don't know if I'd call that simple," Stewart answers, "but I think that could be enough. I personally think there are a lot of couples like us, who really don't expect that those intense urges are ever going to cool off a little and then get so threatened when it happens that they withdraw."

"Well, I don't think it should be that way," Maureen frets. "At least, not from what I've read."

Stewart shrugs. "Listen, since I was a kid, everything I read ended with 'they lived happily ever after.' Nobody writes about boredom or discouragement. That's why we expect everything else *but* that."

"We don't have to accept it, do we?" Maureen asks timidly.

"Damn right, we don't!" Stewart grins. "But it's easier to deal with a problem when you know what to expect."

When things do not proceed the way we expect, we tend to conclude that there is something wrong. We rarely ask ourselves whether it might not be the expectations that are at fault rather than the events that are not fulfilling them. Nobody warns couples to expect a waning of desire; on the contrary, the writings of most experts imply that in good marriages sexual satisfaction and interest grow rather than diminish with time. When couples start probing into their relationship, searching for nonexistent anger or infidelity, they generate hostility that diminishes desire further. While a decrease in desire may make marriages unhappy, it does not necessarily indicate that the marriage is an unhappy one.

In 1976, Drs. Alan Booth and John N. Edwards conducted a study on sexual behavior of 365 husbands and wives and learned that one third had stopped having intercourse for significant periods of time, the average being about eight weeks. Most of the abstainers were between twenty and thirty-nine years old. The most frequently given reason for the cessation of marital relations was discord (40 percent). Physical illness was the second most common cause (20 percent), and 12 percent merely cited a declining interest in sex. Wives were particularly susceptible to the effects of marital dissatisfaction, their sexual desire waning particularly if the husband was perceived as domineering or unaffectionate or if he had threatened to leave.

In 1981, Ellen Frank, Ph.D., of the University of Pittsburgh School of Medicine, reviewed in *Medical Aspects of Human Sexuality* her research involving lack of sexual desire in American marriage. Her research group examined the frequency of lack of sexual desire or sexual interest among married couples experiencing a variety of levels of marital and sexual satisfaction. In a sample of 100 couples, 35 percent of the women and 16 percent of the men reported a lack of interest in sex. What amazed many people was that the couples in question were "happily married"; in other words, they were not in treatment for any type of marital or sexual problem. Predictably, when the same issue was explored with couples who were experiencing marital difficulties, the percentage of those with low sexual desire was higher: 46 percent in women and 34 percent in men.

Since low sexual desire usually comes to our attention only when it is a source of distress for either partner, there is a sizable pool of unrecognized cases among couples who do not feel they have a problem. Particularly in couples married for more than five years, lack of sexual desire appears to be about half as prevalent among the husbands and almost as prevalent among the wives in "happy" marriages as in "troubled" ones.

"It has long been known that lack of sexual desire occurs frequently in troubled marriages," Dr. Frank wrote. "Our research indicates that lack of interest in or desire for sex occurs frequently even among happily married couples."

We are constantly exposed to statistics about what the average couple is doing sexually, but rarely is any mention made of the couple who is doing *nothing* sexually. People are more likely to talk about what they're doing than what they are not doing. While it is scarcely a cause for rejoicing, couples who find themselves going for weeks at a time without sexual interaction can take some consolation in knowing that their situation is far from unique and that the absence of sexual activity is not necessarily indicative of some deep and irreparable flaw in the union.

Maureen, our concerned patient, feels that no "normal" husband could go weeks without wanting to have sex with his wife or be more interested in football than sex. Such a situation can, indeed, exist in the course of "normal" marriages. Steps can be taken to increase sexual desire, but we should discard the false expectation that sexual desire will always be strong in a "good" relationship; otherwise, we will falsely conclude that our relationships are not good whenever sexual desire diminishes.

Sheila Jackman, Ph.D., who directs the Division of Human Sexuality at Albert Einstein Medical Center, reminds us, "When you get used to something, you stop paying attention to it. A new car is gorgeous, and the first week you keep it shining. By the second week, however, you are not washing it as much. You just get into it and you stop appreciating it."

Dr. Jackman has seen many cases where the failure to accept the tendency of waning desire led the couple to blame one another, putting a severe strain on the relationship. Instead of acknowledging that things have slowed down and resolving to expend a little effort to revitalize desire, the partners start flinging accusations at one another, citing perhaps his inability to prolong intercourse or her sexual unresponsiveness. They blame their lack of sexual interest on anger, even if they weren't angry to begin with; in the course of mutual recriminations, anger develops.

Dr. Jackman calls these charges and countercharges "tag-ons." The issues were never really related to decreased sexual desire, but they get "tagged on," one after the other until a relatively light-weight problem has become hopelessly bogged down by a load of grievances, real or imagined.

THE COKE GENERATION
Overly "High" Expectations

Thomas D. Stewart, M.D., a Harvard psychiatrist who directs the Beth Israel Men's Program in Boston, says there is a prevailing belief in our sex-saturated culture that we should constantly feel stimulated. "It's not unlike the addiction to cocaine; people think they ought to feel good all the time. If you and I sniffed coke, there is no doubt that for the next thirty minutes we'd feel great. Then there would be a 'crash' and a hole in our nose and other sorts of things. The attitude that, in spite of our responsibilities, we should be in a constant state of cosmic, orgastic bliss or on the verge thereof is a fantasy. That's not the way life is!"

When it comes to diminished sexual desire, Dr. Stewart feels that unrealistic expectations are often at the root of problems in a couple's relationship. "People tend to overlook that even animals aren't busy having sex each time they can," he comments. "So the idea that there is this 'animal' in us that ought to be either having sex or wanting to at every available opportunity is not based on fact."

Dr. Peter Hoon, co-director of the sexual dysfunction clinic at the University of Tennessee College of Medicine, says that single and married people alike have some very unrealistic expectations about sexual desire. "Maybe this exciting, intense, romantic, physical-desire stage of a relationship can be only that: a stage. Maybe that is something you experience when you fall in love and the sex is terrific, but that intensity and high level of erotic desire is normally only going to be part of the relationship for six to twelve months," he says. "It doesn't mean that sex can't be very exciting, but it's going to change in the way it is emotionally experienced by the couple."

So in the beginning of a relationship, both partners tend to start at a desire level higher than their usual norm, with the possible exception of those with very little sexual experience. Just as there are hot-tempered and even-tempered people, high-pressured and laid-back people, there are people with high desire levels, low desire levels, and levels of every intervening gradation. People tend to lose sight of this spectrum and have the unrealistic expectation that sexual desire in any given person will rise or fall according to how attracted they are to a specific partner.

We are not fixed at one absolute level by our libidinal thermo-stats, but just as a wall thermostat will not allow you to heat your house to 100 degrees, we do have our limitations. A woman with a potentially high desire level inhibited by restrictive parents might become a late-blooming "cactus flower" in her thirties or early forties after years of celibacy. Or a dependent woman forced into a pattern of multiple sexual partners in her quest for a male provider might be sexually indifferent after marriage. In these cases, the true desire level was masked by behavior impelled by circumstances. Men can also be affected by social pressures that induce them to pursue or avoid sexual contact in a manner contrary to their natural inclinations.

One of the reasons there are so many cases of sexual desire disorder among "happily married" couples is that men and women with low desire deliberately choose one another as mates. While a pair of low-desire partners will have less conflict than a pair ill-matched for desire levels, problems will occur. Even in couples with average levels of desire, rarely will *both* partners experience the same degree of desire at a given time. Assuming low-desire spouses want sex at least occasionally, the odds that both will have sufficient interest at the same point in time are prohibitive. Compliance, rather than true desire, may ensure some ongoing sexual interac-tion, but satisfaction is likely to be low.

Confusion between compliance and desire may mislead some-one with high-level desire into a relationship with a low-desire person who is meeting the high-frequency demands for sex in return for affection or security. Later in the relationship, disap-pointment in the payback or increased pressure in nonsexual areas will cause the low-desire partner to stop complying unless desire is truly present, a rare occurrence.

Overvaluation of premarital virginity may influence a high-de-sire man to marry an inexperienced woman, figuring that once he introduces her to the joys of sex, her desire level will quickly rise. Male expertise is no match for an inherently low desire level and some virgin brides never develop an interest in frequent sexual activity, regardless of how often they accommodate their partners. On the other hand, a low-desire man might be dismayed to discover that his sexually repressed bride concealed a high desire level under her veil and that his own libido cannot rise to meet her later expectations.

MAJOR MINOR PROBLEMS
The Effect of Children on Sexual Desire

A major deterrent to sexual desire can be minor problems—those involving people in the household under the age of eighteen.

"Let's face it, frequency drops for almost *everyone* when children come on the scene," says Dr. Sandra Leiblum, co-director of the sexual counseling service at Rutgers Medical School in New Jersey.

Dr. Jackman concurs: "I see so many couples with children who complain of lack of desire. On the female side, the problem is mostly, 'There is so much to do and I'm just exhausted!' or 'One ear is always listening for the children to walk in or my head is wondering, "Are the children okay?"' "

"You are paying so much attention to the children that a man may have to wave a flag and say, 'How about me?' "

Dr. Jackman stresses the interference with female sexual desire that can be caused by the demands of motherhood, but men also frequently experience a loss of sexual desire when they become parents. In some of these cases, the man may be reacting to what he perceives as his wife's loss of interest in him, as the children become her first priority. His reaction may be anger, which he finds difficult to accept, since he, too, cares about his children and does not want to become their rival for his wife's affection. He may feel rejected, like an object that has served its purpose and is no longer needed. Feeling less desired usually means feeling less desire.

On a more complex level, the man may lose sexual desire because he now sees his wife more as a mother than a lover, which aggravates the conflicts engendered by the prostitute-madonna complex. For the man who has not outgrown the simplistic notion that sex is naughty and mothers are nice, he will have to overcome a lot of guilt before he can recast his wife in a provocative role.

In a recent article published in *Medical Aspects of Human Sexuality,* Dr. Bennett Gurian, an associate professor of psychiatry at Harvard Medical School, notes a phenomenon not previously reported: the loss of sexual desire for a period of several months in men following the birth of their children. A loss of sexual desire and responsiveness in women following delivery is common, but the effect on fathers has been neglected.

Dr. Gurian wonders if we might not see more cases of diminished male desire now that fathers are encouraged to be present in the labor and delivery rooms. While some new fathers experience a sense of exhilaration, others feel distress and guilt as they witness their wives enduring hours of pain. The husband may have emotional difficulty dealing with the sight of blood and the cutting of tissues. He may feel like an unwelcome intruder and his insecurity may be aggravated if the obstetrician is male, as he contrasts the supportive, intimate relationship between doctor and woman with his own helplessness.

Dr. Domeena C. Renshaw of Loyola University of Chicago, in her written commentary on Dr. Gurian's article, recalls the case of a man who came with his wife for sex therapy after three years of being in an unconsummated marriage. Observing a gynecological examination performed on his wife as part of the treatment, he became so anxious that he had to leave the room. He was able to trace his anxiety back to watching a sex education film called *Birth of a Baby* from a front-row seat at the age of twelve. The blood and the screams caused him to flee the room and vomit, and he remembered thinking, "If I was a woman, I wouldn't let a man come within forty yards of me."

In cases of mild loss of libido following childbirth, Dr. Renshaw does recommend "early, brief couples therapy to prevent needless entrenchment of sexual avoidance at a time when closeness is essential to nurturing the new family."

Dr. Gurian was prompted to write his article about loss of fathers' libido after childbirth only after he happened to speak with three other colleagues who confided that, as recent parents, they had experienced similar problems. So many common difficulties relating to sexual desire go unrecognized because of our false expectation that sexual desire, as a basic human characteristic, is relatively impervious to the vicissitudes of daily living. Nothing could be farther from the truth. By realizing that the course of desire can be easily impeded, we will be more prepared to deal with deficiencies, without plowing into roadblocks or taking far-ranging detours that lead us off course.

MID-LIFE'S GRAYED EXPECTATIONS
Psychological Effects of Aging

"I just don't have the desire anymore," Ben says. "It just died out in the past few months, and I have no idea why." Ben is a husky, neatly dressed photographer, who sports a trim gray mustache. His unwrinkled face makes him look somewhat younger than his age, but his silver hair adds a few years, the net effect evening out around fifty-one, which is what his birth certificate would show him to be.

"Sandra's five years younger than I and she keeps herself in great shape. I don't think she's gained a pound in the past twenty years," Ben adds. "I care about her as much as ever. Business is okay. I've had a complete physical exam. I just can't figure it out."

"Ben, what exactly do you mean when you say you have no desire?" the therapist inquires. "That you don't want to have sex? That you don't think about it? That something about your wife turns you off?"

"Well, no," Ben replies. "I *want* to have sex, even if only to please Sandy, but there's just no response. Here." Ben points to the zipper on his trousers.

"Are you saying you can't get an erection?" the therapist asks. He is thinking that an erectile dysfunction is really a problem with sexual arousal, not desire.

"Yes and no," Ben clarifies. "I've had an occasional problem with erections before—what honest man hasn't? You have too much to drink, you get opening-night jitters with a new woman (that was before I got married, of course), or you try to go back for seconds a little too soon. But you did get that tingling in your penis, that stirring, even if you could only raise it to half-mast and keep it hard enough to do its job. Now, there's *nothing* stirring. Sandy starts taking off her clothes, I keep watching her, but the old response just isn't there. Less than a year ago, I'd have had a full erection as soon as her hand touched the first button on her dress."

"I hear you talking still about *erections,*" the therapist persists.

"Doc, I wish it *was* an erection problem," Ben protests, his thick fingers running a tortuous path through his hair. "The spirit would be willing even if the flesh is flaccid."

"But you *do* want to make love," the therapist insists.

"Only on an intellectual level. I don't *feel* it in my head."

"Correction," the therapist says. "You don't feel it in your penis. Your head is waiting for the old familiar feedback, and when it isn't transmitted, you conclude that there's no *sexual* desire, just some cerebral wishing. Ben, have you tried masturbating? Do you get erections when you do?"

Ben hesitates, but answers like an honest man. "Yeah, I've done it. And I *do* get erections then. See, Doc, there's the proof that it's not impotence."

"Okay, but *how* does that erection come about?"

Ben gets a little flustered. "Hell, the usual way . . . you know! You grab it, you manipulate it."

"Exactly! You're not getting an erection just by staring at a picture or having a fantasy, right?" the therapist confirms.

"Well, it's kind of simultaneous, isn't it?" Ben says.

"It's the *touching* that's producing the erection now," the therapist emphasizes.

"What do you mean by *now?*" Ben asks.

"I mean, I don't know what was going on last year, but now and henceforth, you're going to have to include your sense of touch in any sexual encounter, in addition to whichever of the other four senses you want to use."

"You're saying it's related to age? Give me a break, Doc, I'm only fifty-one. I'm not ready for Senior City, yet."

"And when you are, you can spend the day making love, like the rest of them," the therapist reassures him. "It's just that those automatic pop-up erections you've been keying in on since the eighth grade will have to be acquired manually. Why, is it so unpleasant if Sandy touches you?"

Ben looks as if it *will* be unpleasant. "I dunno," he mutters. "That's not the way we've been doing it for twenty years."

"Don't you touch her?"

"Of course!" Ben says indignantly. "She'd never have an orgasm if I didn't spend a lot of time touching her . . . erogenous zones."

"So, why can't she do the same for you?"

Ben sighs and hangs his head. "I'm afraid she's going to think I'm not turning on to her anymore, that the erection is just a mechanical reflex that anybody could produce. In the past, I didn't want her to touch me there, for fear I'd climax too soon, you know?"

"Give Sandy a chance, will you, Ben?"

Ben nods slowly. Then, he straightens up and nods in earnest. "Yeah, I will. I think she'll be as relieved as I am to know the situation isn't hopeless. And that I didn't have a desire problem . . . well, I'm still not sure about *that.*"

"It was a desire problem of a sort," the therapist concedes. "A lot of men grow up so preoccupied with their penises that they can't perceive desire unless that erection, or at least the initial stirring, accompanies it. They come to expect that genital cue, and when the expectation fails to materialize, they figure that the desire is gone along with it. And if they worry enough about losing desire, pretty soon they'll be right."

THE SUBWAY SYNDROME
Loss of Spontaneous Erections

Dr. Thomas Stewart of Harvard refers to middle-aged men's consternation over the loss of instant and minimally provoked erections as the "subway syndrome," a metaphor easily appreciated by any New Yorker who's been packed tail-to-tail in the underground rolling sardine cans that transport the masses. "It baffles them, because they have their memories of being eighteen years old and riding on the subway," he explains. "A gal walked by and brushed their jacket and they got an immediate erection. Now, they would read the New York *Times* as soon as look at a gal, and that is confusing."

Why do such men wind up with the *Times* in their hands, not girls on their minds? You certainly don't need an erection just to look. Yet the inadequacy the aging man feels causes him to question his desire, and he feels he is out of his league even in something as nondemanding a spectator sport as girl-watching.

Dr. Herbert Laube of the University of Minnesota has seen men as young as in their late twenties who experience anxiety and confusion when they no longer have frequent spontaneous erections. "If they think about sex, they feel the erection should spontaneously follow," he notes. "When they have the thought and the erection's not there, then confusion reigns. Men don't understand. They interpret that as lack of desire, instead of trying to combine the thought with some physical stimulation."

Dr. Laube has had patients who were very active sexually, but became totally devastated when they lost spontaneous erections. "They had their lifestyles based on it and without that they were really confounded," he says.

If *men* don't understand what is going on, their partners may have a far more difficult time understanding how the unpredictability and force of the teenage erection affects an impressionable young mind. Arousal and desire become practically inseparable early in a man's life. His penis becomes aroused with minimal provocation and his head almost simultaneously becomes flooded with erotic wishes and fantasies. Even by the time the man reaches college age, his physical response has already cooled down to the point where he no longer has to carry a notebook or binder to shield his pelvis when the need suddenly arises. But since the diminution of libido is so gradual, almost imperceptible, and since the young man has more than enough left to keep his sexual interest and performance thriving, he barely notices how his penis comes to react in a more moderate way.

When people talk about the effects of aging on the sexuality of men, we tend to think of the geriatric set, those sixty or even older. To tell a man of thirty-five or forty that his decreased capacity for arousal is a natural consequence of aging may be even less reassuring than confirming his fear that his desire has suddenly evaporated.

The important thing in maintaining a viable sexual relationship is often that the woman not fall into the same trap of mistaking the man's loss of a quick erection for a loss of interest in her. Unfortunately, the waning of visible excitement in the man tends to occur just when his partner is at the age when she fears losing youth and attractiveness. He thinks he has lost desire at the precise time she is feeling undesirable.

If both can accept that desire is still there and the path to arousal merely lies along a different, more time-consuming but pleasant route, they can avoid the failure-panic-avoidance cycle that can lead to a true sexual aversion disorder. Specifically, many men as they get older require some type of penile stimulation, manual or oral, before they can achieve a firm erection. Since younger men, in order to delay ejaculation, may want a minimum of touching during foreplay, couples may find themselves having to break out of the familiar style of lovemaking.

If changes are made in the spirit of novelty and adventure, the couple may actually find their sexual experience enhanced by the greater amount of time spent in lovemaking and precoital intimacy.

THAT OLD FEELING
Sexual Desire and Senior Citizens

Dr. Evalyn S. Gendel, a physician who directs the human sexuality program at the San Francisco School of Medicine, became interested in the sexuality of the elderly as a result of her treatment of chronic illnesses. She views sexual desire as being dependent on many factors, including physical well-being, economic status, and self-esteem, rather than chronological age. "I think desire is strong in many people and it's there forever, unless it's been beaten out of them by their belief in the social myth. Not every male's testosterone falls as he gets older. It's a very individual thing," she maintains.

The "social myth" to which Dr. Gendel refers is the widespread prejudice that regards sex as something the elderly do not or should not engage in. As children, the Oedipal complex causes us to cast Mother in the image of the reluctant virgin and Father as the powerful, heartless satyr. As we become adults, Mother is still the spiritually asexual nurturer, but Father is less formidable to his sons and his image is cut down to their size—or several sizes smaller. Thus, our humor abounds with images of frustrated lecherous old men whose sexual desire is doomed to failure. Occasionally aging women are mocked as man-hungry grannies getting their just repayment for their earlier sexual austerity.

The irony is that these images, simultaneously comic and tragic, of asexual or sexually frustrated elders ultimately serve to deter sexual desire as the youngsters advance in years and sense that they are becoming the elders once ridiculed. They come to believe in the joke, and the fear of advancing age makes them give up sexual functioning and finally leads them to suppress sexual desire.

Not every senior citizen, however, is content to spend the twilight years in a rocking chair. Some have the courage to risk going off their rockers to spend some time in beds that don't have cranking mechanisms. We can think of many instances of rich and successful older men who are photographed with young wives or girlfriends, and older actresses who are escorted with pride by younger mates. And we should not assume that the youthful partners are mere showpieces. As we will discuss in the next section, sex is for winners, and success is a potent aphrodisiac.

But an older person does not have to qualify for "Lifestyles of the Rich and Famous" in order to play "The Dating Game." Some very relevant data on sexual desire has come out of Duke University's twenty-five-year-old ongoing study of men, which began with a sample of forty-five-year-olds. The subjects are now approximately seventy years old and the portion of the study that focused on sexuality revealed that while one third of the men were reporting diminishing interest and activity and one third reported no significant change with the passage of time, fully one third were increasing their sexual awareness and interaction.

THE ULTIMATE LOSS
False Expectations and Self-Esteem

"To the victor belongs the spoils" has been the ancient rule; *Vae victis!* ("Woe to the vanquished!") its older corollary. Conquest has been associated with sex, as the Sabines sorrowfully learned, and while we condemn the flourishing of carnality amid carnage, a rush of testosterone in the victorious might well have accounted for both types of barbarity. Today, our triumphs at the office or on the handball court are less bloody, but often no less conducive to increased libido. For many people, the end of a satisfying day might herald something more erotic than "Miller time."

For the losers, there is only dejection and the depression of desire. But who keeps score? Usually, only we ourselves judge success or failure, and we use our expectations to set the standard. When expectations are unreasonable, failure is inevitable.

Here are some common expectations that were never met because they could never be encountered within the realm of possibility:

*A man expects to bring his sexual partner to orgasm every time and feels like a failure if he does not. Only about 50 percent of women consistently (i.e., nearly always) achieve orgasm during intercourse. Unless such a man is monogamously involved with someone in the top half of the orgasmic population, he's doomed to fail by his standards.

*A woman expects her orgasms to match the descriptions she has read in the self-help books. One book, for example, described orgasm as the high mountaintop on which a couple becomes a full orchestra playing a fortissimo of a glorious symphony. Since the average orgasm lasts 3.5 seconds, won't our subject feel she missed a few notes?

*A couple expects their feelings of love for one another to grow through increased frequency of intercourse, in an effort to bring back the romance of their courtship days. Actually, adolescents and the elderly are most likely to experience romantic feelings, because they are the *least* sexually active people, whereas sexually active couples in their late twenties and the thirties give little thought to romance. Marie, Countess of Champagne and daughter of Eleanor of Aquitaine, presiding over a "court of love" where complex questions on the subject of courtly love were debated and resolved, ruled that romantic love cannot exist between husband and wife. We may appeal that decision, but if a large part of romance *is* simply sexual tension prior to intercourse, we're dealing with a mathematically reciprocal relationship and our couple has not formulated a proper equation.

*A man expects his wife to know how to please him in bed. He wouldn't expect her to know his favorite brand of beer or what teams he roots for, but somehow she's supposed to know his sexual preferences without being told. Maybe beer and baseball are a lot easier to discuss.

*Great Expectations I: Think that mind reading is a tough act for married folk? How about the single person who feels that the first sexual experience with a new partner is an indication of what the rest of the relationship will be like. If the rookie instinctively knows how to bring you to the heights of ecstasy you've been reading about in all the latest books and magazines, he or she passes the test. Is D-minus a pass? Where the dickens do they get these great expectations? As a setup for failure, this one's a pip!

*Great Expectations II: Who said it's lovelier the second time around? The first encounter is all magic, a process that requires suspension of disbelief and selective inattention. As the partner gets more and more real, the magic may disappear—unless you were willing to acknowledge from the start that nothing floats free, least of all the great passions, and there are always some strings attached.

*A woman expects her marriage to reach such a level of psychological intimacy that there will be unrestrained, unreserved communication with her husband at all times. In a recent interview, Masters and Johnson said that in America today only 1 in 100 marriages will become close enough emotionally to reach a "roommate level of intimacy" and only 1 in 100,000 will attain "true bonding." Nothing is worth shooting for if there are going to be 99,999 losers for every winner.

*And if you really want to be a loser, get involved with one. This is a favorite self-defeating ploy for ambitious women, whose rationale is: "I'm too devoted to my career to get involved in a serious relationship right now . . . but of course, being a mature, modern woman, I need sex . . . so, I'll pick someone just for sex, whom I wouldn't possibly consider for anything more serious . . . someone I wouldn't even be *tempted* to get serious about . . . perhaps a married man, one who's hopelessly immature, or who has a drinking problem. . . ." The last portion of this disaster plan is usually subconscious. She may not be serious, but the nature of the ensuing fiasco is.

"Ah, but a man's reach should exceed his grasp, or what's a heaven for?" wrote Robert Browning.

Browning's opinion may have some merit, but with respect to sexual desire, where our expectations are consistently beyond reach, the result can be sheer hell.

On a Role

New Identities in a New World

"Give me the good old days, when men were men and women were women. . . ."

That lament has been echoing for centuries, but it would be difficult to find an era that has encompassed as many dramatic role changes as our generation has seen. Time has made the timeless interaction between the sexes less elementary and more problematic. The physical aspects of sex haven't changed, but the mental part has—and that can have disruptive effects on desire.

"Did you ever play Charades, Doc?" Roger asks with a mischievous smile. "I hadn't played it in years, but a few couples got together and somebody suggested Charades. I'm bringing this up because one of the sayings I had to act out was 'No man is an island.' Now, how would you act out the word 'man'?"

The therapist contemplates the thirty-eight-year-old advertising executive with prematurely graying hair and an offsetting boyish grin. The therapist finally shrugs and simply pokes a finger at his own sternum.

"Naw, that's 'I' or 'me,'" Roger says critically. "Look, without even thinking about it, this is what *I* did." Roger stands up, expands his chest, flexes first one biceps and then the other, and ultimately points to himself, as the therapist did, but not before thumping his fist on his chest, gorilla-style. "Man! One of the guys got it right away. But my wife really let me have it! Laraine said, 'So, *that's* your idea of what a man is, huh? Chest thumping and muscle flexing and smug posturing. Boy, talk about chauvinistic stereotypes! You guys are beyond hope.' Everybody laughed, including Laraine, but I could see her point.

" 'Okay,' I shot back, 'let's see you do "woman." ' Laraine put her head down and wouldn't do anything. Finally, one of the other women kind of sheepishly waved her two hands to outline a curvy, hourglass shape. Everybody howled. That was just as sexist as what I did. Still, what the hell else could you have done? Maybe the world has changed and roles have changed, but I don't think our basic notions of what a man or a woman is have kept pace.

"I don't think that the sexual problem between Laraine and me has anything to do with us as individuals. She's still the person I married fourteen years ago and I still love her. I don't think I've changed all that much. What's changed over the years are the roles we play. I almost said, 'in the bedroom,' but it's not just in the bedroom, although it sure carries over. Before Laraine went to work five years ago, the marriage ran like clockwork. There were little problems, sure. Sometimes I had to work late, sometimes we had trouble meeting expenses on just one salary, sometimes she'd get bored with the household routine. It wasn't perfect, but it wasn't bad.

"Our sex life wasn't bad either. I thought we pretty much mutually agreed on when we were going to have sex, although Laraine has since pointed out to me that I was the one controlling it. For example, if I got home late from work or brought home assignments, we never had sex. If I got home by six-thirty and smiled a lot, Laraine was ready with the perfume and the negligee. At the time, I'd interpret this as 'Great, she wants to have sex,' and my desire always rose to the occasion; I didn't realize that she was cuing in on me. Laraine didn't have orgasms as regularly as she does now, but she never seemed very concerned about it and I never felt she was unhappy with our sex life.

"When both kids started going to school all day and Laraine said she wanted to go back to work, I was all for it. She's a bright gal; I didn't marry her just because . . ." Roger paused to form the Charades hourglass before resuming. "I mean, she had worked before we got married and before the children came, so I just assumed she'd have a simple nine-to-five routine, bring home a little money, and things would go on the same as always.

"But, as I said, Laraine's a bright gal. She just took off. She'd be bringing home work from the office, sometimes staying late, occasionally putting in a Saturday. So much changed. The babysitter we'd originally hired just to put in a couple of hours with the kids after school wasn't enough. With both of our schedules so unpredictable, we needed a live-in homemaker. And that meant moving to a bigger place. Laraine's salary more than offset the expense, but the kids and I had to adjust to some heavy changes.

"Our sex life got better and worse. We were having sex less often, because now there were two of us that might come home too tired or overwhelmed to want sex. Laraine was having orgasms more often, though, because now she was more open about telling me what turned her on and what didn't, instead of leaving everything up to me. Sometimes this would interfere with my getting into it myself and once, when she made some suggestion in the middle of things, I said, 'Yes, boss.' Then I tried to laugh it off as a little joke, but I guess both of us became aware then that I wasn't finding it all that easy to learn that I'd been doing things wrong for years.

"I realize that there are other things I resent, too, that don't deal strictly with Laraine. There's been quite a change in the advertising field during the past twenty years, where we've now actually got more women employed at my agency than men. Initially, I didn't mind and even thought it was rather nice to have all these smart, pretty young women surrounding me. Now—and I know it's unfair—I find myself often thinking, 'Why the hell don't they get married and stay home, or become schoolteachers or nurses? Why are they invading my world? Whatever happened to home and mother?' They tell women they can 'have it all,' but Laraine couldn't pull it off without delegating her mothering responsibilities to the homemaker—or to me, when the homemaker is on vacation or sick. Picking up a sick kid from school, driving one to a dental appointment, attending a PTA meeting means taking time away from our careers and we try to alternate that loss of time, but if there were only one career to worry about, there wouldn't be a problem.

"Once Laraine even came home talking about how people were accepting promotions to work in a new branch in Houston. My heart almost stopped. Laraine didn't push it, because, hell, I would have nothing to gain and a whole life's work to lose by leaving here.

See, there's just no way two people can be married and have both able to take every advantage at work."

Roger slumps in his chair and confesses, "It really was much nicer when I could come from work and know that Laraine would have food on the stove and perfume on her earlobes. My desire would begin perking around four o'clock, rev up when I walked through the door, and be in high gear by bedtime. Now, I don't know what to expect when I get home—whether Laraine will be tired or even whether she'll be there at all. I don't know whether I'm going to be greeted by a sexy wench or an exasperated executive. I'm working without a goddamn script and I guess I'm just not very good at improvising. I *like* playing a role I can be comfortable in, even if it does get predictable or corny. Man!" Roger thumps his chest, then drops his hands into his lap and shakes his head sadly. "Oh, man!"

Sexual desire flourishes best in a stress-free atmosphere. We turn our attention to sex when there are no pressing matters making demands on our attention. Nobody thinks about sex in a time of crisis.

Life, fortunately, is not a series of nonstop crises, but even routine periods may be characterized by low or high stress levels. It is people blessed with a relaxed domestic atmosphere who will experience the least interference with sexual desire. Spouses or lovers who are comfortable in one another's presence are apt to have better sex lives than those whose relationship is in conflict, even if the more stable couples often complain of boredom and predictability.

Roles are comforting, even if they sometimes limit our potential for personal growth and satisfaction. When a man and a woman know exactly what's expected of them, they can interact with a minimum of anxiety and insecurity. The abolition of—or, at least, the attempt to abolish—traditional roles that this generation has witnessed contributed in no small degree to the increase in sexual desire disorder.

"I think men's desire is much more vulnerable and delicate than women's," says Jerry M. Friedman, Ph.D., an assistant professor in the Department of Psychiatry at the State University of New York in Stony Brook, "and the only reason men have been able to survive as well as they have is because of the place women had in their lives."

If many men are not surviving as well, it's because the women who have had a place in their lives have been changing places. With the new fear of sexually transmitted diseases, men don't want to turn to sex outside the relationship for solace. Whereas their previous images of women were limited to the sexy bedmate and the nurturing mother, men now have to contend with a new breed of woman, one who is a competitor at work and who may take charge in the bedroom. Even if they don't view their spouses or girlfriends as rivals, they may carry over the hostility they feel in the workplace to their mates, unconsciously venting their anger in subtle ways, such as sulking, quarreling, or withholding sexual gratification.

Dr. Shirley Zussman points out, "You know what's expected of you at work, but not at home or in the bedroom anymore. Not only in the bedroom, but in the whole interaction. You don't know how to function in a relationship as a man or a woman, how much to give, how much to hold back for other things, whereas before it was very clearly defined. The relationship, for the woman, was the focus of her world, and the man expected that and the woman was there for it. Now, it's so changed, and in a way, it's easier to know what is expected of you at work."

Male-female roles have apparently entered a new stage and there seems to be no director. On first impression, roles may seem to be a pretty flimsy base for a relationship. If people are always expected to act in a certain way, it limits their options and personal achievements. Tasks may be unfairly distributed and talents underutilized, for in life, just as in the theater, there are meaty starring roles and less significant supporting roles.

Yet, roles make things flow a lot more smoothly both on stage and off, if you think of a role not so much as the unvarying words written for one character, but as a set of predictable attitudes and behaviors for that character: the role of the hero, the villain, the ruler, the fool. If a man approaches a woman at a singles dance, she will not reproach him for undue familiarity, as she might if he acted the same way on the street. The couple is allowed to stand closer than usual, prolong eye contact, and make subtly suggestive remarks (even though they are strangers who may never see one another again) because they are relating in the traditional roles of man and woman, not as two complex individuals. Both understand what they may do and may not do in this initial encounter, thanks to decades of precedents. Couples who cannot even speak one another's language have frequently courted and married by using the shorthand communication and techniques of male-female role-playing, which effectively traverse cultural and ethnic barriers.

Increasingly, couples are choosing to share control of all aspects of a relationship rather than divide everything according to traditional male and female roles. The new arrangement may ultimately prove superior to the old constricting patterns, but at present the abandoned old roles are familiar and the new flexibility is not. This affects desire because strong desire for another person makes us vulnerable to them, dependent on their meeting our wants; we suffer intense pains of rejection and jealousy when we cannot predict what they will do.

Uncertainty breeds anxiety and anxiety destroys desire. The anxiety may arise in the bedroom because of the loss of the old roles of male initiator and female receptor, or the anxiety may already be present because of role conflicts that are not directly related to sex.

FROM BREAD MAKER TO BREADWINNER
Female Careers and Sexual Desire Disorder

One prominent benefit of the Sexual Revolution was an increase in successful careers for women; that is, employment that offered substantial remuneration and true accomplishment, not merely a modest salary and unstimulating work. Some of the newest research to come out of the Masters and Johnson Institute focuses on sexual desire disorder in career women and makes an important distinction between those who consider their careers meaningful and those whose primary reward is a paycheck.

While careers have raised the self-esteem of achievement-oriented women, they have exacted a toll on female sexual desire. Dr. Constance Avery-Clark has noted over the course of more than five years at the Masters and Johnson Institute that there is twice as high a rate of sexual desire disorder in married women pursuing careers compared with wives who are either not employed or who are engaged in jobs that offer little challenge or chance for advancement. In analyzing the records of 218 married couples treated at the Institute, she found that 22 percent of the career women complained of low desire, versus 11 percent of the other wives.

On the other hand, the career wives had less trouble reaching orgasm once they did get sexually involved. Dr. Avery-Clark found that 17 percent of them had difficulty reaching orgasm, compared with 25 percent of homemakers and 29 percent of women with less demanding jobs.

Dr. Avery-Clark told us that the interpersonal dynamics between husband and wife may very well play a role, because women with an achievement-oriented mode of thinking perceive themselves as competing with their husbands much more so than wives who are not involved in a career. The career woman is also vulnerable to the "overload dilemma" of handling the multiple responsibilities of worker, wife, and mother in a limited number of hours. The career wife makes demands on herself in a sexual situation, much as she does at her job. She feels she should be very involved and perform well, but is usually too tired to be involved in much of anything. Through low desire, she stops things before they can even get started. Once they get going, she does very well, but getting into the sexual encounter is much more the problem.

Women with orgasmic dysfunction do not have the same difficulty about engaging in sex. According to Dr. Avery-Clark, they have the feeling that sex is primarily to satisfy men and that men are more knowledgeable about techniques. They feel their role is to satisfy the man without being much concerned about their own gratification. Self-esteem is not very high in the women with orgasm failure and they do not feel they have a right to inform their partners about their specific likes and dislikes in sexual situations.

The wife with a career gets more enjoyment out of sex not only because she feels confident about conveying her preferences to her partner, but also because she has developed skills in asserting herself and communicating her needs and desires directly. Dr. Avery-Clark believes that equal rights in the bedroom are very much possible, but can be obtained only by developing good verbal and nonverbal communication. Without such skills, the situation becomes so frustrating that people lose the desire to attempt sexual relations.

BUSINESS: THE ULTIMATE KIND OF TRIP
When Work Is More Fun than Sex

"So, Mike keeps staring at me, droning at me every fifteen minutes or so, 'Charlene, don't you want to go to bed, sugar? It's eleven-fifteen.' And I'm diving through piles of papers, making calculations, with bed the very last thing I'm interested in, especially since Mike only calls me 'sugar' when he wants to have sex. A real great communicator, that Mike! 'Mike, love,' I say, 'I'm really too hyper to sleep or even go near a bed, and I really have to finish this,' " Charlene recounts.

Charlene is a tiny brunette, no more than five feet one, with saucerlike eyes and an infectious smile. Even as she is talking to the therapist, she is fidgeting in her chair with the happy excitement that must be only a fraction of what was keeping her wide-eyed on the night being discussed. She is forty-two and divorced her husband five years ago after a ten-year childless marriage. Mike has been her live-in lover for three years.

"Everything was coming beautifully together at once," Charlene tries to explain. "First, I had gotten my own software dealership. My friend, the union rep, was helping line up deals with this town's whole damn construction industry. And then I got to meet Wyndanch, who's got a dozen of the most lucrative projects under construction and he's in the market for an overhaul of his entire computer system." Her muscles tense, her eyes close, and her lips part silently for a moment. She may be on the verge of an orgasm. "I wanted to open a bottle of champagne, but I didn't dare, because the work wasn't over yet, but it was like coming down the homestretch with a twelve-length lead, knowing nothing was going to stop me. It was the most hectic and wonderful day of my life. Later, I thought back on all my previous 'best days'—the senior prom, college graduation, my wedding day—they were nothing compared to this, in spite of the tension and fear of some last-minute glitch killing the deal.

"But there was Mike, who had been sulking like a lonely puppy ever since I burst through the door. He gave me dinner and I wolfed it down while talking on the phone. He asked if he could do anything to help, and I waved him off. Finally, after another invitation to bed, I just snapped, 'Look, if you're tired, go ahead without me.' He said, 'I didn't want to go to bed to sleep. I had something else in mind.' At which point, I said, 'Then go ahead without me.' He threw a sofa pillow at the wall.

"Well, I'm still on a roll, but things have simmered down a little and I finally got to spend a little time talking to Mike. The problem is that he wants to analyze what's wrong in our relationship, and he doesn't believe me when I insist that there's nothing wrong. He says that maybe I'm angry at him for something he doesn't realize he did or maybe there's something he could be doing to satisfy me more, sexually. Maybe I've met a more interesting man and I feel too committed to him to pursue it. And he doesn't understand when I tell him that I've been just too busy to think about sex—as if *nobody* could be that busy. 'You're becoming a bloody workaholic,' he said.

"And then, Mike gave me a funny look. 'No, Charlene,' he said, 'a workaholic lives for his work, but he's a dull, obsessive little mole, digging away, no fun to be with. You seem to be on a trip of some sort, a real high. You come home radiant and excited. It's unnatural!' I asked Mike if he ever got excited about work and he said not really, not like the way he would get excited about sex. Then, he asked me the big one, whether I could get a better high from work than sex.

" 'God, yes,' I said honestly. 'Not regularly, of course, but when things are really building to a peak or when you cut a super deal and know that everything you've been struggling to do for months is going to pay off—nothing can match that!' I think that really hurt him. 'Well, maybe women are different,' he said. 'Maybe you're in the wrong line of work,' I said.

"I mean, Doc, sex is okay, but it's got its limits. I don't believe that it's always the greatest high for men either. Women are just beginning to get a taste of the excitement a real career can give you, one that carries power and money. I think I always knew what the ultimate trip was, even before I split with my husband to have more freedom to pursue things.

"Remember several years back, when there were all those stories about the business executive who was a mentor to this younger blonde, and there was such a stink because he stood up at a stockholders' meeting to announce that there was *not* anything sexual between them? Everybody seemed convinced that there *had* to be hanky-panky and she left the corporation and he eventually did. And I kept thinking, 'What's wrong with everybody? These two brilliant, dynamic people are flying around the country together, plotting and pulling off billion-dollar takeovers and mergers, the wealth of an entire nation practically in their hands. How could sex possibly compare to the tiniest extent with that sort of excitement? God, what a wretched anticlimax!'

"As I remember, they did get married and she had a baby and that's the last I recall reading about them," Charlene says, a bit sadly. "I really hope they found happiness and success; I know neither of them will ever starve, but I mean *real* happiness." Her face breaks into an impish grin. "Why the hell would a couple bother to screw each other when they could be screwing half the country's corporations?"

Dr. Shirley Zussman quotes Pablo Picasso as saying that the ultimate aphrodisiac is your work. Dr. Zussman believes that in today's world, many women's major interest is their job, the most exciting, gratifying, and ego-enhancing part of their life.

Involvement in work for some of Dr. Zussman's female patients, however, offers neither blissful self-absorption nor sexual arousal. Rather, the effect is one of anxiety. Occasionally the anxiety is related to long-term psychological conflicts, but usually it can be the simple result of getting overwhelmed by the combined demands of children, husband, and job. The therapist must then help the woman either to see how she can reduce some of the demands on herself or lower her self-expectations. The sexual relationship suffers in such cases; when the woman has a long agenda, sex goes to the bottom of the list.

It's not that the woman doesn't expect to get around to sex, even though, in reality, she never does. She expects to be able to manage it all; she *has* to manage it all. She has the idea that all the other women in the new "Wonder Woman" role are able to accomplish everything, and when she does not, she begins to think of herself as inadequate and incompetent.

Thus, the career woman can suffer a loss of sexual desire either from an excessive elevation or lowering of mood. We have read for years about the "workaholic" male with a low sex drive, the man who lives for his work, an obsessive, joyless sort who represses all types of emotion. The industrious career woman may occasionally fall into this pattern, but more likely she is truly excited and emotional about her work, experiencing the genuine "high" that power, money, and success can bring. She is on the ultimate trip, beside which sex rates a dull and distant second place. Lacking the male physiological need for periodic physical release even amid the euphoria of cutting a deal, women in the throes of such a power trip are quite likely to forget they ever had a sex drive.

A woman who gets so involved in her career that she expends energy close to her limits may become genuinely fatigued, anxious, and depressed, and these emotional states will sap sexual desire even more than an overly zealous preoccupation with exciting work. Like Ulysses navigating between Scylla and Charybdis, the career woman must chart an emotional course between the excessively heady atmosphere of corporate climbing and the whirlpool of depression that forms in the wake of attempting and expecting more than one can reasonably achieve.

THE FRIGID MAN
Putting Men in Contact with Feelings

The "frigid man" is a term coined by Herbert H. Laube, Ph.D., assistant professor of family practice and community health at the University of Minnesota Medical School, to describe a typical male patient. Unlike the age-old "frigid woman," who is incapable of orgasm, Laube's male patient is unable to express emotion or affection.

"Frigid men," according to Dr. Laube, use rationalization as a means of coping, denying their own feelings as well as those of people around them whom they abuse psychologically. They lack compassion and a sense of responsibility. Some build their lifestyles around mechanical techniques, so intercourse, rather than intimacy, becomes the primary goal. They often make sexual overtures when, unconsciously, they would prefer emotional closeness.

Others have "workaholic" personalities and are driven toward goals of achievement, power, and control. They find it difficult to relax and be playful, so that even sex is regarded as a task to be completed or a goal to be attained.

Frigid men tend to form a competitive view of their surroundings and find it necessary to maintain strong defenses in order to ward off real or imaginary threats. They block out any type of emotion because they fear that feelings will make them vulnerable. They are threatened by modern women's greater expectations and demands, from which they emotionally withdraw.

Treatment involves guiding the frigid man in learning to identify and express his emotions. Once he is able to identify his feelings and examine the reasons for his behavior, he can begin to modify his actions. Treatment also consists of exploring self-destructive patterns and analyzing how he cares for his own needs. Acceptance of his own body and psyche must precede an ability to relate in a meaningful way to others.

Dr. Sheila Jackman of Albert Einstein Medical Center emphasizes that sometimes a man's reluctance to enter therapy for a sexual desire problem is not because he is ashamed to talk about a sexual deficiency but, on a more basic level, he resists admitting that he needs help of any sort, preferring instead to deal with the situation in a "manly" way by doing everything himself.

Yet, when the distress in a relationship caused by a desire problem becomes intense enough, men will accept help, even those from cultures where the male-dominant role is more firmly entrenched than in America. Dr. Jackman shared a case history about a patient of hers from Iran. "I told him what therapy was going to be like," she said, "and he begged me not to give him any instructions in front of his wife. *Begged* me. At least, he said, I should do it in a way so she wouldn't know they were being told what to do. So, I handled it in that way during the first session, kind of casually, but by the second session he didn't care, because the conflict was so great. 'Tell me what to do!' he said. Letting down—that was actually what the whole problem was about. It's *very* difficult for men."

There is a story that during World War II an American soldier in North Africa was amazed to see an Arabian woman walking across the sand several paces ahead of her husband. Knowing the ancient tradition of the tribe that required the woman to walk always behind her master, the soldier wondered what modern influence could have effected this revolutionary role reversal.

The soldier hurried to question the man, who explained very simply, "Land mines."

Sometimes the behavior changes quickly, but long-held attitudes take much longer to catch up.

ON AN "I"-LAND
The Era of Narcissism

"Doc, I'm going backward, instead of making progress," Rod says. "My goal was to find the right woman, get married, and have children. After years of looking, I'm not even interested anymore in a simple sexual relationship and I sure as hell won't have children if *that's* missing. And time's running out. I'm almost forty, even though I know I don't look it."

Rod looks it. Rod visits a tanning parlor, works out at a health club, and shops in the campus department, but while the carefully placed wisps of hair cover most of his bald spot, they can't cover his age.

"You do have a child," the therapist reminds him.

"Rachel? Sure, but she's with her mother in Boston, so I never see her. She might as well be somebody else's kid," Rod says.

"Boston was on this continent the last time I checked a map," the therapist says. "You could invite her for a visit."

"Nah, what's a twelve-year-old going to do hanging around my art gallery all day?" Rod scoffs.

"You might take a few days off," the therapist suggests.

"Aw, come on, Doc," Rod protests, "the gallery is my *life*. My friends come there. I meet my women there. Suppose some really terrific girl comes in. How can I ask her out, with a kid on my neck? Besides, Rachel is a stranger to me now. I send support checks, but I haven't spoken to her or written in years. She's as much past history as my ex is."

"You want a wife and child. You *had* a wife and child," the therapist notes. "Why did you divorce Sally?"

"Because she was holding me back," Rod explains. "I wasn't accomplishing anything. I could have been a great artist. I won a prize in college. Then, I got married and I was wasting my time on bullshit: driving Rachel to ballet class, picking up the dry cleaning, spending Saturdays at the zoo.

"I knew I was dissatisfied, but it wasn't until I got into therapy with this group that my eyes were really opened. The leader was this very charismatic guy, who could make you believe in yourself.

He said that we all had *infinite* potential, that we could be anything we wanted, but it was up to us to make it happen. Your main responsibility was 'looking out for number one' and not letting anybody deter you with guilt trips. Nobody could make you happy; you had to make yourself happy. Likewise, you couldn't make anyone else happy, so let them look out for themselves. I knew I needed my freedom to reach self-actualization and achieve my true potential."

"So, how's the artwork coming along?" the therapist asks casually.

Rod seems flustered. "Uh, well, I'm able to dab a bit here and there, but the gallery makes so many demands on my time. Of course, I have to draw on my own artistic talent in purchasing works, displaying them to best advantage, and pointing out their merits to customers."

Recovering his composure a little, Rod continues, "And then there's my apartment. *That's* a work of art in itself. You've got to visit it sometime! I've got this sumptuous circular bed, a magnificent ornate bar, dynamite rugs and drapes, and breathtaking erotic statues—in perfect taste, of course. When I take women there, they just fall onto that bed!"

"Have you taken any there lately?"

Rod shakes his head. "Like I said, Doc, I've just been getting less and less interested. That gallery of mine is a perfect girl-trap for the best of the breed. The women who come in are all wealthy, well dressed, smart, and beautiful. I feel like a vegetarian in a meat market now."

"Just what *do* you want in a wife?" the therapist probes.

"A beautiful face, a gorgeous figure, a bright intellect, a really nice personality," Rod enumerates. "Is that too much to ask?"

"What about Anita?" the therapist recalls. "You came close to marrying her . . . several times."

Rod frowns. "She's history. The final straw was when she went off and got a nose job she didn't need and silicone implants in her breasts. Her chest was so hard I felt like I was screwing the Venus de Milo."

The therapist silently wonders whether Anita's reconstruction might have been influenced by Rod's often-voiced praises of women with large busts and perfect features. Rod has a propensity for superlatives, whether describing merchandise or dating partners.

"About this desire problem of yours," the therapist says, "I know it's become acute lately, but has it been going on for a while? There's been a pattern to your interaction with women. You'll come in very excited about this beautiful woman you've met, then you'll come in describing the terrific lovemaking session you had with her, and a week or so later, you're raving about an entirely different woman. Do you lose desire for a woman after you've been to bed with her a couple of times?"

Rod looks perturbed. "No," he answers softly.

"Well, I just don't understand," the therapist presses. "There's something obviously wrong here. You've been on some kind of sexual carousel, three times around and changing mounts without ever getting anywhere, and now, not surprisingly, you want to get off. But if you truly found these women you dated so desirable and if the sex was really that great, why did you always stop seeing them after a few dates?"

"Don't you understand, Doc?" Rod pleads, almost in tears. "I show them the gallery, I show them the apartment, I take them to my favorite restaurants and museums—and that's it! That's the whole show! I'm suave, I'm relaxed up to that point, but I don't know what to do *next*. I'd have to show them the real me, and I'm nowhere near that good!"

When the Sexual Revolution merged with the Women's Liberation Movement, the Age of Narcissism was born. Its true parentage can be debated, although what was popularly called "The Me Generation" showed unmistakable characteristics that derived from those male-gratifying and female-emancipating movements.

The Sexual Revolution deemphasized, directly or indirectly, the importance of interpersonal relationships in sex. With its centerfolds and porn stars, it legitimized the "sex object," a person with no identity or purpose other than within the context of the sex act, even one single sex act. An object requires a subject to act upon it, to use it or take a stance with regard to it. Instead of people viewing the sex act as the joint responsibility of two people, without either of which nothing meaningful could occur, people saw it in terms of one person doing something to another and vice versa, alternately or concurrently.

The Women's Liberation Movement was, of course, absolutely

opposed to the idea of women being sex objects. But as feminist Midge Decter observed with some dismay, women had been converted from sexual objects to sexual subjects, with such frequently quoted imperatives from the Movement as "You are responsible for your own orgasms" and "Men don't give women orgasms, women have orgasms." Even Masters and Johnson wrote such sentiments as "Masturbating women concentrate on their own sexual demand without the distraction of a coital partner," demoting what was once termed a "lover" to a potential hindrance to sexual satisfaction.

The Age of Narcissism was not only concerned with sex. In the hot tubs of Esalen, people shed not only sexual inhibitions, but any hang-ups about coveting their neighbor's wives or goods, or about actually acquiring them. The est leaders preached, "You are responsible for everything that happens to you." Best-sellers bore titles like *Pulling Your Own Strings* and *Looking Out for Number One*— and by then everyone knew who "number one" was without having to consult a scorecard.

They used to say that no man is an island, but America had become an "I"-land, immersed in the greatest wave of egocentricity since Narcissus took the plunge. Suddenly, self-absorption was laudable, and if the new era eradicated hypocrisy among those who had always lived by the narcissistic code, it confused those who had always believed in a brothers'-keepers, not finders'-keepers, ethic.

While the spirit of narcissism might have helped some people increase their success in the business realm, nobody profited from it in the sexual area. Sex is a two-party endeavor, and when one person tries to go it alone without much concern for his partner, he generally gets as far as a one-wheeled bicyclist. Sex becomes superficial at best and conflicted at worst, with the inevitable result that people stop wanting it.

CATCH-44

The Problem of Being a Sexual Spectator

"What *do* women want?" Charles asks, exasperated. "I thought I was being considerate. I thought I was being a sensitive lover. I asked Alice if she enjoyed it. She gave me this little 'mmmm.' So, I said, 'I mean *really* enjoy it. Did you, uh, climax?'

"And instead of being appreciative that I care about her, Alice gets this attitude, like do I *have* to have an orgasm for you. 'No, not for me, for *you,*' I say. 'Oh, bullshit!' she says. 'You just want your masculinity validated by my orgasms!'

"Can you believe it? Before I split up with Laura, she was always complaining that I was so preoccupied with my own erections and orgasms that I was ignoring her. So, now I've got Alice and when I focus on *her,* I still get accused of being in this thing all for myself. Who wants this aggravation?

"Remember *Catch-22?* 'Catch-22' was that you couldn't be relieved of flying missions unless you were crazy, but you had to ask in order to be relieved, and anybody who asked to be relieved was obviously not crazy. It was a no-win situation. Well, what I'm caught in is twice as bad—it's 'Catch-44'!"

"We do seem to be confronted with a paradox here, don't we?" the therapist says. "Both of these ladies of yours were basically claiming you were narcissistic, not concerned about them, even though you tried to treat Alice quite differently. Okay, the situation with Laura seems to be the simpler of the two to understand. Even though you were ultimately concerned with Laura's satisfaction, you apparently got so preoccupied with what you were doing that you lost track of her. Maybe, in order to delay your orgasm, you even tried to detach yourself, do multiplication tables in your head to decrease your excitement."

"I recited the alphabet backward," Charles confesses.

"And maybe Laura was less concerned with your delaying ejaculation than she was in feeling close to you, being really united with you," the therapist points out.

"I don't doubt that," Charles agrees. "I learned my lesson with Laura, only I learned it too late to save the relationship. And I was determined not to make the same mistake with Alice. So I deliberately head in the opposite direction and I find myself up that old beloved creek again. Go figure! I can see how concentrating entirely on your own body, even with the best intentions, can be narcissistic. But don't tell me it's narcissistic to be concerned about what you're doing to someone else!"

"I think you just hit on something," the therapist says. "The essence of narcissism is a focus entirely on the self, right? *I* want, *I* think, *I* do. There's no sense of kinship with others, no real sharing.

The person is in the center of a lonely little world where others are only objects. Now, with Alice, your only thought was 'I want her to have an orgasm,' and you probably thought you were being unselfish. *You* wanted her to have an orgasm, more than anything else. And instead of feeling very close to her and merging with her, you were probably pulling back so you could observe her response carefully and make sure you achieved your aim. With Laura you were focusing exclusively on yourself, with Alice you were focusing exclusively on her. It was the same scenario, you were just shooting it with the camera at opposite ends."

Charles whistles. "Wow. No wonder I couldn't win. So, where do I put the camera now?"

"Scrap the camera," the therapist advises. "If you're always standing behind a lens, you can never really be in the picture. Once you start experiencing things in the 'we' frame, you'll forget all about yourself. When 'we' are responsible for what happens in bed, it's really impossible to place the blame on one person, the pressure goes down, and the desire goes up.

"Sex should be something you *lose* yourself in, not use as a vehicle for self-achievement. I guess sex is the only area in the world where you can escape from your self and all its demands. It would be a shame to waste that opportunity."

How can you tell whether you're acting in a healthy way or a narcissistic way in a sexual relationship? The watch word is the word "watch." To be truly involved, you must be a participant, not a spectator. A person who is marching in a parade is not watching the parade. A player in a game is not watching the game.

Are you watching your erection, your arousal, your orgasm? If you're watching your partner's erection, arousal, or orgasm, it's just as bad. Occasionally, this type of objective spectating does lead to improved performance, but it's invariably obtained at the exorbitant price of decreased intimacy.

Spectating, although it is done by crowds, is a lonely occupation, where one is passive and uninvolved in the action going on. Sex is a partnership activity, with the emphasis on "active."

Narcissists watch alone, partners act together. The two are really incompatible.

LA DIFFÉRENCE
Male versus Female Desire

"I am *really* ashamed of this," Leslie says, reaching into her saddlebag-sized purse. Leslie is a steely-eyed, self-assured, thirty-seven-year-old divorced public relations director. The therapist waits apprehensively to view the source of Leslie's embarrassment.

After a moment of rummaging, she withdraws a well-worn paperback, no more than two hundred pages long. Its cover depicts a bare-chested young man with a bandanna on his head and one gold earring, grasping a flame-haired young woman in a blouse that exposes the top 40 percent of her bosom. Her back arched, the damsel gazes at the man through heavy-lidded eyes, as though in a drug-induced stupor. His expression seems to reflect an incongruous mixture of overpowering lust and unshakable self-control. The title of the book, in scarlet, flourishing script, is *Bride of the Marauder.*

"After twenty years, I am still getting turned on by this garbage!" she exclaims angrily. "What's worse, it's the *only* thing that turns me on now. Me, the woman who organized a campus chapter of NOW, who volunteered time in a women's center, who actively campaigned for the passage of the ERA. I divorced a husband because I felt he was too locked into playing male and female stereotyped roles.

"And now I've got Conrad. I've been living with Conrad for eight months. When he comes home from work, Conrad picks up groceries. Most nights he does the cooking. He does the laundry on Saturdays. He's gentle and considerate in bed. He is the *ideal* man for the liberated woman, but I have just lost all sexual desire for him.

"A few weeks ago, Conrad and I went out to dinner with my friend, Margie, and this new guy she's been seeing. The man was an absolute pig. He kept pawing at her, even grabbing her bottom at one point, and making these lame jokes about male superiority. And Margie would just titter like a schoolgirl. He made a crack about her needing to be tamed and she wiggled and dared him to try it, obviously encouraging him. Intellectually, I was disgusted with Margie and with him, but so help me, on some level I was actually *envying* her. Margie's no pushover and I had fantasies of the two of them fighting, actually grappling physically, and him finally overpowering her and them making love in the middle of all this conflict and just having a marvelous time.

"After that, I was an absolute bitch to Conrad. I sulked. I criticized, I rejected him sexually. He finally exploded briefly, the only time he's ever lost control of his temper in all the time I've known him. And to my horror, I caught myself thinking, 'At last, he's acting like a *man.*' But Conrad turned and walked out, not even slamming the door. He returned with flowers in his hand and tears in his eyes, apologizing for the way he acted. And I forgave him and praised his being so sensitive and understanding, but this nasty little voice inside me kept saying, 'God, what a wimp!'

"Doctor, you are looking at a sick girl . . . I mean, *woman.* My sex drive and my head are on opposite courses. I can accept an occasional fantasy about being swept away by some male brute, but when the *only* time I feel sexual desire is in these masochistic daydreams, I've got a problem."

"Did you think you were a sick girl with a problem when you decided to divorce your husband?" the therapist asks casually.

Leslie looks at him skeptically. "No! It was probably the healthiest thing I've ever done. We were always fighting about his macho values and he was making my life miserable."

"So, why can't you accept your objections to Conrad, without chastising yourself for being 'masochistic'?"

"Because," Leslie explains patiently, "Conrad acts the way men *should* act."

The therapist shakes his head. "Not all the time. When he's unjustifiably provoked, a man, just like a woman, should get angry. You tried to test that, didn't you? A man should show enough independence to make his wishes at least known and enough strength to be able to back up his partner in a crisis. You'd certainly expect that much from a female friend, so why not from your man? Your ex-husband was too domineering and that was no good, but Conrad is too far at the other end of the scale."

Leslie jabs her index finger at the image of the paperback pirate. "And where is this guy on your scale, my fantasy lover? He makes my 'ex' look like PeeWee Herman."

"The pirate captain?" the therapist answers. "Actually, he's a rather sensitive sort, isn't he? He's vulnerable, empathetic, and *hopelessly* in love with the heroine."

"You've read this?" Leslie gasps.

"Oh, not that particular romance. But I'm familiar with the genre. According to the unvarying formula, the heroes are always tough and forceful but never really brutal, and they're wonderful lovers. Is it wrong for women to want take-charge men?"

"Women should want men who are equals," Leslie retorts.

"Equal in rights, maybe, but the idea of males and females being identical otherwise is ludicrous," the therapist says. "The core of heterosexuality is *heteros,* the differences, isn't it?"

"So, women should be passive, while men are aggressive?"

"You can be *receptive* without being passive," the therapist points out. "Women have a lot of power in determining which men they'll accept as lovers and when. Or would you prefer to be out pursuing as many partners as possible?"

"No!" Leslie says. "That would be aping the brainless macho behavior we've been putting down in men. Still, I shouldn't be looking for a powerful daddy to protect me."

"Men never want mothers to look after them?" the therapist counters.

Leslie explodes into a laugh. "Hah! All the time! No matter how strong they act or how much power they wield at work, they still want to be coddled whenever they catch a cold or bruise an ego."

"Well, love isn't just caring for someone, it's having someone who can take care of you. It's natural not to want to be a tigress twenty-four hours a day, but you have to love and trust someone to let yourself become a kitten with him for a while. A partner, male or female, should have some strength, or you might as well fight your way through life alone. The Women's Liberation Movement didn't mean to maintain the old male and female roles with the two sexes simply switching parts. Liberation means freedom to want—whatever attracts you, whatever turns you on, not what someone tells you that you should want," he says.

"So, what do I do with Conrad?" Leslie asks.

"Raise his consciousness," the therapist answers. "Sometimes men have to be encouraged to assert themselves, just as they have to be taught to consider what women want."

"Men wish women were as turned on as they are, as often as they are, but it looks like there is something physiologically differ-

ent in terms of male desire, a 'physical mood,' " observed Dr.
Sheila Jackman. "Men seem to have more of a desire for sex. Their
bodies are telling them they want it, not just their heads; it's not just
the psychological interest.

"For women, the attitude seems to be, 'If my head is into it, then
my body can get into it. If I feel okay about you, that makes me
amenable to wanting sex.' I hear it all the time from women: 'Once
I'm into it, it's fine, but until I get into it I couldn't care less.' So, it's
'Turn me on and I'm responsive, but if that doesn't happen to me, I
wouldn't even think about it.' "

Of the twenty-two sex therapists we interviewed in the course of
writing this book, eleven were women. While Masters and Johnson,
in their research on the arousal and orgasm stages of sexual response, emphasized the similarity between male and female physiological reactions, the therapists we spoke to about desire were more
impressed with the *difference* between the sexes.

While desire is mental, the physical changes in arousal (erection
and lubrication) can follow so quickly that they seem to be occurring simultaneously with the mental perceptions of desire. Therefore, it may seem, as Dr. Jackman puts it, that men's "bodies are
telling them they want it."

Men are prone to physical sensations in the genital area that
have nothing to do with the sexual response cycle, which begins
with desire. Unlike women, who produce a single mature egg per
month, men are constantly manufacturing sperm cells in their testicles. The sperm are stored in convoluted seminiferous tubules with
a combined length of several hundred *yards.* The periodic "horni-
ness" that men feel after several days (the number depending on
age, among other factors) results from this pressure buildup, as
newly formed cells are channeled into the packed tubules. Most
men would have extreme difficulty in turning off sexual desire in
the absence of a suitable partner, unless they were depressed or
experiencing very stressful circumstances. (Depression and stress
decrease testosterone secretion, which is what stimulates sperm
formation.) Thus, men without partners will usually indulge in
masturbation at least every few days, although those who are morally or esthetically opposed to masturbation might get their release
through spontaneous nocturnal emissions ("wet dreams").

As Dr. Jackman observes, women whose only desire fluctuation
may be a once-a-month premenstrual rise are "very different from

men, who say, 'If it isn't every three days, I am going to go off the wall.' "

Sandra Leiblum, Ph.D., co-director of the sexual counseling service at Rutgers Medical School in New Jersey, says that, in talking to women who were *not* in treatment for any type of sexual problem, she found that women can comfortably do without sex when there is no access to sexual partners and there is a period of enforced abstinence. Some of these women revert to masturbation, but others do not. When there is opportunity again in the form of a new lover, the women show a dramatic increase in sexual desire. "These were people who had adequate desire," she explains, "then simply didn't have an opportunity for sex, and they got along very comfortably for a year, two years, five years without any sexual partners just because of a lack of opportunity. Then suddenly they meet someone new and find their desire is extremely high."

A SOFTER PRODUCT
Dual Desires in the Modern Woman

Yang and Yin are the earth's two elemental forms, as conceived by the ancient Chinese, dividing the entire world between them. Yang holds sway over what is positive, spiritual, active, light, lively —and male. Yin holds dominion over the negative, earthy, passive, dark, dead—and female. It should be apparent how, with this sort of underlying philosophy, women in China held little authority.

The famous psychoanalyst, Carl Jung, subscribed to the notion of male and female principles, but believed that each man carried within him elements of a female personality (the *anima*) and every woman had her male side (the *animus*). Feminists generally oppose the notion that specific traits can be designated as male or female, particularly since the so-called male traits, such as assertiveness, strength, and action, seem patently more desirable than "female" traits such as sensitivity, passivity, and softness. They have encouraged a movement toward androgyny in both men and women, an attitude that would incorporate the best traits traditionally attributed to either one sex or the other.

There would have been less controversy if people had regarded the two sets of complementary traits under headings other than "masculine" and "feminine." Jung, for example, might have easily utilized his *logos* principle (the rational, organizing force) and *eros* principle (the intuitive, loving, emotional force) to designate the two groups of traits, rather than equating *logos* with male and *eros* with female. Certainly all of us, regardless of sex, need a full set of these principles in order to deal with our introspective inner world and our intellectually challenging, diversely populated environment. Considering that the major European languages (English excepted, of course) divide all the world's objects and qualities into masculine and feminine genders, it seems impossible to escape the legacy of Yang and Yin. Many of us go on speaking of masculine and feminine traits with never a pang of guilt.

Constance Avery-Clark, Ph.D., a therapist at the Masters and Johnson Institute in St. Louis, feels that working women are more likely than homemakers to develop both types of approaches to life. Yet, while this duality is a healthy one, it poses problems. "They've got a frame of reference for both and they need to express both. And the only time they can express the more feminine, less-task-oriented approach is when they get home," Dr. Avery-Clark explains. "I think they may go from one extreme to the other."

These women have developed the two sets of attitudes, but they have difficulty integrating them. When they are in touch with their "masculine" side, they shut down the "feminine," and vice versa. When they get home, they want to discard the tough, dynamic personality and slip into their more passive, sensitive identity. If a woman's mate originally came to know her in her work role, the man might be understandably perplexed by the seeming dependency. She, likewise, may not be able to understand why he is having so much difficulty meeting her needs.

Dr. Avery-Clark comments, "We often see women who are powerful and smart and who say they want a male who is more androgynous—a working man who is able to be sensitive to her feelings. He should like to spend time with her in nondemanding activities, such as cuddling and holding, without necessarily going on to intercourse.

"And yet, when the guy actually does that and is more sensitive and emotional with her, she has trouble seeing him as a man. Many women report they've lost interest in a man once he did give up that high-powered job to spend a little more time at home with her and the kids, because she is having a hard time now labeling him as a 'real man.' She has difficulty getting excited around him."

Why is there this apparent paradox between the professed wish of many modern women for a sensitive, empathetic man and their sexual attraction to the powerful, dominant man who embodies all the traditional "virile" traits? The paradox disappears if we combine the two images and produce a man who retains the paternal power and dominance, but exercises it in a way that protects and contributes to the welfare of the woman he loves.

Such a man would allow a woman to regress into blissful, secure dependency at the end of a hard day's employment, a dependency that was far less discouraged during *her* childhood and adolescence than in her brothers, who would have been indoctrinated with the virtues of male self-sufficiency. Unfortunately, the tough-tender blend of traits that would enable a man to meet the complex demands for both providing empathetic love and care as well as maintaining the highest standards of earning power by outworking his competitors is difficult for the male to achieve and the female to perceive. Too often a man's decision to ease up on his hard-driving ambition and spend more time doing housework and child care results in a lowering of his own self-esteem and, even worse, his mate's view of him as being less adequate as a husband.

Women who respect the sensitive, noncompetitive man but who can turn on only to a more aggressive, domineering type are not so terribly different from men who can love and respect a maternal, mature woman but get sexually excited only over a lingerie-clad seductress. If the images that excite us in fantasy seem to be immature object choices, it is because we first encountered desire when we *were* immature, as adolescents. As we grow older, we develop our mental appreciation of those traits in the opposite sex that are found only in the mature: empathy, intellect, fidelity, achievement. The figures that fuel our desire, however, often fail to keep pace with our intellectual ideals. Why? Because the old fantasy images are still exciting, and we don't change what works. So, for many, a split develops between people we respect and people we desire.

To resolve the split, it is necessary to include consciously the more mature, admirable types in our fantasies. There will be an initial resistance, a feeling that they somehow do not belong in the primitive realm of desire, accustomed as we are to having that region populated by the long-term inhabitants present since our early adolescence. But if we let the professor replace the football hero in real life, one must replace the other in fantasy as well. Sex acts are part of real life, but desire resides in fantasy and our lovers must have access to both places.

❦ 5 ❦

Two to Tangle

Problems in Relationships

The old axiom says that women give sex in exchange for love and men give love in exchange for sex. In reality, men and women need both sex and love. Sometimes love leads to sex and sometimes sex leads to love. Often, a couple on the long road between sex and love ends up stranded someplace where there doesn't seem to be much of either.

Would any sane person *not* want sex and love? By now, we obviously know that a lack of desire for sex is very common; avoiding intimacy may be almost as prevalent a malady in our complex society. When emotional issues involving anger or a need to control are encountered on the route to sexual fulfillment, the journey is interrupted until these conflicts are resolved. And sometimes couples find themselves on an endless rocky road that seems to be leading nowhere.

"I think I figured out Jennifer's problem. It's because of the unusual spot where her desire is located," Mark says. Mark is a thirty-one-year-old pharmacist, a burly, bearded man with a gentle, teasing sense of humor. He and Jennifer have been living together for about ten months. "It's in her finger. See, most people would say sexual desire is located somewhere in the head. I guess some very sexy people might claim they feel it somewhere in the pelvic area first, and someone very romantic might say desire is in the heart.

"But not Jennifer. Oh no, she's a very rare, very challenging case. *Her* sexual desire is focused right here." Mark holds up his left hand, fingers spread, and with his right index finger, points at the fourth finger of the extended hand. "I think it's that ring. It must be too tight. As soon as I put that engagement ring on her finger, it choked off the sexual desire that usually flows out from there and circulates all over her body. That ring just cut off all the desire, as if I had closed the valve on a water pipe."

Jennifer, a thirty-year-old blonde, slightly overweight medical receptionist, squirms and clenches her left fist, the one where a modest diamond twinkles unobtrusively. "Do you want it back?" she asks Mark. "Do you really think it's that simple, off and on like a faucet? I think the problem is a little more complex than that."

"I don't!" Mark insists. "I don't mean, of course, that Jennifer will immediately become overwhelmed with sexual desire if we break the engagement, but that commitment is at the heart of the problem, nothing else. It's a fear of intimacy."

"That's psychological gobbledygook," Jennifer protests. "What the hell does it mean? I haven't seen anybody else in over a year. Even before you moved in with me and gave up your place, you were at my apartment more nights than at your own. Did anything really change since we got engaged? Did I learn anything about you or you about me that we didn't already know? Do we do anything differently?"

"Nevertheless, I'm sure that's it," Mark says bluntly. "I don't think you want to get married and I'm not sure there's anything I can do to change that, although I'd like to. Come on, Jennifer, do you really want to get married, yes or no?"

"I'm not sure," she says honestly. "Is *anybody* ever sure? Maybe the happy idiots in the movies, who gush, 'Oh yes, darling, yes!' Or the person who wants it first. Come to think about it, isn't it always that way with marriage, one person wants it first and gets the other to agree? We've been talking a lot about sexual desire, how one person basically initiates sex and how rarely desire strikes both people at the same instant. One wants it first, then the other either gets into it or, at least, goes along with it.

"Well, I think it's the same with marriage. Most of the time they say the man proposes, but I know from friends and relatives that it's usually the woman who says, 'Listen, where's this relationship going? Are you really serious?' You negotiate sex more than a hundred times a year and marriage maybe once in a lifetime, but it's the same thing. Somebody wants it and the other agrees, even if they *both* really want it."

"And you said yes, but you're not sure you want it," Mark says.

"Mark, how can *you* be sure?" Jennifer sighs. "A woman has so much more to lose when it doesn't work out. She could be stuck with children, like my mom was when my father walked out. If you have kids, you've got to put your career on hold for a little while. Not that I've got any sort of great career, but I do like my job. I've been there for years, and if I left, I don't know if I'd be able to come back. And even discounting kids, it would be a lot harder for me to find a decent man six or ten years from now than it would be for you to find somebody else."

Mark's coarse features break into a grin. "Sure, everybody wants a pharmacist," he chuckles. "The hypochondriacs, the girls from the methadone program, the ladies who work the street and come in for Flagyl and ampicillin. Where would I meet another *healthy* one? You don't trust me, do you?"

"It's not you, Mark, it would be anybody," Jennifer protests. "I'll admit that until I agreed to get married, I did have the feeling that the door was open, that I could leave the relationship anytime I wanted. There were no strings attached. Sometimes I felt a little insecure, wondering if the love we felt for one another was really going to last, if we'd always be there for one another, but it was easier to accept. It didn't *have* to work. Now it does and that scares me. Is *that* what you call 'fear of intimacy'?"

"Sure," Mark readily agrees. Then, less sure, he adds, "Maybe it's a fear of nonintimacy, that you can't sustain the intimacy you know you're going to need." He looks at the therapist. "Not to digress, Doctor, but I see a parallel here with sexual desire and performance. If you go to a massage parlor or have a drunken one-night stand, you really don't give a damn about how well you do, you're just enjoying yourself. When you really want to please a partner, it gets a lot tougher, more like an important job, and desire doesn't come as easily.

"When you're in a relationship, at the beginning you say, 'This is great, and I really hope it's going to stay this way.' But it doesn't *have* to stay that way. Once you make a commitment, then it becomes a 'must,' and that's scary."

"It's hard to feel desire in a scary situation," the therapist notes.

Mark turns to Jennifer again. "Yeah, but it wasn't as if the minute you put that ring on, the door was locked. First of all, you couldn't have just walked out that door—it's *your* apartment! I'd have to move out, and that might take a little time, at least to remove all my stuff, if not my body. What about the things we've bought for the house since we've been living together? We'd have to work something out there. No strings attached? Hell, we've got more strings than Bil Baird's marionettes backed by Mantovani! Strings get attached one at a time. Chains are formed a link at a time, cages are built one bar at a time. Still, they never built a cage without a door or a lock without a keyhole.

"So, what's the fear about, Jennifer? That I'll escape or that you won't be able to?"

"Maybe . . . maybe the biggest fear of all," Jennifer replies, "is that we'll be unhappy in a situation that we *should* leave, and somehow not be able to do it, even though there's nothing to stop us. Is that too far-out, Doctor?"

The therapist shakes his head. "As a matter of fact, I read a play once with that theme. A man and two women were locked in a comfortable room and began tormenting one another. They desperately came to need one another for psychological validation; their very identities depended on it, but of course, they were doomed to failure. When the locked door suddenly flew open, none of them could walk out. There was nobody else in the universe for them; they were stuck with one another, as hopeless as the situation was. The play was *No Exit* by Jean-Paul Sartre. And the comfortable room was hell."

Fear of intimacy is, at first glance, a very paradoxical term. Almost everyone would agree that intimacy is an unequivocally good thing to have, so why should you be afraid of it? Intimacy means the ability to share openly with another, to know each other's innermost thoughts, feelings, and secrets. It requires trust, respect, and even love.

Are there other positive things that people fear? Do they fear success, wealth, health? In some cases, yes. Most doctors, for example, have seen patients with peptic ulcers or heart attacks who have anxieties about getting better, because the illness has given them a respectable excuse to avoid all manner of stressful or tedious obligations. People fear success, particularly in the case of women, because they fear a corresponding loss of love, nurturing, or desirability; success invariably means increased responsibility, as does wealth.

COSTELLO: I would never marry a pretty girl. A pretty girl might run away.

ABBOTT: A homely girl might run away, too.

COSTELLO: Who cares?

That simple Abbott and Costello routine seems to encapsulate perfectly the essence of the conflict over intimacy, over truly caring for a person. The more satisfying something is, the more excruciating would be the pain of losing it. If you can get by with something in which you have very little emotional investment, you need not fear losing it.

The inherent absurdity in this argument, despite its popularity, is the implication that the ideal state would be not having any feeling at all and the ultimate goal would be coma or death. There might be a few ascetic sects who aspire to a state of spiritual numbness, but most of us want to experience life with a bit of gusto, even if it involves the risk of a few bruises and aches.

The fear of intimacy is basically a fear of failure, rather than fear of a loss of a cherished person. There is, admittedly, a loss of autonomy and independence with increased intimacy. You cannot do whatever you want with total disregard for the partner's feelings once intimacy is achieved, but only a callous cad would be that insensitive in a less intense relationship. As Professor Henry Higgins protested to the newly liberated Eliza Doolittle: "Independence? That's middle-class blasphemy. We are all dependent on one another, every soul of us on earth." Independence is an illusion and no one can go about the world doing and saying exactly what he or she pleases without landing in jail or a mental hospital.

The fear of intimacy is usually rooted in the vulnerability it involves. If you trust a person with your secrets, will he or she betray them? How do you know the person will not abandon you once you have entrusted your happiness to his or her care? And sometimes, can you trust *yourself* not to walk out, not to betray the loved one? Often, the bigger concern is whether *you* can keep such an important commitment.

Fear of intimacy and fear of abandonment may seem to be polar opposites, yet it is usually those who dread intimacy that would be most vulnerable to fear of abandonment should they allow themselves to become emotionally close to another. Once dependency is acknowledged, fear of losing the partner takes hold.

In many cases of sexual desire discrepancy, a fear of intimacy/ abandonment reinforces the interaction. One partner refuses sex because it increases intimacy and the other regards this as abandonment. The rejected partner then presses for sexual activity to gain reassurance that he or she will not be abandoned. This pressure causes the partner who fears intimacy to back off even further and the pursuer to become more threatened and obsessed with sex. At this point, sexual desire is no longer the motivating factor in either the distancer or the pursuer. Desire has been relegated to a distant second place and sexual contact or a lack of it results from attempts to secure the partner's devotion or to escape perceived entrapment.

"Marriage is to me apostasy, profanation of the sanctuary of my soul, violation of my manhood, sale of my birthright, shameful surrender, ignominious capitulation, acceptance of defeat," protests Shaw's John Tanner, moments before he agrees to marry Ann Whitefield. The humor of his speech lies in its vehemence, not its irrelevance, because intimacy does require admitting someone else into the innermost recesses of our souls. As an adolescent, Tanner had broken off a budding love relationship with Ann because he felt himself acquiring a soul, which was something Ann would "never have let me call my own." As a responsible adult, he can no longer run from intimacy; marriage and parenthood require the sacrifice of privacy and the risk of vulnerability.

Therapists frequently see men or women who have carried on affairs for years with someone who is married. The unmarried lovers seem to be inhumanly capable of selfless love and dedication to their married partners, willing to accept limited moments, waiting patiently at their beck and call. Yet, so often, when the married one finally escapes marriage through divorce or widowhood, the partner either balks at marriage or soon after marrying their long-term paramour becomes disenchanted and passionate sexual activity deteriorates into lack of desire. The most extreme example, though not uncommon, is the lover who remains faithful to someone who is in prison for years, but who flees the relationship once the felon is free and able to engage in intimacy.

People who fear intimacy will experience sexual desire only in situations where intimacy has not yet developed or is restricted by the partner's limited availability. Sexual desire wanes in any atmosphere that provokes anxiety, and to the person with fear of intimacy, a truly close relationship holds more terror than a closet does to a claustrophobe.

Intimacy is vital to sexual desire, especially in the later stages of a relationship. It is an unpleasant, unromantic reality, but sexual desire *does* naturally decrease between partners as they become accustomed to one another and other demands and pressures arise. A compatible couple has to be able to shift into second gear and utilize the advantages of intimacy, the antidote to the sexual apathy that plagues long-standing relationships. Intimacy works because it gives the partners the confidence to communicate freely about their sexual likes and dislikes and the courage to experiment with variations and innovations in their lovemaking that can increase excitement.

As we hopefully emerge from the "Me Generation" into the "We Generation," a new emphasis on intimacy would be undoubtedly preferable to the old self-actualization ethic, which inherently blocked compromise and commitment.

Sex is a form of immediate intimacy. The intimacy may be purely physical or imperfect emotionally, but the closeness is inevitable. You can see how avoidance of intimacy quickly translates to avoidance of sex and a lack of desire for it. A sympathetic partner who is capable of providing true emotional intimacy is, unfortunately, not the perfect solution when intimacy is precisely what is being avoided.

The solution must start with old "number one," even if these days "one" doesn't rank as high as it used to.

SO CLOSE AND YET SO FAR APART
Male and Female Attitudes About Closeness

"If you take a look at the people who don't want to have sex, the sex that they are having hasn't been worth having," says Dr. David M. Schnarch of Louisiana State University. "When you have something good, you don't have to sell it to people—they will knock you down to get two helpings of it."

What constitutes good sex? It's a very subjective judgment, and skillful technique culminating in mutual orgasm might not be sufficient to qualify. When we speak of desire discrepancy, we refer to the frequencies with which the respective partners prefer sexual activity to occur. There can also be discrepancy between the *type* of sexual interaction partners desire, with regard to the amount of psychological intimacy they bring to the bedroom.

Much has been said about how women's new assertiveness concerning their sexual desire has led to decreased desire in men who are threatened by a perceived demand that they cannot meet. This fear is usually interpreted as the man's inability to meet the desired frequency of relations in a partner with a higher level of libido. Overlooked is the issue of the *quality* of sex women want. Women have learned not only to ask for sex, but to ask for it on their terms, to require involvement of an emotional as well as a physical nature. This is more likely to threaten men than a request for increased frequency. While sex without emotional intimacy may be considered shallow and unsatisfying to some, for others too much emphasis on the personal relationship during sex can reduce its erotic appeal and subsequently lower desire.

Couples who are able to integrate the need for emotional closeness with their sexual desire will probably engage in sex more frequently, since they crave physical closeness even without a wish to have intercourse and this very closeness will often evoke desire of a more erotic nature.

Despite the efforts of the Women's Liberation Movement to get us to view men and women as essentially the same, there are experts who feel there are some basic, pervasive differences in the emotional needs of men and women that can interfere with sexual desire.

Dr. Daniel Goldberg, a psychologist at the Center for Sexual Health in Cherry Hill, New Jersey, sees men as preoccupied with autonomy and women with intimacy. "Women are toxic to distance and men are toxic to overcloseness," he observes. "While men have a hard time with intimacy, women have a hard time with independence, with boundaries and separateness. Women can't tolerate breathing space."

According to Dr. Goldberg's observations, if men get claustrophobic in a committed relationship, women seem to have a corresponding agoraphobia, a fear of spaces in the togetherness. Dr. Goldberg feels that women are always pushing forward and men pushing away, and "that movement is the central issue of low sexual desire."

Dr. Goldberg does not believe that men are incapable of experiencing intimacy, but rather they cannot verbally express what the experience is. He views this as analogous to the development of speech in children, who develop a receptive (understanding) form of language before they can express themselves in words.

Peter Kilmann, Ph.D., director of the Human Sexuality Project at the University of South Carolina, likewise thinks that men and women differ categorically in their use of sex as part of a relationship. He says that women are focused more on emotional closeness, a feeling of reassurance about themselves being loved. For men, it seems to be a sense of reinforcing their masculinity, feeling they are important as men. According to Dr. Kilmann, the type of validation a man wants would increase his ability to be self-sufficient, apart from others. Women want to be validated in the context of a loving union with one significant other person.

Is the apparent difference in the emotional attitudes men and women bring to a sexual relationship based on some sort of inherent physical difference, the product of centuries of discriminatory attitudes in raising male and female children, or inaccurate sexist stereotyping? It is interesting that males and females differ not only in sexual organs, but in skeletal structure and even brain function. In the left (dominant) hemisphere of the brain, verbal and logical processes are stored sequentially in time; the right hemisphere is more specialized for the processing of visual patterns or spatial relationships as they exist at any particular time. Women seem to be more left-hemisphere-influenced than men, who are more adept at the functions under the control of the right hemisphere.

Men are far more attracted to specific physical features of a partner, whether heterosexual or homosexual, and fetishism, an erotic attraction to objects, seems to be an exclusively male deviation. Women, in an apparent correlation with the left hemisphere's time sequences, are less impressed by physical attributes and more concerned with what a partner has said or done in the past, or promises to do in the future. Men would thus be expected to be more emotionally detached from sex partners, while women would incorporate sexual attraction into the context of an ongoing or prospective relationship.

This difference in the wiring of the neuroanatomical apparatus helps to explain some of the characteristics of sexual desire more peculiar to one sex than the other. One female patient said about her husband, "All I have to do is start putting on my stockings in front of him. He immediately gets turned on and wants me to stop getting dressed so we can have sex." Many men who seem impervious to candlelight, soft music, and affectionate words will become instantly aroused by the sight of a pair of naked breasts or buttocks or by a black lace garter belt. On the other hand, while women may appreciate a trim male physique, rarely will they feel instant desire at the sight of an erect penis, a hairy chest, or black silk pajamas. It is the women who report erotic feelings that develop over the course of a leisurely evening of intimate conversation, relaxation, and nonsexual caresses.

If there are truly differences in male and female brains (the organs of sexual desire) comparable to the differences in the genitals (the organs of arousal and orgasm) then the treatment of desire disorder cannot ignore them in hopes of promoting an ideologically credible but unnatural equality of desire between the sexes. We do not mean to imply that the surest course toward lasting sexual desire is for men and women to follow passively their biological proclivities. If men continually isolate desire from intimacy and if women demand an excessive amount of intimacy to validate their desire, dissatisfaction and hostility will soon develop in relationships, and nothing is more detrimental to sexual desire than an unhappy relationship. When lack of desire results from failure to achieve intimacy or avoidance of it through fear of loss of autonomy, the focus of treatment must be on the interpersonal relationship.

THE EIGHT-LEGGED HERMAPHRODITE
The Problem of Excessive Togetherness

The ancient Greeks believed that humans were once two-headed creatures with both male and female body parts, possessing four legs and four arms. In the course of time, they split apart into separate beings, male and female. This loss of half their bodies caused them great distress and ever since there has been an incessant longing and constant attempt to merge the bodies again, which accounts for the intense power of sexual attraction and the sexual desire it universally evokes.

According to this legend, there was no sexual desire before the split into two separate sexes. There was no autoerotic activity because the male and female parts were already merged, entirely contained within the boundaries of one self.

Ironically, couples who have too much emotional intimacy can suffer as much from desire disorder as those who have no emotional intimacy. By "too much" we mean those who never seem to be apart from one another. Take, for example, two college students who share the same bed, eat all their meals together, take as many of the same courses as they can, share the same friends, and participate in the same recreational activities. They are one another's best friend and they reach the stage where they can practically communicate by mind reading. Strangely enough, sexual desire wanes and evaporates, although they truly love one another. One sex therapist wrote that a young woman involved in such a relationship said, "When I kiss him, it's like kissing a mirror."

Sexual desire involves a certain amount of tension. While occasionally someone might experience an overwhelming "lust at first sight" desire for a person he or she has just met, the feeling usually grows with time, whether we are talking about time between first meeting and first intercourse or simply the time from the first twinges of desire on a given day to its fulfillment with one's steady partner. This accounts for the difficulty where a low-desire partner is trying to increase desire (the psychological wish, not the physical arousal) for a partner who has been thinking about it for hours.

Emotional intimacy also depends on tension to some extent. Looking forward to being with a special person, telling that someone about the things you've been doing since your last time together, learning about a loved one's experiences and feelings shared with no one else bring about a flooding of warm sensations and ego enhancement that just are not possible if you already know one another's every thought and action.

This explains the paradox of intimacy through independence. Dr. Peter Fagan, associate director for the Sexual Behavior Consultation Unit at Johns Hopkins Medical Center, says that intimacy is being able to share blurring of the boundaries. This cannot happen if the boundaries are too sharp and rigid to allow blurring nor can it occur if there are no real boundaries because dependency has eroded them away. Men, in general, are more often guilty of keeping distance, while women "crowd" their men, but there are certainly significant numbers of women who defend against closeness and men who seek dependency in a relationship.

Kahlil Gibran, in *The Prophet,* advises newlyweds to allow for spaces in their togetherness, pointing out that one tree cannot flourish if it is forever in the shade of another. When it comes to sound counsel about keeping a union vital and thriving, the prophet is never at a loss for words.

THE CONTROLLING PARTNER
Sexual Pursuit and Avoidance

Garry looks like a pudgy, scared rabbit. "Look," he appeals to Ruth, his spouse, "I am trying to improve things, but it doesn't help when I get home, still keyed up from work, without a chance to unwind, and you're already making sexual advances, with that green peignoir."

Ruth wrinkles her tiny freckled nose with a sniff of disdain. "*I* work, too, after all, and I don't think that a little closeness is such a bad way to unwind. Besides, what's so sexy about a loose-fitting gown?"

"She knows what I mean," Garry assures the therapist. "Come on, Ruth, you know that green dress is a signal: 'Okay, you've got the green light! Go, baby, go!' "

"You seem to feel that Ruth pressures you," the therapist observes.

Garry nods. "She's making overtures at least four times a week now. If it's not the green peignoir, it's a bottle of wine or a 'let's go to bed early, honey.' "

"And you want me to settle for 'Saturday Night Live' and the rest of the week dead?" Ruth asks.

"I didn't say that," Garry moans. "But look, I'll admit I'm at fault. We were making love as little as once or twice a month, and you usually had to initiate it. Things have been improving—slowly, I'll concede, but they're better. At this stage, don't you think twice a week would be a fair compromise?"

"More than fair," she agrees patiently. "But if I ask twice, I'm not going to score twice. You've got to say no two or three times before you feel guilty enough to make the effort. With that sort of batting average, I have to try to interest you just about *every* night to ensure succeeding twice."

Garry considers this for a moment. "What you're saying sort of makes sense; yet, if you think back, I was actually getting into it more when you weren't trying so hard. Hell, Ruth, do you think I enjoy saying, 'Maybe later,' when I know that I'm feeling absolutely nothing but a little queasy?"

"You know that once we actually get into the bedroom you can relax and get interested," she responds. "It's happened before and it can happen again."

Garry sighs. "Yeah, but you've got such a head start that I never really am able to catch up." Ruth looks puzzled, so Garry explains, "You've been feeling desire for an hour or more, so you get aroused in no time flat. I'm just beginning to feel desire and start-ing to get aroused and by then you're really hot and I can tell you want me to go in. I'm wishing I had a little more time to *get* into it before I *go* into it and worried about whether I'm really ready. You climax and most of the time I'm relieved to just withdraw."

"I guess the head start should go to the one with the handicap," Ruth says. "Can I trust you to get things started once in a while, if I don't?"

"I think you can," Garry says. "I don't think I was all that turned off to sex when we got into our rut; maybe just a little pressured by work. But the more I started running away from your advances, the more threatening sex became. Do you think, as a man, I like having you control our sex life?"

"Is that how you feel, Garry?" the therapist asks.

"Sure," he affirms. "Ruth makes all the advances. She's in charge."

"How often would you be having sex if Ruth were in complete control?"

The question stops Garry in his tracks and he senses that he's turning around. "Well, if she had her way, I suppose four times a week, maybe even every night."

"And if you had control?"

"Right now, I guess we'd be having sex once a week, a little more or less."

"And how often *have* you two been making love?" the therapist asks.

Garry nods slowly. "Wow, I see your point. Ruth isn't really in control at all, is she?"

"I would be if I could be," Ruth drawls ruefully.

"Want to give her the reins for a while?" the therapist suggests. "You decide when you might have enough desire to take a risk and she'll decide whether or not to let you."

"Maybe I should buy myself some green pajamas to make my new role easier," Garry says.

Garry and Ruth are a good example of a basically compatible couple who fell into a maladaptive pattern of dealing with desire discrepancy so that the situation got worse instead of better.

Garry got further encumbered by espousing a common fallacy that lowers self-esteem and further inhibits desire. Ask people whether the person in a relationship with the higher or lower desire level determines the frequency of sex and most will automatically blurt, "The one with higher desire." Others might argue that if the low-desire partner always complied, the high-desire partner would be determining the sexual frequency; however, it is the acquiescence rather than the initiation that ultimately sets the standard. A couple will never have sex *more* frequently than either partner wishes, but will nearly always have sex less than what is considered optimal by the more desirous partner.

So, the partner with the lower level of sexual desire *always* controls the frequency of intercourse. Once that is understood and acknowledged, efforts can be made to increase or take maximum advantage of whatever desire the lower-level mate has.

Garry illustrated the futility of his wife's trying to increase the frequency of sexual activity by stepping up her advances. Garry merely stepped up his retreat. What might have begun as a simple discrepancy between Garry's and Ruth's ideal frequencies escalated into a more serious problem as Ruth's pursuit conditioned a sexual aversion response in Garry.

This couple also ran into two common dilemmas: "Catch Up" and "Catch Me." The "Catch Up" paradox occurs because the initiator is already ahead with respect to desire and, with this head start, is also more quickly aroused. The low-desire partner, at a disadvantage already, never really closes the gap. The problem is even worse when the man is running on ahead, because he will usually want to effect penetration and proceed to orgasm before the woman is sufficiently aroused, leaving her frustrated and even less desirous of a repeat engagement.

"Catch Me" is a game of pursuit. The high-desire partner pursues and the low-desire partner retreats. If you ever watch two children run where an obviously faster child keeps taunting and running out of reach, you know what eventually happens: the pursuer gets disgusted and refuses to play, at which point the distancer draws progressively closer to the original pursuer. Unless the low-desire partner has no desire whatsoever or has an aversive disorder, there can be a reversal of pursuit roles, if the high-desire partner has the insight to break up the pattern by stopping the chase.

SEASONS CHANGE, PEOPLE DON'T
Inherent Levels of Sexual Desire

"What you see is what you get!" This laugh line was popularized a couple of decades ago by comedian Flip Wilson and it struck such a responsive chord that it was incorporated into our idiomatic vocabulary. Ironically, Wilson usually delivered the flippant phrase when costumed in "drag" as the sassy female character, Geraldine; anyone who expected to get the curvaceous woman would be shocked at discovering Geraldine's Flip-side.

When a couple, such as Garry and Ruth, have a desire discrepancy, they can work toward a more mutually satisfying sex life by helping the low-desire partner to maximize desire, but it would not be realistic to expect someone like Garry to raise his inherent desire level to that of a high-libido partner like Ruth. When you look at Peter, what you see is what you get, although what you *do* with what you get can improve the situation.

Sometimes couples have sexual problems because the level of desire they saw during courtship was *not* what they got in the partner once he or she was in the home.

Dr. Maj-Britt Rosenbaum, director of the Human Sexuality Center of Long Island Jewish Medical Center in New Hyde Park, New York, observes: "The saying 'what you see is what you get' is true, but sometimes you see *more* than you're going to get during the courtship period when there can be a real wish for bonding, to get close to somebody." This desperate wish for closeness can masquerade as sexual desire, not only to the person being pursued, but even to the mind of the would-be bonder. Once the security of having a committed mate is established, the mask is dropped and desire drops with it. Even without ulterior motivation, sexual desire can be higher in the earliest stages of a relationship because of the novelty and excitement of uncertainty. Familiarity doesn't breed contempt, it breeds apathy.

Dr. Rebecca Liswood, former executive director of the Marriage Counseling Service of Greater New York and one of the first medical experts to discuss sexual problems on radio and television, would say that there are six people in every marriage, two real and four imaginary ones. There's the husband as he is, as the type of husband he would like to be, and the type of husband his wife would love him to be. The wife, likewise, has one real and two imaginary counterparts. The real people are the ones who prevail in most cases and the success of a sexual relationship generally depends on each spouse trying to work things out with the real partner, not with his or her "wannabe."

There are often problems with the marriage contract. If you are or have been married, take out your copy of the contract and check it. You don't have one? Of course you don't, unless you signed a prenuptial agreement, and those deal only with property, not personal relationships. The contract that we carry in our imaginations contains what we promised to put into a union and what we expect to get out of it from our partner. It probably also contains a hidden and unenforceable clause that stipulates the person we marry will change after we marry him.

But people either don't change at all or they change very slowly. High-desire people often harbor unrealistic expectations that their spouses will develop in time the same enthusiasm for frequent sex that comes so naturally to themselves. Most low-desire people (the exception being those with aversive desire disorder) do not have any impairment for enjoyment once sex is engaged in. There are people who truly enjoy movies or Chinese restaurants but never go to one unless someone else suggests it. A spouse with a taste for Oscar-quality roles and egg rolls would simply make sure to invite the partner out and not worry about whose idea it was.

Except for cases in which a major psychological block is removed from someone destined to be a high-desire person, there are limits to the extent to which an inherent desire level can be raised. A man wouldn't marry a woman whose looks rated a 3 on his girl-watchers' 1-to-10 scale and expect her to become a 10 after marriage. Losing a few pounds and coloring her hair might get her up to a 5, but nowhere near a 10 spot. Yet, people somehow expect a miraculous jump in sexual desire to occur after marriage, even though there's nothing you can buy at the cosmetics counter or order from the Sears catalog to help the situation.

Some spouses will not be satisfied with a perfectly acceptable improvement in sexual frequency because they want their partners to initiate sex "spontaneously" and to have as high an interest in sex as their own. Results are more important than enthusiasm, in the bedroom as well as the workplace. There are enthusiastic workers who never accomplish anything significant and placid workers who consistently perform at top level. Smart bosses would choose the latter. Desire is an intention, sex is the result. Results should be our destination; we already know where pathways formed from good intentions tend to lead.

ALL-PURPOSE DESIRE
Substituting Desire for Other Emotional Needs

"I don't know what good it's doing for me to come here, when the one with the problem is my hardheaded husband—the rest of him should only be so hard!" Anne-Marie says, taking a long drag on her cigarette. She is a buxom forty-one-year-old waitress who wears her thick dark hair in a beehive style atop a head buzzing with indignant recriminations.

"I was really aching for sex, too," she complains. "That was the night my boss, Larry, told me Vera was going to take over the hostess job at the Scungilli Shell. Larry knew I had my heart set on that job after Rosie retired and I even had a lot of customers put in a good word for me. But he gave me this bullshit about Vera had worked there longer and knew how to make the customers feel special." Anne-Marie crushes out her half-smoked cigarette, and mutters a curse under her breath.

"It sounds as though you were really disappointed, very sad that night," the therapist says. "Probably angry, too."

"Who wouldn't be? I went into the ladies' room and cried after

he told me," Anne-Marie confesses. "Vera doesn't give a damn
about the place. She calls in sick all the time, gets snotty with the
customers, and is always screwing up orders. There's no justice!
And my husband, when I try to get close that night, he says, 'We had
sex two days ago,' and rolls over."

"Were there other nights this week when you were in the mood
and he wasn't?"

Anne-Marie thinks for a minute. "Sure, Wednesday. My bitchy
sister-in-law, Carol, calls up around nine-thirty at night to say she's
driving to Jersey the next morning to go to Toy Mountain, since our
niece's birthday is coming up, and do I want her to pick up anything. Sure, I said, I was going to buy the kid a talking Wonka-
Wombat, but they go for over a hundred in the city and Toy Mountain's got them for about sixty-eight dollars. But I'm having coffee
with my neighbor, who is just about to leave, so I ask Carol if I can
call back in fifteen minutes with the information. Well, she says, she
is going to bed because she has to get up early, but I should call first
thing in the morning.

"So help me, I'm back on the phone within fifteen minutes, but
her phone just rings and rings, which means she pulled the goddamn jack out of the wall. She's probably screwing with her husband, because who the hell goes to sleep at ten o'clock! Fine, so I
set my alarm for 6 A.M. and every few minutes I dial, but she never
puts the phone back into the wall. So, naturally, she never buys the
Wonka-Wombat because she didn't know exactly what I wanted. I
wanted her tail on a platter, that's what I wanted!"

"And you wanted sex that night?" the therapist asks.

"I was fuming! I was steamed! It really would have helped,"
Anne-Marie says. "But Lou comes home late from his club and he's
'too tired.' "

"Anne-Marie, did you talk to Lou about how angry you were
with his sister? The night you didn't get promoted, did you cry on
Lou's shoulder?"

"I told him Vera got the job and he said, 'Gee, that's tough,
babe,' but that's as far as it went. What's the point about criticizing
his sister? He always stands by his family and tries to justify their
behavior."

"At least he would have known you were angry, maybe help you
let some of the tension out, even if you wound up directing some of
it at him," the therapist explains. "Sex sometimes helps get tension
released, too, whether you're sad or angry, but it's not the only way,

and sometimes not even the best way. You've got to ask yourself, what do I really want to share tonight? Sex may be a second choice, but you might be able to get your first choice."

Anne-Marie ponders his words. "You know, Doctor, I've got customers who have been coming in for years and they always order the same thing. It gets so that, after a while, I just smile and say, 'The usual?' Maybe I've kept them from trying something different and I'm going to start suggesting other items on the menu. They might keep ordering the same stuff, but at least they'll think about it —like I'm going to start thinking about it. At the Scungilli Shell, we've got a hell of a lot more to offer than just scungilli and I guess you can find more in a bedroom than just a bed."

In his writings about therapy for problems of sexual desire, Dr. Bernie Zilbergeld describes Gail, a character from Peter Benchley's *The Deep,* for whom sex was a vehicle for expressing everything from delight and love to frustration and outrage. Gail would use anything, from the first fallen leaf of autumn to the anniversary of Richard Nixon's resignation, as a reason for making love.

Dr. Zilbergeld immediately thought of Gail when we asked him about sexual cues, those situations that typically evoke desire in an individual. "The best answer is related to Peter Benchley's book," he told us. "You made love when you were happy, you made love when you were angry, you made love when you were sad. That is the extreme, of course, but I thought he said it very well, and really captured something."

For people like Gail and Anne-Marie, nearly everything suggests sex and nothing else. Other people have very few cues that put them in a mental frame for sex. Some may have desire only in response to a stimulus they consider "dirty," such as pornographic material or prostitutes. Others may not think about sex unless the situation is very specific, such as being in bed on a Saturday night.

In a relationship, we may be labeling one partner "high desire" because of a tendency to respond to too many situations with sexual desire and the other "low desire" because very few situations will trigger desire.

Whereas once therapists almost routinely sought to resolve such discrepancies by encouraging the partner with lower desire to accommodate the more demanding one, therapists today will try to get the couple to see whether they're asking for sex when in reality something else would be equally or more satisfying, such as verbal communication, nonsexual cuddling, a sympathetic ear, or companionship.

Is there such a thing as too much sexual desire? There is an organization called Sexaholics Anonymous, a self-help group for people whose obsession with sex has ruined marriages, health, and credit ratings. People who pursue sexual gratification constantly and are never satisfied are almost always trying to substitute sex for other emotional needs; if sex were really what they wanted, there would be no need for compulsively repeating the acts intended to bring satisfaction. You don't eat one meal after another to satisfy physical hunger; binge eaters are really trying to assuage an emotional longing.

A partner who seems to want sex constantly may be trying to use it as an inadequate substitute for some other emotional need. Sometimes, such a person may be well aware of what he or she truly wants, but has a partner who is not capable of giving much more than sex. It's therefore important to ask yourself, in the context of the relationship: What do I really want at this time? What is my partner capable of giving me? Can the situation be improved with regard to specific responses to specific desires?

MAD ABOUT YOU—AND A LOT OF OTHER THINGS
Anger's Effects on Sexual Desire

"We had sex three times last week," Barbara, a twenty-eight-year-old nurse, reports with false enthusiasm. Raising her right fist in a victory salute, she says, "Sneaking up on the old national average, Doctor!"

Her husband, Eddie, a muscular ex-Marine ten years her senior who now mans a desk selling office copiers, grumbles, "I don't even want to count the last time. We didn't finish."

"Desire is what we're counting," Barbara argues, "wanting to do it. How it turns out doesn't matter."

"Hah, you didn't really *want* to do it last night!" Eddie scoffs.

"Can we stop talking in numbers," the therapist interrupts,

"and communicate in words? Let's start over. What happened last week?"

"Monday night, we went to Eddie's mother's house for dinner—at his insistence," Barbara, the more loquacious of the pair, begins. "Eddie makes my life miserable unless he drags me over there at least every other week. So my mother-in-law prepares her usual seven-course banquet and Eddie stuffs himself like a Thanksgiving turkey, as if he just came off a week-long fast, while his mother beams proudly at him. Then, dear old mother-in-law says, 'You don't get food like *that* anywhere else, huh?' "

"She didn't mean for you to take it personally," Eddie cajoles.

"No?" Barbara objects. "I suppose she meant that none of this city's thousands of restaurants can match her cooking. You know damn well that was a dig at me, the dumb little girl from Kansas who cooks nothing but hamburgers."

"So Barbara got mad," Eddie tells the therapist, "and naturally, she wasn't interested in sex that night."

"I was *sick,*" Barbara clarifies. "My stomach felt like it was on fire. And *he* was so unsympathetic. He said I had insulted his mother by not eating enough of that poison."

"I *said* I was sorry," Eddie says defensively. "I even bought you the ceramic panda the next night."

Barbara smiles appreciatively. "I collect pandas. It was a really nice one that Eddie got me. He must have paid over fifty dollars for it."

"And you had sex that night," the therapist surmises. They nod.

"Wednesday evening, I suggested to Eddie that I take a computer course," Barbara says, resuming the narration. "As soon as I get the words out, he vetoes it."

"Why do you need a computer course?" Eddie asks. "You're a nurse, not an astrophysicist!"

"Because everything's getting computerized at the hospital," Barbara explains. "Admissions, discharges, scheduled procedures, medications. I could be a better nurse and advance farther if I understood better what I was doing. You still think of me as running around giving needles and fetching bedpans."

"No sex that night?" the therapist ventures. They nod.

"Well, I did give in and say you could take the course," Eddie adds.

"Yeah, the following night," Barbara agrees.

"Sex that night?" the therapist says. They nod.

"Barbara even cooked dinner," Eddie adds. "Wednesday, she was too tired to do even that."

"Which brings us to Friday, the night Melanie came over," Barbara recounts icily.

"Came over!" Eddie scoffs. "She was in our apartment less than ten minutes. She's our neighbor and she wanted to borrow some vanilla extract. Ten minutes, and this one acts as if I'm having an affair! She came to borrow the vanilla from you, not from me."

"You've got to see this tramp, Doc," Barbara explains. "She comes over wearing shorts cut to her inguinal folds, to put it in medical terms. It's March, for God's sake! Who the hell wears short shorts in March? And this ape never takes his eyes off her legs, following us into the kitchen and back again, asking if she wants to borrow anything else. He would have loaned her the refrigerator if she'd asked."

"Barbara had a headache that night," Eddie notes. "Saturday was the last time we had sex—or *almost* had sex, if you count complete acts only. Barbara went out shopping at the mall all day long —I didn't complain. She came home too late to cook, so she sent out for Chinese—I didn't complain. Then, when we go to bed, she says she's tired."

"I *was* tired," Barbara protests.

"From doing what?" Eddie complains. "From shopping for clothes for yourself, from running up big bills on the credit cards?"

"Tired is tired, regardless of what you did," Barbara says. "You spent the day in front of the television set, so you weren't tired."

"But after I let you go out and spend money, why do I have to suffer for it?" Eddie argues.

"That's why I said okay," Barbara says. "I figured, to keep peace, even though I don't really feel like it, we'll have sex. It will be over in a few minutes, Eddie will be happy, and I can get some sleep. But that night, Eddie decides to go for his personal best, to break his own endurance mark. He goes on and on."

Eddie turns to the therapist. "Doctor, I could tell she wasn't really that aroused. I wanted to take more time, give her a chance to get more into it. So, I was holding back on my orgasm."

"Mister Considerate!" Barbara snorts.

"And right in the middle of things," Eddie says, his voice rising in agitation, "she says, 'Finish for God's sake!' Well, I stop dead, as if she'd slapped me. I said, 'Darling, I want you to enjoy yourself, too.' And she said—I still can't believe this—'I don't *want* to enjoy myself!'

"I ask you, Doctor, how can we get anywhere with that kind of an attitude? How can you desire sex if you don't want to enjoy it? What's sex for, if not enjoyment?"

Sex, as Eddie is finding out, can be used for many purposes other than enjoyment. When animosity erupts between a couple, sex can be used as a powerful weapon.

The withholding of sex to win concessions from a mate or to punish the partner is scarcely a form of modern weaponry. In ancient Greece, Aristophanes—the Neil Simon of his day—wrote a play in which Lysistrata and the other Grecian women compelled their husbands to stop waging war by refusing sex, concluding their pledge of abstinence with "If he takes me by force against my will, I shall do it badly and keep from moving."

Homer, in the *Iliad,* recounted how Zeus gently chided Aphrodite for pitching herself ineptly into the midst of a battle: "Fighting, my child, is not for you. *You* are in charge of wedlock and the tender passions. We will leave the enterprising War-god and Athene to look after military affairs." Zeus's sound advice, like that of many fathers, remained unheeded through the subsequent centuries.

This bedroom weaponry can be particularly lethal when the parties are essentially unaware of their employing it. There are many times when one partner will think, "I'm angry and I'll be damned if I'm going to make him [or her] happy by having sex." An angry partner will probably have little sexual desire, although it is entirely possible that desire is present and even strong, its gratification sacrificed in the interest of warfare. In many cases, however, the partners may not even be able to acknowledge that they are angry and they attribute their refusal to have sex to disinterest, a lack of desire.

Why would a person have difficulty recognizing anger? Take, for example, the situations experienced by Barbara and Eddie. When Barbara goes to her mother-in-law's house, she gets furious because she feels Eddie's mother is being competitive with her and denigrates her. Barbara is probably right. Still, she knows it is irrational to take her anger out on Eddie. Sure, he could eat a little less heartily or make a conscious effort to praise Barbara in front of his mother (although this might merely escalate the rivalry), but basically Eddie is not the offender. So Barbara gets indigestion (which is probably real given the relationship between emotional aggravation and stomach acid secretion) which provides her with a more rational reason for losing sexual desire.

With regard to taking the computer course, Barbara could have taken the time to explain to Eddie how the new skills could help her career or she could even have said, "Look, while I'd like your approval, I am earning a salary, and if I feel this course would help me, I'm going to take it, even if you don't see the need for it." Unfortunately, Barbara has learned that losing interest in sex is a more effortless, effective way to win Eddie's consent, even though it neither helps him to understand her work and her needs nor helps her to feel that she doesn't have to get his approval for everything she does. Ultimately, Barbara will be emotionally frustrated because she knows she didn't really obtain any self-validation through Eddie and, by using the sexual "shortcut," bypassed the path to more effective communication.

And while we're on the subject of shortcuts, Barbara's response to the short-cut apparel of neighbor Melanie involved a more conscious level of anger, but the net effect of lowered desire on Barbara's part and sexual frustration for Eddie was the same as when the anger was less conscious. Barbara could have simply acknowledged the casual attraction of the average male toward other women and, instead of feeling threatened by Melanie, said, "She can warm up his engine, but I've got the license and ownership papers."

Finally, there was the Saturday night marathon, sex without end and without climax. Even though she was tired, Barbara was participating clearly because she felt a sense of obligation. Anger can be even more distressing when one feels guilty about it, and Barbara *was* angry, as they both fully realized when she finally exploded at Eddie. Eddie could have accepted her being tired, even though she was fatigued because of an enjoyable shopping trip. He could have either forgone sex or been willing to demand less effort and enthusiasm from Barbara. Instead, he backed her into a corner by provoking guilt in her for shopping and trying to beg off having sex; this, in turn, produced guilt in him, so that he launched into a doomed quest to make the sexual experience enjoyable for her as well. To Barbara, this persistence was a hostile act, breaking her completely unspoken contract with him to have his way and get it over with. By the time they terminated the activity, Eddie had as little desire as Barbara.

When sexual activity is governed by anger rather than desire, desire may become irrelevant and neglected. When we try to adapt an object to a new purpose, it often loses its old purpose. When sex becomes a weapon, a prod, a wedge, a lever, it loses its original identity as a method of experiencing pleasure, achieving intimacy, or expressing love.

Another problem that develops is that even if sex is only used occasionally to reward or punish a partner, a few unpleasant experiences of this type will make one or both partners avoid sex. They don't stop to think, "I was rejected last time, but that was because of the fight we'd been having," they stop at "I was rejected last time." The fear of repeating a negative experience overcomes the desire for a positive one.

A VOICE FROM BELOW
Passive-Aggressive Defenses Against Anger

"He was talking with his phallus," Dr. Thomas D. Stewart of Harvard Medical Center said of a patient. "He was angry at her and didn't want to give her anything." The impotent patient had come in with what he perceived as a problem with desire and arousal. In the course of talking to Dr. Stewart, the man enumerated all his complaints about the way his wife had treated him. Surprisingly, while the man was giving plenty of reasons for being furious, he really wasn't in touch with the anger he was feeling. His flaccid penis seemed to be communicating his anger better than his head.

When we think of anger, our immediate associations are ones of violence, loud words, threats, and loss of control. Yet in most cases, when someone offends us, we resort to subtler reactions, such as avoiding them, speaking to them less, doing less for them, or failing to smile at them. We trust they will get the message, yet we can deny, if need be, that we were acting in a hostile or retaliatory way.

Psychologists call this "passive-aggressive" behavior. It is passive in the sense that there is no explosive, patently hostile action taken, but aggressive because we are, in fact, impeding the other person's satisfaction in some way. If we all expressed anger or frustration in the most direct way, with blunt insults or instruments, civilization would self-destruct. A cold shoulder can accomplish as much as a hot tongue.

This genteel defense becomes less valuable when the person

using it loses awareness and control. The sexual partner who says, "Not tonight, dear, I have a headache," and knows he or she means, "And I'll have one tomorrow night, too, unless you make up for what you did," will be pressuring the partner toward resolution of a problem. But the partner who feels no desire and is unaware of the underlying anger will not be able to communicate the conflict to the mate or monitor the relationship to see if the situation is improving.

People with poorly expressed and poorly perceived anger that results in impaired sexual desire will do the following:

1. **Procrastinate.** They don't say, "I don't want sex until I feel better," they say, "I don't want sex right now, but I'm sure I will by tomorrow." Of course, like the looking-glass jam that the White Queen offered to Alice, it's always "desire yesterday and desire tomorrow, but never desire today."

2. **Sulk.** They are always in an inexplicable bad mood, especially around bedtime. Everything irritates them and they argue about trivia, so that the partner never dares venture a sexual invitation.

3. **Putter.** At bedtime, they suddenly become absorbed in household repairs, engrossed in magazine articles, or fascinated by late-night talk shows. They say they'll come to bed "in a minute." If the Minute Men had been that slow, our chief executive today would be Queen Elizabeth II.

4. **Protest.** They give spouses grief with their grievances. They feel they are overworked, underappreciated, and unfairly treated. There are no specific sexual grievances in some cases, but even then they are so full of complaints that there's no room in which to squeeze desire.

5. **Forget.** If they acknowledge at some point that their sex life needs revitalizing and agree to work on it with the partner, they forget that they were supposed to make arrangements to leave the children with a relative or make arrangements to come home early on a prearranged night.

6. **Blame.** Instead of confronting their low desire, they point out that it's amazing how much desire they have left, given the partner's attitudes and faults.

7. **Praise.** They limit the praise to themselves, of course. Rather than seeing there is a problem that might be solvable, they point

out their remarkable daily accomplishments, beside which desire pales in importance like the moon in the glare of the sun.

Direct anger can be unpleasant to deal with, but it can be dealt with because it is so undeniably accessible. Passive-aggressive maneuvering that stems from repressed anger seems tamer, but is much tougher, because you have to bring the conflict into the open. It's easier to hunt a wolf than a gopher because you don't have to dig out the creature first from wherever it's buried.

DINNER AT 8, FIGHT AT 10, NEWS AT 11
Rules for Marital Fighting

"Okay, Iggy, that's it! I'll meet you at ten after three in the lot back of the schoolyard. Just you and me, bare knucks."

Many males have had the childhood experience of scheduling a fight, but not with a member of the opposite sex. Girls may have had some limited exposure to spontaneous clawing, hair-pulling "cat fights," but they are not the sort of event a young woman would pencil in on her social calendar.

Unfortunately, then, most couples do not seriously consider scheduling a fair fight, which is a very effective way to deal with impaired sexual and nonsexual compatibility when one or both partners are aware there is anger.

Dr. Peter Kilmann of the University of South Carolina believes a couple should set a particular time for a discussion, just as they would make a movie date. He feels this type of prearrangement is especially important for people with children or with a lot of work responsibility who really don't have that much time to deal with domestic issues. The "date" makes it safe to bring up sensitive matters because you know that you are going to be listened to. The partner will not be caught at an inopportune moment.

Dr. Kilmann uses the "Fair Fighting" techniques developed by psychologist Dr. George R. Bach, author of *Creative Aggression* and *The Intimate Enemy.* These principles include, besides setting a definite time for private discussion, limiting the discussion to just one issue, stating what you want your partner to do in definite and direct terms, and clarifying any of your partner's questions. Making specific suggestions, which the partner can then adopt, reject, or modify, is far more constructive than enumerating complaints without any proposed remedy.

Emotional problems are more difficult to solve than nonemotional problems; as with all problems, however, solutions can proceed via a logical thought train, testing specific potential remedies. If you were trying to renovate the basement, you wouldn't limit your discussion to all the things that were wrong without proposing corrections. You wouldn't start considering problems with the upstairs bathroom or the kitchen in the middle of the talk about the basement. Yet, in the usual unstructured fight, couples begin hurling all sorts of irrelevant accusations at one another, which add heat, but no light, to the initial issue. If a wife responds to her husband's criticism about the inadequate meals she serves with criticisms of his sexual performance, both will mentally attach all the negative feelings engendered in the meal argument to the sexual activities, impeding desire in the process.

Dr. Bach's "Fair Fight" techniques did for marital fighting what the Marquis of Queensbury did for boxing. They contained the fight within a manageable area, ensuring the combatants wouldn't be brawling over limitless territory. They prevented unfair below-the-belt blows by limiting the areas to be attacked. They gave the fight a starting time and an approximate ending time. They decreased the sense of vulnerability in the participants and made the encounter a mutually voluntary one where abiding by the rules gave the event an atmosphere of cooperation as well as conflict. In Chapter 15, we will discuss further how couples can fight without damaging their desire and sex lives.

There are many similarities between the boxing ring and the marriage bed; each can be a square circle of combat, big enough for only two adversaries, one trying to get the other horizontal. There is one paramount difference, however: In boxing, there is one winner and one loser. In bedrooms, there are either two winners or two losers.

Personal Problems

Individual Conflicts and Desire Loss

Desire is a highly personal matter. There are people who have desire loss that results from a conflicted relationship with the partner and their situation can be improved by analyzing and resolving the problems. Others may suffer a desire deficit because of stressful circumstances at home or at work and desire will return when the situation improves.

The most challenging cases are problems with desire stemming from personal anxiety, past traumas, or other psychological difficulties. In any endeavor, a person cannot team effectively with a partner unless he or she feels confident and capable. Often the therapist has to divert attention away from sexual matters and focus on more basic problems of self-identity and self-esteem. By exorcising bad feelings, a person can make some room for an influx of sexual desire, a very good feeling.

"So Ray, who works with me in the billing office, hands me this," Barry says, depositing the figurine on the therapist's desk. It's a cheap china image of a doctor with a boyish face, holding a coiled stethoscope in his hand and wearing a reflecting mirror on his forehead. " 'You work in a goddamn hospital, you should know what one looks like,' Ray says to me. 'Now that you know, go see one, 'cause, man, you *need* one!' "

Barry is twenty-seven, lanky, bespectacled, and his cheeks spotted with a few pimples. There's no fatal flaw about his appearance, yet his features are expressionless, his grooming careless. "I suppose I should have come a long time ago. It's been four years since I've had sex, three years since I had a date, and now I just don't even think about sex anymore.

"You won't believe this, but I was actually *popular* once. That was a long time ago, back in high school. Not that I had any more in the way of looks to work with then, but I could always make people laugh and feel relaxed around me. Man, to think, I actually used to complain about going to school! All you had to do if you wanted to meet a chick was to turn your head to either side. A few had steady boyfriends, but there were always some who were unattached and the 'easy makes' let you know who they were—that's why they were easy.

"Even before I dropped out of school, I always had a job, usually pumping gas. With a few dollars in your pocket and an old car of your own, you were a king. Split a pizza and a six-pack with a girl and it was make-out city, no hassle. It was all I ever wanted out of life. I left school because I wanted the extra bread.

"Maybe I should have paid more attention in math class. The expenses add up a lot faster when you have to pay your own rent and buy your own food, not like when I was living with my folks. I left the gas station, but nothing they would hire me for paid much above minimum wage: stockrooms, messenger work, valet parking, fast-food places. So, I came to the city. Big deal, the pay is a little better and the rent is a lot worse!

"But it wasn't just the jobs that made me come to the city. I just couldn't meet available girls. The ones I went to school with either got married or were looking for a guy who could offer them a future, not just a few laughs. I figured in the city there would be a lot more single girls to meet. Well, they're here, but they might as well be in Alaska for all the good it does me. The first thing they want to know is 'What kind of work do you do?' I try to be a little vague, just say, 'I work in a hospital,' but either they want more specifics or they just shy away. One bitchy girl cut me dead with, 'Orderly?'

"I got tired of striking out wherever I went—bars, singles dances, church mixers. I hardly ever meet anybody at the hospital and the women who are available there have their sights on something higher than a billing clerk. My sex life was limited to fantasy, but lately even that's gone. I think it was because I started striking out there, too.

"Is that ridiculous, or what? But it's true. I'd read these bullshit letters and stories in magazines, where the guys had these chicks all over them, panting to get at them, and I'd feel hopeless. I'd watch a porn video and see these cool guys with big organs and I'd say, 'Shit, that sure ain't me.' I couldn't even crack my way into a fantasy world. Then, one day, I stopped wanting to. I just didn't give a damn about sex, not even masturbating. I go back to my one-room apartment and stare at the boob tube all night."

"Barry," the therapist asks, "does your friend, Ray, work in the same office as you? Same job?"

Barry nods. The therapist then asks, "How come he doesn't seem to have the kind of problems with sexual desire you do?"

Barry shakes his head and grins. "Maybe he's too dumb to know what a loser he is. He goes around acting like he's Santa Claus's present to all the women on earth and it takes him all year to get around to everyone. Maybe he's snowing me, but I actually believe him when he tells me he's scoring. He seems to have the girls believing his rap."

"He seems to feel pretty good about himself," the therapist says. "Why do you think that is, considering he's got the same job you have?"

"He sees it as only temporary," Barry explains. "Well, to give him due credit, he is taking some night classes. He works out at a gym and puts in some time as a volunteer for a boys' club."

"Do you think you might feel better about yourself if you did things like that?" the therapist asks.

"Well, it might help," Barry concedes. "I couldn't feel any worse than I do now. But that's not going to help my sex drive any, is it? I can't see what classes and activities have to do with sex."

"What would you think about sex with a loser?"

"I don't think about sex with anybody. But back in my better days, I don't suppose I'd be too keen on having a loser for a partner."

"Suppose *you* were the loser?"

Barry thinks that one over. "I was going to say, 'Who cares, it's what the woman is that counts,' but I don't know if I could really enjoy it knowing I was one."

"Isn't that the way you've been feeling about yourself?"

"Is that the way I come across?" Barry reflects. "Yeah, why try to hide it? Ray knew it, too, that's why he got me to come here."

"The worst team in baseball history, the 1962 New York Mets, still won a quarter of their games," the therapist says. "The only way you can be a guaranteed loser is not to show up on the playing field and forfeit. Before you can score, you've got to be in the game, and before that you've got to want to get out on the playing field."

"The race is not to the swift, nor the battle to the strong." But that's the way the smart money bets.

We live in a competitive society. Not only do people compete with one another for career advancement, but they compete in looks and possessions. They compete indirectly, without even knowing one another. A model with a flabless figure and gold tresses appears on a TV screen and women viewers feel they should match her in appearance. Commercials and advertisements hawk products that seem to be in every home and garage except one's own. Often we cannot afford what is advertised, cannot make ourselves over into the beautiful people who populate the screen, and we feel inadequate for it.

Sex appeal seems ultimately to be determined by an aura of self-confidence. A feeling that you're sexually attractive gets conveyed to those within reach of the aura and you actually become desirable. People who feel sexy *are* sexy to others.

For every action, there is an equal and opposite reaction. Sir Isaac Newton probably didn't care a fig about sexual desire, but his laws of motion have relevance to human emotion. If a positive self-image increases sex appeal, desirability, and desire, a negative self-image just as surely leads to rejection and loss of desire. A confident person takes rejection in stride, because he or she does not equate it with evidence of personal inadequacy. On the other hand, the person with low self-esteem expects rejection and sees it as confirming his or her worthlessness.

When sexual desire evaporates as a result of low self-esteem, it often cannot be restored until the self-image problem is improved. Couldn't it be helped by meeting a partner who finds the self-perceived "loser" interesting and attractive, thus adding to the depleted store of that person's confidence? Only sometimes, because the one who has lost desire might have become a victim of the "Groucho's Club" mentality.

Groucho Marx is reputed to have declined membership in a very prestigious club for celebrities, saying, "I refuse to belong to any club that would have me as a member." Groucho was joking, but many people actually think themselves into a no-win situation by adhering to the principle that anybody who sees any worth in them must be very dumb or mentally disturbed to perceive them so inaccurately, an even worse loser than themselves to settle for someone so worthless. Or at best, someone who has not really had time to get to know them and will reject them once they do get to know them. The "loser" saves time by rejecting relationships before getting rejected.

REMEMBRANCE OF THINGS PAST
Emotional Deprivation and Childhood Trauma

"How come you always call me Stephanie and I call you Doctor?" she asks. "I have a Ph.D., so I'm a doctor, too."

"Would you like me to call you Doctor?" the therapist asks. Stephanie frowns and says no. "Then, do you want to call me by my first name?" the therapist asks. "It's fine by me."

Stephanie does not reply. For the rest of the session, she will not use any name or title. Using whatever designation she wants would ruin her case that women are always put down by men. So she launches a new argument—new for this session, but an old one in terms of her use of it. "I'll probably lose my job by the end of the year," she grumbles. "It's 'publish or perish' and, of course, since I won't have published anything, they'll have the perfect excuse to dump me."

Stephanie sighs angrily. She is a tall, broad-shouldered thirty-three-year-old, with light brown natural curls. Her gray eyes are chronically narrowed in a suspicious squint and her mouth is kept drawn in a straight line.

"Did you start writing something?" the therapist asks, already knowing the answer.

"Of course not!" she snaps. "What's the use? They never accept papers written by women. Why should I waste my time? All the tenure, all the promotions, go to the male faculty members. I'm playing against a stacked deck."

Stephanie has come into treatment, on referral by her internist, for colitis. She complains of diarrhea, although her symptoms have never caused her to miss work or have to walk out on a class or interrupt a movie. Her internist, however, knows that her gastrointestinal tract is the least of her problems, and there are plenty of other issues to deal with in therapy. Stephanie has never had a boyfriend and her social life with men is limited to an occasional lunch or dinner date with a male colleague at the college where she is employed as a history professor. She has no discernible sexual desire.

"You may be playing against a stacked deck, but as long as you're in the game, you might as well play the cards," the therapist says. "Nobody can publish something that's never even been written."

"They wouldn't publish it anyway," she insists. "The men have all the power and they're not going to share it."

"Is that the way you see the relationships between all men and all women, or just the ones where you work?"

"Well, it's surely that way in the academic world," Stephanie says. "But no, I don't think it's that way everywhere. My mother was the domineering one in my family. She was the tough one. Very cold, too."

"And your father? Was he easier to get close to?"

Stephanie's mouth softens and her eyes get a faraway look, as if she is peering into the past. "Yes, he was, at least at times. The problem was that when my mother was around he was so timid that he didn't dare get too close to me, for fear she would accuse him of siding with me against her. God knows, we always had our differences. But when she was away, he'd be able to drink as much as he wanted."

"When she was away?" the therapist inquires.

"Oh, she had a sister in another city," Stephanie says. "By the time I was ten or so, she'd get on a train and go off for a few days, leaving Dad and me to fend for ourselves. I kind of looked forward to it, in the beginning. Until she took that trip when I was fourteen.

"Her sister was sick and Mother figured to be gone longer than usual, a week at least. By then, I was old enough to cook well and take care of things, and I thought my father would be really proud of me. Maybe we hadn't been that close, but this would be a good time to get to know one another, spend a lot of time together.

"The very first day my mother was away, I started cooking dinner as soon as I got home from school. But Dad never came home—at least, not till about ten at night. And when he did get home, he was drunk, and he had this friend with him, who was in even worse shape, so drunk he could hardly stand up. Dad said his friend, who I'd never seen before, was sick and he wanted him to lie down for a while. So Dad managed to maneuver the guy into his bedroom and somehow got him onto the bed. I was disgusted, but I went into the kitchen and started warming up some food for my father. Then, I heard my father let out a yell for me to come.

"His friend was having a convulsion on the bed, and Dad was just staring at him, frozen in terror. 'Call an ambulance,' I said, but he just stood there, so I called. I was looking around for a pencil or a cloth or something to put in the man's mouth, but by then the convulsion stopped, only now he was lying very still. Dad was saying over and over, 'My God, maybe he's dead!' The man had drooled all over the pillow and his face was buried in it, but I turned his head and could see he was breathing, although with little shallow gasps and his lips were blue. I prayed the ambulance would come.

"Dad just wandered out of the bedroom. Then, he called me and he said, 'Steph, listen, he's got some money of mine in his pocket. You've got to get it before they come.' I just didn't understand. Finally, I said, 'Well, *you* get it!' but he started crying and trembling and he shook his head. 'I can't touch a dead man!' he said. I told him the man wasn't dead, but he clung to me and begged me to do it.

"I went back in and the man did look dead. He was lying on his side, and as luck would have it, there was nothing in the pocket facing me but a filthy handkerchief that stank of vomitus. I had to push him over to reach into the other pocket and I found this roll of bills. I don't know how much it was, I didn't even look. Maybe it was just a bunch of ones, maybe a lot more. He still seemed to be breathing. I walked out and shoved the money into my father's hand without a word. To this day, I don't know if the money really was his, or if he'd seen that the man had the cash and I was robbing him. The ambulance came and they took the man to the hospital and I went to my room. Dad stayed drunk the rest of the week. That was my dream week with my father."

"So you never did get close to him?" the therapist asks.

For the first time since she's been in therapy, Stephanie is crying. She keeps her head erect and her hands folded in her lap, but large tears run down her cheeks, neglected, plopping randomly on her blouse. "I visit my parents on the holidays. I telephone every week or so. Now that my father's older, he doesn't drink as much; maybe it's because he's not working and my mother curbs him at home. But we're not close, no. And Mother never changed."

"Who *are* you close to, Stephanie?"

She clenches her hands into fists and rubs away the tears with rough swipes. "Nobody," she says defiantly. "I'm never disappointed anymore. I always expect the worst and it usually happens."

"Like never getting anything published?"

"You can't beat a stacked deck," she says.

"Wrong," the therapist says. "You can cut the cards, you can shuffle, you can even call for a new deck. Cheaters get rich off the fish who expect to lose and blame bad luck."

Stephanie looks at him with tearless eyes, opened wider than he has ever seen them. "So you don't think it's a lot of feminist paranoia when I tell you what I'm up against?"

"No," he replies. "Advancing in your career isn't easy. Finding people you can trust isn't easy. Finding someone you can love— that can be like drawing to a three-card flush. But remember, Stephanie, take a risk here and there. People can bluff their way into a pot or two with losing hands, but nobody ever won anything by throwing in their cards."

The hardest type of desire disorder to treat is one that is rooted in the distant past. It's like dealing with an old tree whose underground roots are interfering with water pipes. In the first place, the source of the problem is buried where you can't see it. In the second place, the point of interference might lie quite a distance from the part of the tree you can see, so it's hard even to connect the trouble with what's visible. In the third place, the problem gets worse with time, because the roots continue to grow, tangling up objects even more. Finally, the tree can't tell you what's going on.

Someone like Stephanie can talk, but it is not easy to talk about unpleasant things. While the passing years dim memory, traumatic events are easier to recall—unless our brains use nature's protective forgetting mechanism, which psychologists call repression. Stephanie has a primary desire disorder, in that she has never had sexual desire. She could respond rather readily that she finds men to be competitive and exploitative and that she really wants no part of them, including sexually. But many women face the same prejudices with which Stephanie must contend; the roots of her difficulty relating to men go much deeper. The hope and disillusionment she experienced in her relationship with her father left her vulnerable to the common complaint of those with traumatic childhoods: "If you can't trust a parent, whom *can* you trust?"

That's fallacious thinking, a cognitive error. The world is filled with untrustworthy humans. Parents are human and some are bound to be untrustworthy. Parenthood, unfortunately, does not automatically make people trustworthy, kind, lovable, or competent. From a child's viewpoint, however, parents are supposed to be the best and most reliable caretakers, and when the child is disillusioned, he becomes sour on the entire human race.

The exception, interestingly enough, occurs when the parents are unequivocally abusive, with no redeeming qualities. Some children of such parents may grow up with chronic depression and deep emotional scars, but they don't seem to suffer half the anxiety of children who are expected to believe that they are loved and that their parents are acting in accordance with the children's best interests.

Sexual desire, as we should all appreciate by now, involves far more than simple drive or natural response. It requires reaching out to another person and nobody wants to reach out to something that hurts them. Since we don't think of our parents or our childhood experiences in sexual terms, it is not surprising that people have difficulty connecting the events of those early asexual years with sexual desire problems. The old traumas are like ghosts, in the sense that they are dead and have no ongoing existence, yet continue to make their presence felt, haunting our current lives, unseen by others and only half-seen by ourselves.

Sometimes these ghosts don't seem frightening or harmful at all. Sometimes, we're like the child who, when asked by a playmate if the devil really exists, answered, "Well, I think he's sort of like Santa Claus. You believe in him for a while, but then you find out it's only your father." Parental ghosts may seem more reassuring than threatening and not even very ghostly if their aged counterparts are still living, but they sometimes wreak more havoc than a poltergeist in a china shop.

Nearly all parents lay down *some* prohibitions about sex. This may involve, in the younger child, instructions not to expose certain body parts around the house and certainly not to show them to playmates or to refrain from "touching" the genital area. Older children are warned against strangers who approach them, the dangers of physical intimacy, and the importance of moral standards. Parents would be irresponsible if they gave carte blanche to their children in sexual matters. Trouble only develops if the parent gives such messages in an inappropriate way, such as preaching dire and unrealistic consequences for sexual offenses, taking an inordinate amount of interest in the child's sexual feelings and practices, or giving inconsistent or overly restrictive commands.

We have talked about the prostitute-madonna complex and its intrusions into relationships. Some men compound the problem by choosing a woman physically like their mother; if the mother was very possessive and sought to prevent the son from seeking a suitable sexual partner, the man has, in his mate, not only someone who resembles the mother physically but embodies the prohibitions, a woman who, from the man's distorted perception, demands *not* to be sexually desired.

As children, we live with make-believe and very quickly learn where the boundaries between fantasy and reality lie. We know that birds fly and horses don't, but we hold on to our belief in Santa's flying reindeer a bit longer until we feel that our parents can no longer believe that we still believe. We take sexual prohibitions with a bit of healthy skepticism and test the limits, like the boy who, when warned that masturbation would cause blindness, decided to continue the practice until he required glasses. Sometimes, though, the demons we dismissed as harmless tales invented to frighten us resurface later in life, more formidable than ever.

Take, for example, two sisters raised by a very puritanical mother who warns them of severe punishment from God if they act in a lustful manner or regard sex as anything more than a marital duty. One sister may grow up with minimal sexual desire and get virtually no pleasure from marital relations. The other sister has a vivid interest in sex, has premarital partners, and establishes a thoroughly enjoyable sexual relationship. Years later, she loses all sexual desire, with no conceivable reason. If you explore the events that preceded the loss of desire, you may find that some adverse event has occurred, possibly unrelated to sex. She might have had a serious illness, lost some money, or been disappointed in her love life. Subconsciously, she may view this as the punishment her mother had always predicted, come belatedly to fruition. She had been able to scoff at the doomsaying, unlike her more repressed sister, but now she cannot help but feel that mother was right after all.

Sexual abuse in childhood, physical beatings, or any type of insecurity can take its toll. Since many deprived children may seek love through sexual relations as they mature, we may get a confusing history of excessive interest in sex and even promiscuity. A later decrease in sexual interest may be a more accurate reflection of their true mental attitude.

When these dispiriting recollections emerge from the past to haunt us, who you gonna call? Professional therapists deal best with firmly entrenched problems, but a person can make some headway on his or her own by venturing outside of the present circumstances that seem to be impeding desire and reflecting on the past. Not all causes of desire disorder lie in the immediate surroundings or in the person beside you in bed. Relive your past with the aid of photo albums, home movies, old letters—any memorabilia that can make the memories more vivid. Talk over the distant years with people who shared them with you—a brother or sister, a childhood friend, or a cousin—and compare their perspective with your own.

It isn't only people who have had traumatic experiences or unhappy childhoods that can have desire adversely affected by their pasts; a puritanical parent or other authority figure may have done damage with prohibitive pronouncements that are only dimly recalled. Think back not only to early sexual experiences, but also to anything you heard or learned about sex at an early age.

In Chapter 10, pay particular attention to the autohypnotic techniques developed by Dr. Daniel Araoz and Dr. Arnold Lazarus, who encourage their patients to travel mentally backward in time to confront past significant figures and to get in touch with themselves as impressionable children.

You cannot change the past, but you *can* change the past's effect on your present.

WHEN HEARTS ARE YOUNG AND SAD
Conflicts over Heterosexual Object Choice

"I don't know if it's so much sex *per se,* Doctor, as it is women in general." Joshua sighs. His thin face is nearly obscured by his thick, black beard and he is impeccably dressed in a close-fitting three-piece suit. "I think that's why I got out of directing and into production. It was such a strain trying to work with them. Actresses!" Joshua is only twenty-six and already has produced a few off-off-Broadway shows and some summer stock productions, although most of his regular employment is in scenic design or lighting.

"It's true our sex life has been lousy," he confesses. "I know I'm avoiding Meredith." He tries to adjust his perfectly positioned necktie. "There's so much tension I feel around her. We've been married nearly three years and I still feel I don't have a handle on her, what's going to please her and what's going to annoy her."

"Annoy?" the therapist asks.

Joshua smiles feebly. "Well, she's high-strung and sometimes, even though she complains about wanting more sex, when I try she doesn't seem to get into it. I guess she's slow to get aroused and I wish she could tell me exactly what she's experiencing and what she wants. As I said, I never was much of a director myself. But I'm at a loss, as if I'm trying to relate to a whole other species that I can't communicate with." He laughs nervously. "Maybe women *are* a whole different species."

"You find men a lot easier to relate to?" the therapist asks.

"Lord, yes!" Joshua exclaims. "You can tell what they're thinking, where they're coming from. I'd much rather work with men than women, even the most temperamental ones. They make much better friends, too."

"Do you think they're easier to relate to sexually?"

Joshua looks flustered and gives the therapist a hurt, questioning glance. "Well, I really can't speak from direct experience there. Or, did you mean do women have an easier time with men in bed than vice versa?"

"Either," the therapist says.

Joshua ponders the question. "I suppose Meredith doesn't have an easy time with me, although I think men are simple enough creatures. I meet a lot of gay men, of course, and some I would even consider friends. I'll say this about gay sex, and I certainly don't mean that homosexuals aren't capable of intimate, loving relationships, but if what you're looking for is straightforward, no-nonsense sexual gratification, you can easily find it, without all the games and bullshit that women put you through."

"Do you know any bisexual men?"

"Oh, sure," Joshua says. "One I know quite well, his name is Cliff. He enjoys women, but he's single and he tells me if he's really horny and looking for some quick release, he'll just drive to the West Side and find some guy to give him a blow job. It costs him nothing, maybe the price of a beer. Even the sleaziest hookers want fifteen bucks a head." Joshua snickers at his pun.

"Do Cliff and the other bisexual or gay men ever come on to you?"

Joshua fidgets in his chair nervously. "Oh, once in a while. You know, 'Try it, you'll like it. What can you lose?' I've always been thin and even with the beard I look young, the kind of appearance most of the gays go for, but believe me, Doctor, I could *never* get into that! I'm no stud with women, but I'm unalterably straight-arrow."

"Then, let's work on the kind of sex you *do* have," the therapist says. "Can you tell me about what you and your wife do?"

"As I said, I'm kind of straight-arrow, direct, no frills, you know," Joshua says. "I guess I save my off-beat stuff for the stage. Meredith is pretty conservative, too. I mean, there's foreplay, not just in and out, on and off."

"Is there anything about your sex life that tends to turn you off?"

Joshua shrugs, but looks concerned. "One problem is that, for some inexplicable reason, Meredith seems to want sex just when her period starts, which is something I can't fathom at all. Well, there's no way I could go along with that. Meredith said with her diaphragm in I wouldn't even know she was menstruating, but . . ." He sighs. "I was always squeamish when it comes to blood and stuff like that. I was the kind of kid who couldn't put a hook in a worm or dissect a frog in biology class. And I'm a scrupulously clean person. I'd *never* go to bed without showering.

"Meredith can be, to put it bluntly, a slob. When she's working on a modeling job, she's immaculate, but between assignments, she's tearing the house apart, climbing ladders, putting up wallpaper, going barefoot with filthy feet. She'll go a week without shaving her underarms. Gross!"

"You mentioned foreplay," the therapist notes. "Does that include oral sex?"

"Rarely," Joshua admits. "Call me prudish, if you want, but I really can't understand why anyone would want to put his mouth *there.* She doesn't mind going down on me, but then a penis can be so much cleaner, not so close to everything else, you know; I don't feel right not reciprocating, so I find that sticking with straight intercourse saves a lot of hassles."

"What turns *you* on, Joshua? Seeing a woman, touching her, or what?"

"I'd say I'm what you might call a sensualist. It's what I *feel,* a mood, I suppose. I never went in for those magazines or dirty movies. I prefer the lights low and some filmy covering to nakedness. A little illusion is always more appealing than stark reality, as those in my profession know. I like having my body touched and stroked. They always write articles about how important it is for a man to give a woman adequate stimulation before intercourse, but they never mention its importance for men, too."

Then, he adds, "But I suppose I'm not the typical man. Meredith certainly doesn't think I am. Can you make me typical, Doctor?"

Joshua is not homosexual. The problem is that he isn't terribly heterosexual either. He has aversive attitudes toward females, both physically and psychologically. Even though he is more comfortable around men, his aversion to homosexuality, mostly on an intellectual basis, is even stronger, so the overall effect is a desire level fast approaching zero.

There are two types of bisexual people. The first, like Joshua's friend Cliff, enjoys sexual activity with members of either sex and lives by the credo, "If it feels good, do it!" These people rarely have problems with sexual desire, except possibly an excess of it. The second type is someone who really prefers homosexual activity, but tries as much as possible to settle for heterosexual gratification and lifestyle because of the increased social acceptance and security (conventional marriage and family life) it entails. They are more likely to have desire problems because they are struggling against their preferences.

Dr. Jerry Friedman of the State University of New York at Stony Brook suspects that some of the low-desire males he treats have a conscious or unconscious concern over sexual-object choices. "In other words," he explains, "a lot of these men may be bisexual or homosexually oriented. It is usually the wife who brings them in. I have never had anyone admit it. They may suppress all desire rather than face this possibility."

Since nearly all such men have some degree of heterosexual desire and are capable of intercourse, and would not be psychologically comfortable with homosexual activity, treatment can be successfully focused on overcoming their sense of inadequacy and becoming more at ease with the female body and mind. Men who feel inferior to other males sometimes develop a syndrome that has been termed "pseudohomosexuality," in which they suspect they are homosexual, have erotic fantasies or even dreams of a homosexual nature, feel compelled to look at other men's genitals, and are uneasy around homosexuals. They never actually engage in homosexuality, but are afraid of competing with other men for women and idealize their perceived superiors in a homoerotic manner.

While it is very unusual to see a man past the age of forty turn from heterosexual to homosexual behavior for the first time, the phenomenon seems more common among middle-aged, divorced women. Their primary motivation for entering a lesbian relationship is to secure a sense of emotional intimacy they never were or are no longer able to get from a man. Ironically, many women who were previously very conservative will get homosexually involved because, after a divorce, they cannot accept the casual approach to premarital sex that men now tend to expect. Or with fewer prospective male partners than younger women, they cannot find a man who meets their emotional, as well as physical, needs.

A woman need not be divorced to turn to homosexuality later in life. Unsatisfied homemakers who are unwilling to jeopardize a marriage with an extramarital heterosexual affair can often successfully cover a homosexual relationship that appears to be only a casual friendship. An experienced homosexual woman will usually initiate the novice, rather than two disgruntled women mutually sharing their first homosexual experience.

Lesbian liaisons involving an age gap of twenty or more years are more common than such relationships in males, where, if they do occur, the younger man is benefiting from the wealth or prestige of the elder, who is more a "sugar daddy" than a true father figure. Women tend to be more intimate, which facilitates development of a mother-daughter bond that is mutually satisfying, despite the Oedipal (or Electra-cal) hazards.

It is far easier for women with homosexual experience or strivings to settle in a conventional marriage than a homosexually oriented man, since sexual compliance is easier for a woman. Sexual desire will obviously pose a problem for women who attempt a sexual adjustment at odds with their primary orientation.

Given the small fraction of homosexuals in the population and the much smaller percentage who will not pursue their inclinations, it is unlikely that many of the numerous cases of desire disorder can be attributed to conflict over sexual-object choice. It should be borne in mind, however, that while mystery and novelty draw men and women together, there are a few who are more threatened than intrigued by the differences between the sexes and these are candidates for desire disorder.

GOING STRAIGHT
Increasing Heterosexual Desire Through Therapy

If, as Dr. Friedman contends, a substantial percentage of men with desire disorder have conflicts over heterosexual object choice, we would expect to encounter at least three different types: men, like Joshua, who are opposed to homosexuality and who feel no conscious desire toward members of the same sex; men who do have secret homosexual fantasies, but who have never acted on them; and men who have had homosexual experience to which they will not admit. What these types have in common is some degree of desire toward women, even though it is too low to maintain a satisfactory heterosexual relationship.

Can homosexuality or homosexual tendencies be treated? We are not asking whether such conditions *should* be treated and today nearly all reputable therapists would agree that treatment should not be foisted upon anyone happy with his orientation, both on ethical grounds and on the practical grounds that the efforts would be almost certain to fail. Many homosexuals or bisexuals will request help in promoting heterosexual desire, either to achieve a thorough change in sexual orientation or to satisfy a partner of the opposite sex. Among patients motivated to change their preference, therapists report a success rate ranging from 20 to 50 percent of cases.

About forty years ago, Dr. Alfred Kinsey pointed out that homosexuality is not an all-or-none pattern and recommended that the degree of homosexuality be graded on a six-point scale. Patients with a history of heterosexual attraction and responsiveness do better in therapy than those who have been exclusively homosexual, and younger men or those with a recent onset of homosexual activity will find it easier to change than older men with long-established homosexual preferences.

In cases where a man is capable of feeling desire toward a woman, but is more strongly attracted toward men, therapists have been able to strengthen heterosexual desire by a technique called orgasmic reconditioning. Sex therapists have observed that no matter what fantasy provides the most arousal, it is the fantasy present at the moment of orgasm that strongly reinforces subsequent arousal patterns.

Dr. Joseph LoPiccolo has described a case at the University of Oregon Psychology Clinic where this technique was used successfully in a male who had been an overt homosexual since early adolescence. He was living with a highly experienced female graduate student who did not object to his homosexual relationships provided he could satisfy her sexually as well. He had been involved in half a dozen heterosexual relationships, all of which failed because of his inability to maintain erections during intercourse.

The man was able to increase his desire for his female partner by incorporating images of her into his masturbatory fantasies at the point where he felt ejaculation was inevitable. Because homosexual males have difficulty visualizing heterosexual stimuli during masturbation, he was provided with provocative Polaroid photographs of his girlfriend to view at the point of orgasm. As the therapy progressed, the man was able to switch to the heterosexual fantasy progressively earlier in the masturbatory process until he was able to feel desire only for the girlfriend from the start of the arousal process. When intercourse was attempted, a similar procedure was used, whereby homosexual fantasies could be employed, as long as he switched to "heterosexual reality" at the moment of

orgasm. Again, in time, there was no need for homosexual fantasies.

This particular patient achieved his goal of improving his sexual
relationship with his girlfriend, although he continued to have homosexual relationships as well. Note that the therapists worked
backward in the sexual response cycle, from orgasm to arousal to
desire; in other words, the man was ultimately able to become
aroused and proceed to orgasm as a result of exclusively heterosexual desire.

What about the patient who does not feel any conscious sexual
attraction toward men, but feels anxiety or repugnance in the presence of women? When a heterosexual man is able to admit to
homosexual desire, the therapist can work on intensifying heterosexual desire at the expense of same-sex attraction, as described
above. When the therapist has only the negative attitudes toward
women to work with, the treatment can be focused on making the
man more comfortable in threatening nonsexual situations with
women.

There have been many different theories about the cause of
homosexuality and probably there are several causes. Fear of
women, sexually prohibitive parents, and seductive mothers have
been implicated, and some men may, indeed, turn to other males
for sexual gratification because they are too threatened by women
to approach them sexually.

In treating passive, insecure men, the therapist has them imagine themselves dealing with hostile or aggressive women in a variety of situations, beginning with the most innocuous. The man may
practice asserting himself with a sarcastic saleswoman or an unco-
operative waitress. He may use a female therapist with whom he can
role-play scenes involving a critical relative or an aloof colleague.
Finally, he may accept assignments to try assertive techniques in
real situations between treatment sessions. The patient is rewarded
with praise not only by the therapist, but also by the women in his
life for his more confident attitude. As anxiety associated with
women diminishes, his sexual desire can increase without inhibi-
tion.

George Bernard Shaw noted that, while people are free to go
either to concerts or the racetrack, "At every one of those concerts
in England you will find rows of weary people who are there, not
because they really like classical music, but because they think they
ought to like it. Well, there is the same thing in heaven. A number of

people sit there in glory, not because they are happy, but because they think they owe it to their position to be in heaven."

In a similar vein, there are undoubtedly many people who would find more sexual satisfaction with members of their own sex, but resist their inclinations because of how they think they ought to be. Still, some people can cultivate an appreciation and desire for classical music where there was initially little interest, and thanks to our growing understanding of the process, some can attain hetero-sexual desire through motivation and effort.

TEARDROPS ON THE PILLOW, DESIRE DROPS IN BED

Depression as a Cause of Desire Disorder

"I've got a *depression?*" Carol says incredulously. Her voice, pre-viously monotonous, picks up a welcome note of animation, but her face remains frozen in its expressionless mask. Her high cheek-bones and finely chiseled nose make her attractive, but the therapist remembers her as even more attractive on the arm of her husband, a radiologist, when he escorted her to hospital parties in happier times. Carol is thirty-two and has a nine-year-old daughter and a four-year-old son.

"I don't feel *that* depressed," she protests. "Sure, everything is an effort and sometimes I'll sit in a chair and watch the clock go around for three hours till it's time to pick up Jonathan from nurs-ery school. And it's nearly Thanksgiving and I haven't finished my Christmas shopping, which I usually have completed by August. But I don't cry myself to sleep every night."

"Do you cry?" the therapist asks.

She nods slowly. "Sometimes. I just get so frustrated because I know I'm not functioning anymore."

"Do you sleep every night?"

"Some," she says. "I wake up a lot. I get up early."

"How early?"

"Oh, 5 or 5:30 A.M.," she says casually. "Then I don't do a damn thing."

"How's your appetite? Have you lost weight?"

"Not much. Five, six pounds maybe. Listen, I could afford to lose it."

"And not much sexual desire," the therapist adds.

"Well, you know *that,*" Carol agrees. "That's why Mel sent me here. I could fake the rest: getting the kids off to school, throwing a meal together, doing the laundry. I couldn't pull it off in bed. He said if I didn't come here and do something about it, he was going to swap me as a bedmate for our daughter's Raggedy Ann. But what have I got to be depressed about?"

"Just from what we've talked about today," the therapist says, "it seems as if you've been under a lot of stress. Jonathan just started nursery school. Your father's been sick off and on. You've had some unexpected home repairs. Mel has been adding new equipment to his office, which means more work for him and some temporary budget-tightening."

"Sure, but you're talking to Supermom," Carol says. "I've had it a lot tougher than this. When my father was in the hospital two years ago, I was constantly driving back and forth, and my son was a lot harder to manage then. Moving away from my parents four years ago was tough for me after living within blocks of them all my life, but I got through that. Why now?"

"Carol, we don't understand depression all that well, although we're learning more," he says. "Tough situations can depress anybody, but some people get depressed for no particular reason. Somewhere along the line, there's a biochemical change in the brain, where certain substances that maintain a normal mood get depleted or inactivated too quickly. Maybe the difference between sadness and depression is only a matter of degree—how much of these chemical mediators are in operation. But when depression sets in, people not only feel sad, but their sleep, appetite, and sexual functioning are disturbed."

"So, if I've got some biochemical disorder, why was I okay for the first thirty years of my life?" she persists.

"Some might take a strictly physical approach to this," he says, "but I see it as a combination of factors. You know what adrenaline is, right? Suppose I give you an injection of it, right into your vein? Your heart will race, your breathing will get rapid, and your blood pressure will rise. If you've got a rare adrenaline-secreting tumor in your adrenal gland, you'll get the same effect, with no apparent reason for the physical change. Now, suppose a vicious pit bull charges you, barking and snarling. Your body pours out adrenaline, same physical sensations. If your lovable, 150-pound wolfhound, Shep, comes bounding into this room, barking his head off, my adrenaline would probably go up because I don't know old Shep, but yours wouldn't. See what I mean? In every case, there's a chemical involved, but the trigger is different."

Carol shakes her head. "I knew there was *something* wrong with me. Even my friends and my kids said I just wasn't the same. Still, I figured depression meant sitting on a window ledge."

"We can deal with depression long before it ever gets to that," the therapist says.

"What do you mean by 'deal with it'?" Carol asks skeptically. "Do I have to take medicine?"

"You don't *have* to, but I'd certainly recommend it," he replies. "An antidepressant won't make everything better overnight, but it should help your sleep pattern, your appetite, your mood, and even your sexual desire. I also want to see you on a regular basis to work on some of these nonphysical stresses and how you're coping with them. And I *don't* gauge improvement by how many chores you accomplish, so let's put away the Supermom costume for a while."

The lower half of Carol's mask curls into a tiny smile. "Wait till Mel finds out he blew a diagnosis. And he was right on top of the case, too!"

Depression is a common cause of low sexual desire, particularly in people who have previously had a normal desire level. At any point in time, about 3 percent of men and 7 percent of women in the United States are in the throes of a major depressive episode. It is estimated that as many as one in ten males and one in four females will have a depression at some time in their lives.

The most severe depressives will come to medical attention either because they stop functioning totally or become suicidal, but many fail to get any treatment or even evaluation because their symptoms take the form of vague physical complaints, excessive fatigue, or a lack of energy. Untreated depressions are usually self-limiting and get better after six months or so—a very difficult six months to endure.

Some of the symptoms of depression, such as crying spells and thoughts of suicide, are easy to identify as hallmarks of a serious mood disorder. Others, such as difficulty concentrating; sleep dis-

turbance, often with early wakening; appetite disturbance with
weight loss; loss of interest in formerly pleasurable activities; and
low self-esteem or feelings of guilt are more subtle and might be
dismissed by the patient, his doctor, and his relatives as a mere
nervous reaction to stress.

Some psychiatrists feel that depressions which seem to come on
spontaneously have a better chance of responding to antidepressant medication, while those that arise when there is stress can be
better helped by psychotherapy. One cannot predict with certainty
when antidepressants will be of value, but generally the patients
who have appetite and sleep disturbances and whose speech and
movements are either noticeably slowed or associated with agitation (pacing or restlessness) will show a good response to medication. Patients whose depression comes and goes, who are able to
joke and laugh and who maintain a fair degree of functioning might
show less improvement through medication alone than those with
more disabling symptoms.

Loss of sexual desire is a frequent symptom of depression;
however, it will not be the *only* symptom. It might be the only
symptom that concerns the partner, who will dismiss the depressed
person's other difficulties as mere nervousness or moodiness.

Just as one can shed tears without having a depression, one can
have a depression with dry eyes.

STUDIES IN BLUE
Research on Depression and Desire

Psychologist Patricia Schreiner-Engel and psychiatrist Raul
Schiavi are working on a four-year study of desire disorder at
Mount Sinai Medical Center in New York City. Funded by government grants, the research project focuses exclusively on men and
women with *global* loss of desire.

Subjects with global desire disorder might be highly arousable,
have orgasms, and even enjoy sex, but they lack the desire to
initiate or engage in sex. They participate because their partners
insist, or they do it to please their partners or to keep marriages
intact.

The researchers screened more than three hundred people

from their own clinic plus another one hundred referred through other sources. About one quarter of these were found to have an emotional depression that had not been recognized or treated and these were dropped from the study. Drs. Schreiner-Engel and Schiavi wound up with 46 men and women who met the criteria for having global desire disorder. The people in this group desired and engaged in sexual activity no more than twice a month. Masturbation counted as sexual experience, since people with global desire disorder have no interest in any form of sexual gratification.

The subjects with desire disorder were matched with control subjects; that is, people who were similar to them in such characteristics as age, length of marriage, and religion, and who desired sex at least once a week if over age forty-five and at least twice a week if under forty-five. The researchers were looking for differences that might account for the desire disorder in the one group and not the other. Extensive psychological questionnaires were administered to both the desire disorder subjects and the controls.

"We have the psychopathology report and the findings were a knockout. . . . they absolutely took us away!" Dr. Schreiner-Engel comments.

It was found that, even though they were not currently depressed, the men and women with desire disorder tended to have past histories of depression far more often than the control group. Exactly half of the 24 women with impaired desire and 55 percent of the 22 men with low desire had past episodes of major depression, nearly twice the number of control subjects who reported depressive symptoms in the past. About 70 percent of the men and women with desire disorder had some type of past mood disorder, although not necessarily a major depressive episode.

In nine out of ten men who had lost sexual desire, the loss occurred concurrently with or following the onset of their initial depressive episode. Every woman with desire disorder had lost her interest in all sexual activity during or subsequent to her first episode of depression and the ten women (42 percent) who had *never* experienced sexual desire all had depressions that began in adolescence.

The major conclusion that can be drawn from this study is that depression and desire disorder may have a common cause. We know that loss of desire frequently accompanies current depressions, but the subjects in this study had a global loss of desire without current or recent depression and a high incidence of past depressions. The onset of the desire disorder invariably occurred during or subsequent to the first depressive episode. There may be an identical or similar biochemical abnormality contributing to both depression and global desire disorder.

Dr. Schreiner-Engel's group has been studying other possible contributory factors to desire disorder, including the effect of early trauma or developmental deficits in childhood, hormonal imbalances, deficits in the arousal stage of sexual response, and problems in interpersonal aspects of sexual relationships. Only through comprehensive, carefully designed and controlled research of this type will we learn all there is to know about sexual desire disorder, and it is heartening to see funds being made available so that we can better understand and help a condition that affects the happiness of so many people.

✻ 7 ✻

Any Body Can Fail—
But Most Don't

Physical Factors Affecting Sexual Desire

There was a time when a man or woman who had lost interest in sex would eventually consult the family doctor with the conviction that there must be something physically wrong—maybe a slight anemia, a sluggish thyroid, lack of vitamins, or "something wrong down there." The expectation, or at least the hope, on the part of the patient or the frustrated spouse was that the medical man would fix things through some pill or injection.

Today, people are far more likely to equate low sexual desire with some sort of psychological problem and hie themselves to a psychologist, psychiatrist, or if fortunate enough to live in a large city, to some clinic or hospital-based program specializing in sexual desire disorders. A good psychotherapist, however, never immediately assumes that the problem is "all in the mind." A thorough medical history, a comprehensive physical examination, and usually some blood tests should be part of the initial evaluation.

Since this is not a medical textbook, we will not provide many details about the various things that could go wrong in the body and affect sexual desire. Still, we would be remiss if we left you with the impression that a loss of sexual desire stems exclusively from nonphysical causes, whether of a situational, interpersonal, or personal nature. In this chapter we'll answer the most common questions people have (we won't say "ask," because there's usually no one to ask), correct frequently held misconceptions, and give a few clues that might point to a physical cause in certain cases.

The first point to bear in mind is that few physical disorders affect *only* sexual desire. If the problem is not strictly limited to the sex glands (testicles in the male, ovaries in the female), we would expect to see symptoms that affect the body in general, such as fatigue, headaches, or nausea. If the problem is limited to the sex glands, we would expect difficulties in sexual function, as well as with sexual desire.

THE GLAND RUSH
Endocrine Organs

Remember how the mother of the fattest kid in school would always say, "His weight problem is 'glandular' "? (Sure, his digestive glands were working overtime and his sweat glands were underemployed.) People usually have only a vague notion of what glands are and how they affect our bodies; the role of the sex glands is probably the most misunderstood of all. All glands produce some type of chemical substance that the body needs. Some glands are microscopic, like the tiny pockets of cells in the stomach that secrete digestive juices or the sweat glands in our skin. Others are sizable organs, such as the pancreas or thymus, while the pituitary and adrenal glands are really composites of different types of tissue, each producing a different secretion.

If a gland lies close to the site where its attention is needed, it delivers its secretions through a duct, and it's called an exocrine gland. The mammary glands (breasts), sweat glands, and sebaceous (oil) glands are of this type; they deliver their products to one spot, not throughout the body.

But if a gland is manufacturing one or more substances needed by more distant "target organs," it uses the most direct and fastest route by releasing the chemicals into the bloodstream. Glands which rush their products without pipelines are called endocrine glands and we usually speak of their products as *hormones* rather than secretions.

The pituitary is a small but very powerful master gland, securely nested in a bony chamber at the base of the brain. It controls growth in children and adolescents and monitors the work of the adrenal, thyroid, and sex glands. If the bloodstream flowing by shows that some of those distant glands are not producing according to expectations, the pituitary sends out a chemical messenger to tell them to step things up. An underproductive thyroid or, much more rarely, an underproductive adrenal will diminish desire, but will also produce more general symptoms, ranging from low energy to sluggishness and malaise (a nonspecific term, meaning "feeling sick"). Underactive thyroids are not uncommon, particularly in women, and in many cases the condition is easily treated with pills.

Another uncommon problem can be failure of the pituitary. Sometimes it is not able to give the routine orders that keep the body's metabolism running or it may produce excessive amounts of a hormone that slows down the other glands. Dr. Domeena Renshaw of Loyola Medical Center in Illinois told us about an interesting case where a formerly athletic thirty-one-year-old man had complaints of no sexual desire, no ejaculate, and constant fatigue. Although he had no headaches or blurred vision, typical of brain tumors, the man's wife was convinced there was a physical problem because his whole personality had changed from an active, outgoing one to an expressionless one, all of his actions having a mechanical quality. He was found to have an inoperable but medically treatable pituitary tumor that was producing excessive amounts of prolactin, a hormone that stimulates milk production in women and interferes with male sexual desire and function.

THE JUICE OF DESIRE
The Role of Testosterone

The hormone that most directly affects desire is testosterone. It's known as "the male hormone" and it affects male sexual desire and functioning. Produced by the testes (a term used for the male sex glands in all creatures; when the testes are palpably present in the scrotal sac outside the body instead of within the body cavity, they are called testicles), testosterone is secreted directly into the bloodstream, not transported out through ducts the way the constantly manufactured sperm cells are.

When testosterone is low, a man will probably have erectile failure as well as low sexual desire, but he may not be aware of his impotence because he considers himself just too disinterested to "try." In such cases, testosterone treatment will nearly always be effective in restoring desire and function. Giving more testosterone to someone who already has a normal level will *not* produce an increase in desire; there is no "more is better" rule involved here.

Sex drive in all creatures seems constitutionally determined with respect to *level.* You need hormones to let you reach that ceiling, but that's as high as hormones alone can get you. Administering testosterone to a castrated rat will restore the animal's interest in sex, but no matter how high the dose, the treated rat will never be more sexually active than it originally was. As you realize by now, humans are such complex creatures that many are below their maximum potential for sexual desire because so many extraneous and internal factors interfere.

About thirty-five years ago, Dr. Fuller Albright pointed out that even "a patient who complains of lifelong impotence or lack of libido does not suffer from hormonal lack; a patient with real endocrine insufficiency has impotence and absent libido, but does not complain of them, but of something more trivial, such as being mistaken for a girl over the telephone."

Dr. Kay Peterson of the Men's Program for the Treatment of Sexual Dysfunction, and instructor in medicine at Harvard Medical School, Cambridge, discussed with us the physical causes of low desire in men. The rarer conditions, such as pituitary tumors, may be insidious, so that the patient is not aware that something is physically wrong, but when the testes are directly affected, the man invariably knows about it. If the man was born with shrunken, nonfunctional testes because of a chromosomal abnormality, his body will show signs of feminization as he grows, such as absence of body hair, abnormally long arms and legs (eunochism) or female body contours because of fat deposition in the hips. Such men never have sexual libido and would only complain about its absence as they became aware of their difference from other men in this regard.

Mumps, particularly if it is contracted after puberty, can cause viral infection of the testicles (orchitis) and may damage sperm and/or testosterone production, resulting in sterility, low desire, or both. Trauma to the testicles could impair the blood supply enough to cause permanent damage and irreversible inability to produce testosterone. Obviously, any man who had endured the pain of orchitis or the horror of testicular trauma would probably readily relate any change in sexual desire and function to those events.

One cause of testicular damage that is overlooked frequently is alcoholism. The drunken porter in Shakespeare's *Macbeth* observed that alcohol increases sexual desire, though it decreases performance. While alcohol's tendency to reduce inhibitions in general might cause an apparent increase of desire after a few drinks, many drinks over many years may poison the testicular cells (just as alcohol poisons the liver and brain cells), which will shut off desire permanently, once the tissue damage is done. Because the alcoholic's body has already been formed, even those with severe testicular atrophy (shrinkage) usually will not show signs of feminization; however, sometimes you will observe loss of hair on the chest and breast development (gynecomastia). Testosterone treatment may restore desire to male alcoholics, but the prognosis is uncertain because there are so many psychological factors involved.

Can a testosterone level be low without the doctors' ever being able to pinpoint the cause? Emphatically, yes. This is called idiopathic hypogonadism, a term meaning "we don't know why the sex glands are underactive." Middle-aged men may have untreated desire problems for years, falsely attributed to the inevitable stresses of life, until someone decides to test the blood for testosterone and finds it deficient. Any large laboratory is able to perform this test, and if the testosterone level is normal, the reassurance alone may help the man's desire. If the level is low, an injection every two-to-four weeks of testosterone can produce a dramatic improvement in sexual desire; therefore, even though low testosterone is not as common a problem as the average person may think, the cost of a blood test is usually a worthwhile investment, especially when low desire is associated with erectile failure.

FEMALE PEAKS AND VALLEYS
Hormones Affecting Women's Desire

There are two exclusively female (i.e., males don't have them) hormones, estrogen and progesterone. Both are produced by the ovaries, progesterone chiefly during the half of the menstrual cycle that follows ovulation. Estrogen causes and maintains the development of female body characteristics, such as breasts, pubic hair, and thickening of the vaginal lining. Progesterone is essential for pregnancy and is formed in the follicle from which the ovum (egg) was released until the fertilized egg can supply a placenta to take over. It does not seem that progesterone has anything to do with enhancing sexual desire and may even offset whatever positive effect estrogen has ("Not tonight, dear, I've got morning sickness!").

We know that estrogen is very vital for sexual activity in animals, since only when the female is in the high-estrogen (estrus) phase of her hormonal cycle will she be receptive (i.e., allow a male to approach her sexually). However, usually the male will not even be attracted to her at other times, so the estrogen seems to be working as much on his nose as her body. Human females, fortunately, are far more flexible with respect to sexual desire, so estrogen is of minor importance compared to its role in other creatures. Some studies, including those on the role of the sense of smell, have indicated that men do find women more attractive during the pre-ovulatory, high-estrogen phase of the menstrual cycle, but not exclusively or remarkably so.

The big surprise is that the hormone which most affects female sexual desire is the *male* hormone, produced in small amounts by the adrenal cortex. We will speak of it as androgen *(andros* is Greek for male), rather than testosterone, because some of its forms may differ slightly in chemical formula from the testosterone produced in the testes, although the action is practically identical. We know this, partly, from reports of women suffering from tumors of the adrenal cortex which produce excessive androgen and women given testosterone for treatment of breast cancer.

The scoresheet, then, with the effect of hormones on female sexual desire: androgens—very stimulating; estrogen—mildly to moderately stimulating; progesterone—neutral or possibly inhibitory. Progesterone antagonizes estrogen and both female hormones antagonize androgen. While the increase in sexual desire reported to occur in some women after menopause might be psychological (e.g., less worry about contraception and the demands of child raising), it is likely that the loss of estrogenic opposition to androgen plays a major role.

Some women—and only some—will say that they definitely feel an increase in sexual desire at certain times in their menstrual cycles. The most frequently cited point is just prior to menstruation, which confused earlier scientists, who couldn't figure out why Nature would have made women most eager for sex at a time they were least able to become pregnant. The second peak in sexual interest is experienced just before ovulation, the optimum time for getting pregnant.

Is estrogen highest at times of women's greatest desire? Actually, estrogen secretion peaks twice during the menstrual cycle, once just before ovulation and again in the middle of the postovulatory phase. The preovulatory rise in estrogen correlates with the increase in female desire, even if a large part of that might be a woman's response to the increased attention she gets from her mate because of the estrogen's effect on *him.* (Apparently the effect on males is mediated through subliminal scents, the pheromones.) The second estrogen rise, after ovulation, may not be effectual because it is antagonized by the even greater flood of progesterone.

The premenstrual desire peak would coincide with the lowest levels of both female hormones; this dearth may permit the androgens, in their small but potent quantity, to exert their full effect on libido without opposition.

As in the case of men, women also seem to have some sort of inherent constitutional level of desire. *Playboy* once published a cartoon in which a young woman, having just entered an apartment, was saying to another woman who looked exactly like her, "Well, we're not identical twins anymore." According to one research study, pairs of identical twin girls have their first sexual experiences at much closer ages than nonidentical twins. Age of first intercourse is not a foolproof measure of libido level, but the difference between types of twins would tend to rule out age, upbringing, and social status as the most important determinant of virginity loss.

Postmenopausal women are often treated with estrogen, but this does not raise their level of sexual desire. Estrogen will restore thickness and blood supply in the vaginal lining of a hormone-deficient woman and correct the conditions of thinning and dryness that lead to infection and discomfort on intercourse, which would secondarily affect desire for sexual activity. Estrogen may help relieve "hot flashes." It does not restore hot blood.

Can treatment of women with androgens increase their sexual desire? Some sex therapy centers do give male hormone in small amounts, although such treatment is not widely used because of the virilizing side effects, such as beard growth, deepening of the voice, and clitoral enlargement, which would tend to lower the woman's self-esteem and her partner's sexual desire.

BAD MEDICINE FOR DESIRE
Side Effects of Medication

The trouble with medications is that they follow the rapid transit route of the bloodstream, along with the hormones. The chemical couriers that Nature sets loose are more efficient than prescribed drugs because the hormones have very selective destinations and do not tamper with extraneous organs along the route. Nearly every medication has a desired effect and several potential side effects on organs and systems that were not the intended targets.

Any drug that makes you sleepy or lethargic is bound to affect your sexual desire to some extent, particularly tranquilizers and sleeping pills, but also antihistamines. If a pill makes you nauseated, gives you cramps, or causes diarrhea, you are not going to feel very sexy.

Even more specific are certain commonly prescribed drugs that have a deleterious effect on sexual desire without causing physical discomfort. The prime offenders here are probably the antihypertensive agents, medication prescribed for high blood pressure. While the simpler and less potent antihypertensives, such as those that work exclusively by increasing loss of water through urination (the diuretics), have no inhibiting action, agents containing reserpine or methyldopa may. These drugs can interfere with erection as well, and men are more likely to complain of impotence rather than low desire, although, as we have discussed, men often equate erection with desire and loss of the former can soon result in absence of desire. Reserpine can exert a double-whammy because it can cause psychological depression, one symptom of which is loss of sexual desire.

Most patients taking antihypertensive agents are males and most are in their late fifties or older. Since a natural weakening of erectile ability tends to occur around this age, loss of desire as a side effect of antihypertensive medication may be overlooked. A man may say, "I must be getting old." His decreasing potency increases his sense of failure, so his desire for more of the same will obviously decrease.

Another type of commonly prescribed drugs that can inhibit desire is the beta-blockers, such as propanalol. Their chief use is controlling irregular heart rhythms or rapid heartbeat, although they can also be helpful in lowering blood pressure. Because of the occurrence of frightening racing of the heart in certain nervous conditions without much preliminary subjective anxiety, beta-blocking agents have recently been used to control panic attacks and have been prescribed for social phobia (where there is a terror of having to speak in public) or "stage fright" on the part of accomplished performers. Propanalol and its relatives will affect potency in men, but in about 1 case in 20 they will lower desire without a noticeable effect on erection.

Some of the drugs that decrease acid secretion in stomach conditions, including peptic ulcers, have been implicated in desire disorders. Since doctors very often prescribe such agents even without documented ulcer disease, cimetidine and similar drugs are high on the list of most-used medications. However the incidence of interference with desire is far lower than with the cardiovascular drugs discussed above.

Women seem far less likely to suffer from loss of desire as a result of medication. However the male-female difference is probably not truly as wide as we might be led to believe. High blood pressure and heart conditions are far more common among males, so they take most of the prescribed problematic drugs. Desire disorder in women is often masked by a pattern of automatic compliance with male desire that characterizes a large percentage of marriages; perhaps with younger women's willingness to take the sexual initiative, more cases of sexual desire disorder in middle-aged women will be coming to light. Women probably take more prescribed tranquilizers than men, but diminished desire gets blamed on nervousness, not the medication.

Sexual arousal holds a key position midway between desire and orgasm. Note that when arousal is impaired, men tend to project the complaint backward and women forward. In other words, a man with a failed erection will say that he has lost his desire and a woman who fails to have vaginal tissue swelling and lubrication (so that intercourse is uncomfortable) will say that she cannot have orgasms. Where medication is the culprit in desire loss, you will rarely hear the person say, "But I'm fine once I get involved in sex."

ON THE HORN OF A UNICORN
Fabled Aphrodisiacs

We've talked about medicinal substances that interfere with sexual desire, but has medical science come up with anything, other than testosterone for men who lack their own supply, to increase desire—a true aphrodisiac?

Back in the Middle Ages, your friendly local apothecary would have sold you his satisfaction-guaranteed brand of powdered unicorn horn. If he saw from your raiment and retinue that you were a person of wealth, he might offer to sell you a complete horn. (In case you're wondering how apothecaries got real spiral, ivory horns from mythological animals, these impressive appendages came from narwhals, small Arctic whales that have a single long tusk that looks just like what you'd expect of a unicorn horn. People found it easier to believe in unicorns than narwhals.)

Placebos, or remedies that work only through the power of suggestion, have always had an important place in the practice of medicine and even today any decent drug study will compare patients who take an experimental drug not with a group who don't take anything but with those given a placebo; a percentage always will report improvement with the placebo. Thus, some responded because they expected the unicorn horn to work, based, no doubt, on the belief that their penises would take on the long, rigid properties of the ingested horn. Orientals have taken great stock in rhinoceros horn for the same reason, and contributed to the primeval creature's position on the endangered species list by hunting it nearly to extinction.

The unconscious association of their shape with certain sexual parts led to the use of some foods as aphrodisiacs. Asparagus and celery were expected to induce the penis to emulate them. Oysters, olives, and eggs gained their unreliable reputations through their resemblance to the testes. "Prairie oysters" (bull's testicles) still have a limited vogue among Westerners who consume them to bolster virility. As loaded with testosterone as these glands are, cooking destroys any of the hormone that might have helped the limited few with a hormone deficiency.

"Spanish fly" is a fabled aphrodisiac actually used by animal breeders to make prudish cattle add a few head to the herd. The drug is made from the dried bodies of iridescent beetles found (of course) in Spain, which are pulverized to extract an active substance, cantharidin. The drug is concentrated in the urine, causing intense irritation of the bladder and urethra, with reflex stimulation of the labia and clitoris in females. Most of the stories about slipping it in a woman's drink to turn her into an insatiable nymphomaniac are apocryphal boasts, since cantharidin is highly toxic to the central nervous system and can cause fatal convulsions.

Ginseng is a natural substance long valued by the Orientals as a desire stimulant, which has found its way onto the shelves of the health food stores that sprang up alongside the health clubs. Ginseng is usually sold as a powder or a tea. It grows as a twisted root, resembling horseradish or ginger, and like the fabled mandrake with alleged magical properties, the uncut ginseng looks like a man, with head and paired limbs extending from its "torso." Although its fans swear to its efficacy, the notion that something that looks like a man will make one more virile smacks of horn worship.

OVER THE COUNTER AND UNDER THE TABLE
Searching for a Modern Aphrodisiac

Is there *nothing*, legal or illegal, in the way of drugs that works as a reliable aphrodisiac in these modern times?

There is no medication sanctioned by the Federal Drug Administration as a stimulant to sexual desire although today's alchemists continue to search for a true aphrodisiac long after they stopped trying to turn base metals into gold. The nearest thing we have to a prescribable drug that is reputed to promote, in some cases, sexual arousal and desire only in males is yohimbine hydrochloride. Yohimbine is not a new drug and was formerly used to treat high blood pressure before more effective medications were developed. It is extracted from the bark of the Rubaceae tree, which grows in

Africa. Yohimbine's principal action is to dilate, or widen, blood vessels. Erections occur when blood floods into the spongy tissues of the penis and yohimbine seems a little more selective than other vasodilators with respect to the pelvic arteries. Since male desire drops when self-esteem drops, the restoration of a good erection (as Dr. Thomas Stewart likes to pun, a "ressur-erection") will, in retrograde fashion, renew sexual desire. The problem is that yohimbine's ability to reverse impotence is far from predictable and its ability to restore sexual desire is even less successful.

Levodopa, used in the treatment of Parkinson's disease, has been reputed to cause an increase in sexual desire in the men who receive it, primarily elderly patients. Levodopa (or l-dopa) can cause erections or even priapism (persistent erections) and it is likely that the men who suddenly start acting seductive or lecherous around their nurses are responding enthusiastically to this totally unexpected return of genital sensation. Desire was probably always there, but beaten down by the loss of capacity for physical arousal.

Trazedone is one of the newer antidepressant drugs and there have been a few reported cases of its causing priapism, a problem not encountered with other drugs of this type. Priapus, the god with the organ that was eternally on the rise, was worshipped by the ancients, but priapism is a painful, not stimulating, condition. Surgery to correct it has even resulted in permanent loss of erectile ability, so with all the available alternative drugs, few psychiatrists would give trazedone to a male patient, however rare this complication.

How about illegal aphrodisiacs, substances that you can't get over the counter but might get under the table? Reputable authorities will answer the question in the negative, but some consumers of "recreational drugs" cannot "just say no." They will extol marijuana, cocaine, and perhaps the hallucinogens, like LSD, as enhancers of sexual desire and gratification.

To the extent that these substances work at all, their mechanism is similar to that of an addicting drug that is perfectly legal and can be obtained over the counter at your local "package store," where the products are packaged in glass containers. We mean alcohol, of course, which you don't have to obtain under the table, although consumers often end up there anyway.

To assess the ability of alcohol to augment sexual desire consistently, just ask the wife of any alcoholic about their sex life. Generally, the bed is used for passing out, not making out. What a moderate amount of alcohol does accomplish is to reduce anxiety or fear, which is why it is more effectively employed by adventurous singles than the married folk who would be more expected to need some prodding in the desire department. Good judgment can override strong desire and alcohol impairs judgment, so that an apparent increase in desire may actually be the removal of a sensible obstacle.

Is the quest for improved sexual desire worth an arrest or a possible bad trip? Marijuana devotees claim a relaxing, euphoric effect that makes sexual activity more pleasant, but at least as many experimenters have found that the drug causes irritability, agitation, and paranoia. You can't unconvert the converted, but those mired in the shoals of low desire cannot expect to sail into deeper levels by getting themselves hooked on the reefer.

LSD does not mean "low sexual desire," but it doesn't mean higher desire either. Some night-trippers have claimed to experience great sexual desire and excitement; they have also experienced great elephant parades and dragon flights, which can distract you from your sexual activity. LSD, STP, DMT, and the other three-letter drugs that were often ingested during four-letter activities in the 1960s have, fortunately, gone out of vogue, except for, possibly, PCP or "angel dust," a hellish hallucinogen with potentially fatal effects on the brain.

Cocaine is the latest drug to be touted as a potent igniter of desire, although Sigmund Freud was hooked on the stuff and we know how tame his libido was—it was virtually domesticated. Cocaine produces a short-lived feeling of euphoria, and when you're euphoric you can get pretty enthusiastic about anything, from having sex to clipping your toenails. Cocaine has less staying power than a premature ejaculator and soon its euphoriant effect lasts as long as snow on a hot tin roof. Any regular user of cocaine will develop a constant strong desire—only it's exclusively a desire for more cocaine.

As far as formulating an overall rule regarding drugs and desire: your sexual desire level will never be high as long as you are.

While we eagerly await the results of new research, we have already learned much during the past decade about the causes and treatment of sexual desire disorder, not so very long ago a condition without a name.

The time to apply what we have already learned is now.

❧ *III* ❧

SELF-EVALUATION

❧ 8 ❧

Check It Out

Evaluating Your Desire

There are many reasons for loss of desire and there are many different remedies. So when desire lags, how do we know which is the right prescription for us?

Our sexuality is as much a part of our basic personality as our sociability, our work habits, and our temperament. Desire, the non-physical part of our sexual response cycle, takes its form, direction, and intensity from our individual makeup and is unique for each person. To understand your sexual desire, you must understand your personality and the type of desire pattern that goes with it.

In this section, you will be able to assess some aspects of your psychological makeup to which you probably haven't given much thought before. By answering the questions the way your partner might, you may understand the factors that adversely affect his or her interest in sex.

There are four factors that shape our desire and determine its intensity:

1. Experience. We begin having sexual experiences in childhood; even though we don't engage in mature sexual behavior, we become curious about and learn about the sex organs and form some impressions about what adults do sexually. In adolescence, we greatly increase our awareness and information, feel sexual desire, and have physical perceptions of arousal and gratification. All of these early experiences color our feelings about sex in adulthood, even when we are not consciously aware of them.

2. Personality type. Some people are cautious and emotionally restrained, while others are impulsive and emotionally expressive. Some are governed by their heads and others lead with their hearts. How they handle desire is markedly different.

3. Attitudes. Life offers a wide variety of options, but most of us quickly limit our sexual activities to what corresponds with our personal philosophies. Conservatives, moderates, and liberals all feel desire, but are likely to express it in contrasting ways.

4. Sensuality. What turns you on the most? Do you bring all five of your senses to sexual encounters or do you find that focusing on genital sensation is most exciting and gratifying? Do you like some romantic preliminaries or do you find them phony and unnecessary? When you understand what really turns you on, you'll be better able to understand what turns your desire off.

First, we want to call your attention to certain cognitive errors that impede desire. We have discussed how false expectations can cause someone to regard a basically normal situation as a hopeless catastrophe. False expectations are one type of cognitive error. There are others, equally hazardous, and identifying and eliminating them may be enough to restore desire.

THINKING STRAIGHT
Correcting Cognitive Errors

> *"But I am quite content with brain enough to know that I'm enjoying myself. I don't want to understand why. In fact, I'd rather not. My experience is that one's pleasures don't bear thinking about."*
> —GEORGE BERNARD SHAW,
> *Man and Superman*

The elderly Commander, who expresses these popular sentiments in Shaw's play, speaks for many who feel that pleasure and serious thought are natural enemies. There is a grain of truth to this. Most of us will recall that the things that were the most fun for us, including some sexual adventures, were those in which we abandoned ourselves to sheer enjoyment and conducted ourselves like carefree children, quite differently from the day-to-day way in which supervisors or subordinates view us.

When we intellectualize sex, as opposed to fantasizing about it, we don't think about desire the way we think about the subsequent phases in the sexual response cycle. We apply our intellects to sexual techniques that ensure adequate stimulation and orgasm, but not to improving desire, because we feel the two processes, rational thought and desire, are totally incompatible and mutually inhibitory.

Sometime in the seventies, our society acquired an incestuous infatuation with Mother Nature. Natural foods, natural beverages, natural vitamins, and natural cosmetics became bestsellers. If it came directly from Nature, it had to be healthy, we were led to believe, forgetting that the typhoid bacillus, the mosquito, and typhoons are also part of Nature.

How often did you hear the media mavens say, "Sex is a *natural* drive, a *natural* function, a *natural* process!" Nobody dared ask them what the hell they meant, but the implication was that if you just get down to it, sex will take care of itself and things will be wonderful.

To give Nature her due, humans are capable of having sex 365¼ days per year, unlike other creatures who are motivated to mate only at certain times during their hormonal cycles. Since desire is so obviously associated with volition or will, using our intellects to augment, as well as curb, desire would seem to be more in keeping with Nature than opposing her.

DEMYSTIFYING AND DEMYTHIFYING DESIRE
Common Misconceptions About Sex

What we believe about and expect sexual desire to be is related to our beliefs and attitudes in general. Over the past two decades, we have become better informed about sex than any previous generation. Yet our increasing preoccupation with sexuality has also fostered myths.

Read the ten brief statements below, most of which you have seen or heard before, and without any deep thought, honestly and impulsively blurt out "true" or "false."

1. An active, satisfying sex life is important for emotional health.
2. Since the sex urge is a basic biological drive, people *need* sexual outlets.
3. Lack of sexual desire indicates deep psychological problems.
4. People who have frequent sexual relations are more well adjusted than other people.
5. Normal married couples have intercourse at least once a week, usually two or three times a week.
6. Couples who have infrequent sexual relations have deep conflicts in their relationship.
7. Couples who are compatible sexually are usually highly compatible in other aspects of their relationship as well.
8. Lack of interest in having sexual relations with one's partner indicates a strong element of unconscious anger.
9. Love is invariably associated with strong sexual attraction.
10. One's desirability as a person is reflected by one's sex appeal.

Here are the answers:

1.   *An active, satisfying sex life is important for emotional health.*
False. Some people gain considerable emotional satisfaction from sexual activity. For others, sexual activity has brought misery and ruin. Many people, such as priests, nuns, teenagers, prudent single persons, widows and widowers, and even some married people are celibate by choice or because of the absence of an appropriate sex partner and are perfectly well adjusted. At last we've escaped the centuries-old myth that excessive sexual activity causes insanity, but now we seem to be erring at the opposite extreme. The idea that one's mental health depends on sexual activity is poppycock.

2.   *Since the sex urge is a basic biological drive, people need sexual outlets.*
False. Freud referred to sex as a "drive," but is it? *Human* sex is entirely under voluntary control. The fallacy that once you feel desire there must be some corresponding activity to release the urge leads many people to repress desire. Lacking a suitable outlet, they choose a life devoid of desire rather than risk the frustration of searching for love and sexual fulfillment. Finding that appropriate partner might take a little time, but it's worth the wait—nothing disastrous will happen in the interim when there is desire without sex. Maybe fish gotta swim and birds gotta fly, but humans don't

gotta do anything, least of all have sex. The notion that we *need* an outlet is tommyrot.

3. *Lack of sexual desire indicates deep psychological problems.*

False. People with secondary lack of sexual desire (i.e., who have experienced sexual desire at some time in the past) are often just reacting to environmental pressures. Stress on the job, a conflict with a family member, or financial worries are nonsexual concerns that can decrease desire markedly. People with a primary lack may have been influenced by overly strict or prudish parents or teachers, but they need not have problems in other areas. While some of these people require prolonged therapy, others respond very quickly to short-term treatment, which might consist chiefly of the therapist's giving them some long-neglected sex education and, through his frankness and acceptance, permission to do what had been prohibited in the past. A lack of sexual desire does not necessarily indicate complex emotional problems.

4. *People who have frequent sexual relations are more well adjusted than other people.*

False. This is the ever-popular "more is better" fallacy. Coupled with the myth that sex is necessary for healthy mental adjustment, this emphasis on quantity assumes that whatever benefits you get from sex will be multiplied by the number of times you have sex. Some people turn to sex as a release for *every* sort of emotional need, from insecurity to anger and this does not make them well adjusted.

5. *Normal married couples have intercourse at least once a week, usually two or three times a week.*

False. This statement confuses "normal" with "average." It is true that on average married couples of all ages have sex twice a week. It is also true, according to our nationwide survey, *Husbands and Wives,* that 10 percent of all couples and 3 percent between the ages of forty and fifty don't have sex at all. For every couple having sex four times a week, there are two couples having sex once. For every pair of newlyweds having sex six times a week, two couples are having sex once a month. "Normal" behavior covers the whole frequency range, producing an average.

6. *Couples who have infrequent sexual relations have deep conflicts in their relationship.*

False. While couples who constantly quarrel may have infrequent sex, couples may also be having sex infrequently simply because it suits their individual temperaments. Given the tension that desire discrepancy can cause, a pair of low-desire spouses might have far fewer potential causes of friction than a couple in which one partner presses the other for more frequent sex. The assumption that infrequent sex indicates conflict is balderdash.

7. *Couples who are compatible sexually are usually highly compatible in other aspects of their relationship as well.*

False. One would have to assume that people with similar sexual desire and favorite practices would share qualities such as intelligence, temperament, empathy, sensitivity, etc., because these traits correlated in some way with sexuality. Unfortunately, there is no such link and many couples who marry because of their great sexual attraction are dismayed to discover they have nothing else in common. A genuine liking for one another usually improves sexual compatibility, but sexual and overall compatibility do not invariably go together.

8. *Lack of interest in having sexual relations with one's partner indicates a strong element of unconscious anger.*

False. People who believe that deep conflicts are associated with infrequent sex may argue that, if conflicts are not apparent, it is because the anger is repressed, but still operative. Sometimes unconscious anger is the motive behind refusal of a spouse's invitation to sex, but more often lack of desire may be related to personal problems, such as depression, entirely independent of the relationship.

9. *Love is invariably associated with strong sexual attraction.*

False. It's bad enough when a spouse feels that a partner is sexually disinterested, but far worse when the disinterest is interpreted as a lack of love. Many men caught in the grip of the ubiquitous prostitute-madonna complex find the exact opposite is true. At the beginning of the relationship, the man finds the woman to be the object of his sexual urges. As he gets to know her and appreciate her more, especially after she adds the role of motherhood to her complex image, he acquires new respect and concern for her as a human being and, unfortunately, often a desire disorder as well.

The stereotypical *macho* man, associated with Latin cultures, is known not only for his lascivious, impersonal pursuit of women, but also for his devotion to his mother. He is prepared to engage in mortal combat with anyone who dares impugn his mother's virtue. Psychoanalysts attribute the split image of bad, sexy women and good, asexual women to a defense against unacceptable Oedipal sexual feelings. True or not, it's the most feasible explanation anyone has come up with. The taboo extends, of course, to sisters, aunts, housekeepers, and any other respectable woman encountered in the environment of a sex-obsessed adolescent male. Hence, boys' early masturbatory fantasies usually focus on impersonal pinups, not real women.

The flip side of the fallacy is that a strong sexual attraction means love. Thus, a man may convince not only a woman but himself that he feels true love, simply because his desire is so great. If he hardly knows the woman, the existence of true love is highly unlikely. Looking at the equation from either side, the belief that love and strong sexual attraction are virtually synonymous is rubbish.

10. *One's desirability as a person is reflected by one's sex appeal.*

False. We're not even sure we can define "sex appeal," but we take it to mean an aura about a person which makes you feel he or she is attractive, not necessarily physically, as a *man* or a *woman.* Hollywood started this nebulous nonsense decades ago, but it got out of hand when the press applied the term "sex symbol" to a paunchy, bespectacled cabinet member who dated an aging actress. Now, even septuagenarian statesmen and octagenarian grand dames are embarrassed (or should be) by that designation and only Mother Teresa seems remotely safe. So it is not surprising that a man or woman who feels unattractive as a sex partner would extend that image to other facets of the personality.

This tendency to generalize sets up a self-perpetuating cycle. The key element of sex appeal, which obviously does not depend strictly on physical attractiveness or accomplishments, seems to be the person's ability to exude a sense of self-confidence, the carriage and demeanor of a winner. Think about it: How many homely people have you known who could attract others, while prettier individuals consistently blend in with the formica?

Some people complain that, where meeting people is concerned, it's feast or famine. Just when they find a boyfriend, they suddenly find eligible men flocking around them. They break up with a boyfriend and men avoid them the way Greta Garbo would react to Robin Leach. They fail to realize that they *are* more attractive when they're feeling happy and confident and less attractive when they feel down and unsexy. But the equation of that elusive quality called sex appeal with one's overall worth is twaddle.

What do the above myths have to do with sexual desire? As our analysis of Fallacy 10 indicates, a person who feels inadequate sexually soon transposes this sense of inferiority to his or her entire self. Subscribing to any of these myths can undermine one's self-confidence, for no valid reason. Thinking that there is something wrong with yourself or your relationship because your frequency of sexual relations is not up to some meaningless standard or fearing that if things haven't yet gone wrong they soon will can make you feel depressed. Nothing kills sexual desire like depression. Feeling like a winner and feeling sexy are not identical, but they do reinforce one another.

MENTAL BLOCKS OF THE STUMBLING KIND
Cognitive Errors That Impede Desire

"I'm a sexual *klutz,"* Lester moans. He's twenty-four, single, and has just launched a promising career in computer program design after compiling an exceptional academic record in college and graduate school. While not movie-idol material, he is trim, exercises regularly, and except for a shyness that causes him to date only women who approach him (and many do), he could have a very active social life. For several months he has been dating Cheryl, a twenty-two-year-old music student.

"We had sex again last Saturday, and as always, it was a disaster. I was so afraid I'd lose my erection if I tried to penetrate her that I kept going with foreplay to the point that she must have been wondering what the hell I was waiting for. When we finally got down to it, I just couldn't give her an orgasm. I wanted to try again and she said she was really tired. Hah! You know that was her polite way of showing she was disgusted with the whole thing."

"Did she really seem all that disappointed?" the therapist asks.

"Oh, she was very cuddly and affectionate afterward and said how much she liked my making love to her," Lester says with a shrug, "but she was just trying to make me feel good. Anyway, I'm the first man she went all the way with, so how would she know the difference anyway? Not that I'm all that experienced myself, as I've told you, but the few times I've managed to go to bed with a girl, it was the same sad story. I never really satisfy them and I always do something to louse things up.

"I ought to be able to prolong intercourse long enough for a girl to have a real good climax. I've tried reading books on the subject, but I can't seem to put it into practice. I'm a loser in bed. I'm gutless. I keep thinking how Cheryl would rather be making it with some tall, muscular guy with a bigger penis than mine and how miserable she must be having to settle for me. Well, next time I see her, I'm sure she'll invent some excuse so that she doesn't have to go to bed with me. Maybe I should just stop calling her and save her the trouble of breaking up with me. I just feel in my gut that I've blown it for good."

Remember those puzzles you used to solve in magazines when you were a kid, the ones where you had to find ten things wrong with this picture? Well, Lester's mournful account of his last attempt at lovemaking, brief as it is, contains at least ten self-defeating cognitive pitfalls, or *mental stumbling blocks*.

The casual listener will perceive that Lester is really down on himself, and at the rate he's going, he soon will lose all desire for sex, since his encounters lead to frustration and unhappiness. What is not so obvious is that Lester is *thinking* himself into this predicament. This highly intelligent, usually logical young man is stumbling from one mental error into another, too emotionally upset to realize that he would never make such patent errors in programming his computers, for fear they would melt down their microchips.

Desire is lodged in the brain—exclusively in the brain. So, many therapists now rely heavily on a cognitive approach to treat desire disorder. Believing you are unsuccessful will make you feel like a chronic loser and perceiving experiences as negative will make you lose the desire to repeat them. Your distorted perception of your sexual potential becomes your reality. Correction of mental errors leads to a more positive perception and ultimately to a happier reality.

THE TEN TRIPWIRES

Here are ten cognitive pitfalls, all of which Lester, the computer programmer, nicely demonstrates. See if you can spot the flaws in this "logic."

1. "Eliminate the Positive"
Whenever you spot something positive about your sexual experience, think of some way to disqualify it. If your wife seemed to enjoy your last encounter, say, "She's had so little experience with other men, she wouldn't know the difference between a good lover and a bad one [like me]." If your husband seemed happy, tell yourself, "He thought I had an orgasm. If he knew I faked it, he would have been devastated."

2. "Accentuate the Negative"
Search very hard to find at least one negative thing about your sexual experience. Then, make this the hallmark of the entire encounter. If she didn't have an orgasm, the evening was a total disappointment. If she did, she should have had multiple orgasms. Maybe the two of you should have had simultaneous, multiple orgasms.

3. "Molehill Development"
With a little effort, a minor mishap can be built up into a catastrophe of tragic proportions. If a man feels he ejaculated prematurely, he can tell himself that his partner is so furious she will never want to have sex with him again. If he failed to get an erection, his new partner has concluded that he is gay, and will tell all her friends, and no one will ever go to bed with him again.

4. "Name Calling"

This involves labeling yourself. Don't say, "I have difficulty reaching orgasm," say, "I'm frigid." It saves time and identifies you as a deficient person, not just someone with a particular problem. Seeing yourself as a "lousy lover," "prude," "wimp," or "dog" will save you the trouble of constructively addressing the problem, and even though members of the opposite sex aren't aware of your pet name for yourself, you'll be amazed how you're suddenly conveying that image to them.

5. "Personal Account"

If your partner doesn't seem satisfied, who's to blame? *You,* of course! If he has erectile dysfunction, it must be because you're so unexciting. If she doesn't have an orgasm, you don't know how to satisfy a woman.

6. "Skipping and Jumping"

This mental exercise involves skipping over logical steps and jumping to conclusions. If your partner complains that she is too tired for sex, you can't know what's going on in her head, so skip any attempt to discern reality and jump to the conclusion that she is angry at you because you were so inadequate the last time you made love. Always conclude the worst.

7. "Now and Forever"

Just qualify everything that happens with *always* and everything that fails to happen with *never;* for example, "I *always* let some worry distract me during sex," or "I *never* satisfy my partner." If things don't seem to be going right, assume that they will stay that way forever. If things haven't improved, assume they will never improve.

8. "The Black Whole"

Think in absolutes. Black and white. Yes and no. All or nothing. If you're not wholly satisfied, then you're unsatisfied. If you don't have a full measure of desire, you have no desire. If you had a little of something, you might be able to work with it, but how can you get a grip on nothing?

9. "All for Ought"

Look at what you're doing and then tell yourself what you *ought* to be doing. You've heard that a man *should* be interested in sex whenever the opportunity arises or that a man *should* bring his partner to orgasm every time. No matter what you're doing, you should be able to find something you've failed to do.

10. "Dread Feelings"

Trust your feelings. If you *feel* you are unattractive, why let anyone convince you otherwise? If you *feel* you're inadequate as a lover, what difference does it make what your partners think? The ultimate resistance against rational thinking is to deny the importance of such things and insist, "But that's not the way I *feel!*"

These mental stumbling blocks can transform a sexual experience that is 90 percent satisfying into a total disappointment. What's the effect on desire? Obviously, nobody desires negative experiences, so with these illogical mind-sets, desire soon dies out.

Cognitive pitfalls can even prevent desire from ever developing. People raised by prohibitive, sexually repressed parents fall prey to the "ought" fallacy, or more specifically, its "ought not" variation. Any twinge of desire immediately evokes the words *dirty* and *sinful.* The persistent illogical sanctions against desire reduce any sexual activities to dispassionate compliance.

"Name calling" can also be a source of primary global desire disorder. A person who is self-conscious about awkwardness or some physical imperfection may, in early adolescence, assume the self-label of "loser" or "dog." Rather than subject themselves to certain rejection, such people may never let desire be felt.

Secondary desire disorder can occur if a person habitually overreacts to any negative aspect of sexual experience—and *some* negative experiences are inevitable. Developing a molehill of disappointment into a mountainous obstacle to future satisfaction or making an unpleasant part of an experience into a "black whole" will extinguish desire for what was previously anticipated with eagerness.

Jumping to unjustified conclusions about a partner's dissatisfaction and holding yourself personally accountable for anything less than a flawless encounter will lead to increasing tension in a relationship and development of a selective desire disorder, with retreat from your partner to fantasy, masturbation, or extramarital affairs.

Desire is a mental process that aims at sexual satisfaction. You can't aim straight unless you think straight.

TAKING A SEXUAL INVENTORY

"I am a part of all that I have met. . . ."
—ALFRED LORD TENNYSON, *Ulysses*

It would be more accurate to say, "All that I have met is part of me." It pleases us to think that we have made some subtle impression on every person we have ever met or have influenced the outcome of every event at which we were present. This is occasionally true; however, we can say with certainty that everything we have ever experienced is incorporated into our being in some way, even if only as a dimly perceived memory.

Everybody's sexuality is unique; desire is the most individualized component of human sexual response. We might do a quick survey of men and women, asking, "How often do you want sex?" and conclude that a vast majority want sex four to twelve times a month. That might lead us to conclude that most people are similar in their desire level, but we would be ignoring such factors as the circumstances (time, atmosphere, preliminaries), specific activities, and the kind of partner that each person would prefer under ideal conditions.

Every sex therapist must assess his or her patient's sexual attitudes and sexual preferences during the course of treatment by taking a sexual history. It encompasses not only sexual experiences in adulthood, but also all the events and sources of influence during childhood and adolescence that molded one's ideas and feelings about sex and one's sexual preferences and aversions.

Can you take and assess your own sexual history? Yes. In fact, the advantages of self-evaluation are considerable. There is no problem of self-consciousness or embarrassment. There is no time pressure; in an interview, there is a tendency to respond as quickly as possible. Once you give an interviewer an answer, you are unlikely to change it, but you are free to reconsider things in a self-assessment. Verbal communication is often an inadequate way to convey our most intimate thoughts and a listener can misinterpret what we really want to say. Finally, interviewers gather data but rarely discuss its implications with the person interviewed, so that information flows in only one direction.

The sexual history is *your* history, a very personal odyssey that began even before you were aware that you had embarked on it. The questions below are drawn from those routinely used by prominent sex therapists. Answering these questions will help you relive your past and get in touch with the things that have made you the sort of sexual person you are today. There will be happy memories and probably a few unpleasant ones; times you would love to reexperience and others you would have rather avoided. But since desire is heightened or diminished by all we have encountered in the past, it is important to take inventory of the positive and negative forces that have made an impact on our sexual attitudes and practices.

YOUR SEXUAL INVENTORY

Childhood

1. How old were your parents when you were born? Was one parent older than the other? Were they older or younger than the parents of most of your friends?
2. Do you have brothers and sisters? How many the same sex as you and how many of the opposite sex?
3. Where do you rank in age among the children in your family?
4. Where do you rank among siblings of the same sex?
5. Are any siblings of the opposite sex older or younger than you?
6. Are both of your parents still living? If either or both are deceased, how old were you when they died?
7. Were you raised to an appreciable extent by people other than your parents (relatives, foster parents, housekeepers), either in your parents' home or in outside homes? Did any of these people have a significant effect on your education or experience about sex?
8. Did your parents stay together throughout your childhood

and adolescence, or did they separate or divorce at some point?

9. Were either of your parents previously married? Did you have any contact with their former spouses? Did either parent have children by other marriages, and how much contact did you have with these children?

10. At what age (if any) did you think about your parents' sex life? What was your conception of their sex life?

11. Did your parents openly show physical affection for one another? Did they show affection by direct verbal expression? Did they show affection by the way they behaved toward one another, even though they didn't speak openly in affectionate terms?

12. Did your parents ever engage openly in behavior that was frankly sexual in intent, as opposed to merely affectionate (i.e., joking about sex, making sexual comments, touching each other intimately)?

13. Was your mother an affectionate person? How did she show it? Would you have wanted more affection from her, or preferred that she showed affection in a different way?

14. Was your father an affectionate person? How did he show it? Would you have wanted more affection from him, or preferred that he showed affection in a different way?

15. What do you think were your mother's attitudes, feelings, and activities with regard to sex? Did she ever talk to you about this, or did you have to form your opinions by supposing how she felt?

16. What do you think were your father's attitudes, feelings, and activities with regard to sex? Did he ever talk to you about this, or did you have to form your opinions by supposing how he felt?

17. Do you think your parents were well suited to one another? Why or why not?

18. Was religion an important factor in your early attitudes toward sex? Did you ever have strong feelings about what you should or shouldn't do on the basis of religious beliefs or religious role models (e.g., priest, rabbi, teacher, etc.)?

19. Did you see your parent of the same sex naked? Was this a chance occurrence, or did the parent make no attempt to avoid being nude in your presence (e.g., bathing, changing in

a locker room, undressing for bed, etc.)? At what ages did this occur?

20. Did you see your parent of the opposite sex naked? Was this a chance occurrence, or did the parent make no attempt to avoid being nude in your presence? At what ages did this occur?

21. Prior to adolescence, do you recall having asked either parent about pregnancy, sex, or interactions between men and women? How willing were they to respond? What information did they share?

22. Did you talk about sex, look at the naked body, or engage in any type of body exploration with a sibling of the same sex?

23. Did you talk about sex, look at the naked body, or engage in any type of body exploration with a sibling of the opposite sex?

24. If you engaged in any talk or actions with a brother or sister about sex, did you or they usually initiate it?

25. Do you recall, prior to adolescence, having exchanged sexual information or engaged in physical exploration with a friend or friends of the same sex?

26. Do you recall, prior to adolescence, having exchanged sexual information or engaged in physical exploration with a friend or friends of the opposite sex?

27. Did any adult other than a parent talk to you about or contribute to your ideas about sex, such as a teacher, relative, neighbor, etc.?

28. Did you ever intensely admire a person of the same sex when you were a child? Did you want physical contact with that person?

29. Did you have a "crush" on or strong feelings for a person of the opposite sex prior to your adolescence? Was it someone your own age or an adult? Did you want physical contact with that person?

30. At what age did you first think you were in love? Did the object of your affections know about it? Did he or she reciprocate in any way?

31. Did an adult or teenager ever kiss or fondle you in a way that you then or later, in retrospect, recognized to be sexual? Was it done with your consent? Did you ever resist such an attempt?

32. Did you ever report to your parents an older person's successful or unsuccessful attempt to engage you in some type of sexual activity? What was their reaction?

33. Did you go through a phase in childhood where you strongly disliked children of the opposite sex?

34. Did you ever feel, as a child, that a parent violated your privacy by overconcern with your bowel habits, bathing you when you felt old enough to bathe yourself, dressing you, or inspecting your body?

35. Did your parents ever embarrass you by exposing your body during spankings or other punishment?

Adolescence

1. At what age did you first become aware of sexual relations between men and women? How did you first find out about it? When did you first receive sufficient information and how did you acquire that information?

2. In retrospect, how much misinformation about sex did you acquire during your teen years?

3. At what age do your remember being aware of sexual urges within your body? How did it happen?

4. When did you first notice body changes associated with puberty and what was your reaction?

5. When did you first masturbate? Was the physical pleasure associated with masturbation an accidental discovery, or had you learned about masturbation from others? When did you first have an orgasm through masturbation?

6. Did you feel guilty about masturbation? Did you have any specific fears about the effect of masturbation on your body or mind? Were you afraid of being punished by your parents? Did you feel any guilt because of religious beliefs?

7. Did you ever masturbate in the presence of others of the same sex? Did they directly touch or stimulate you?

8. When were you first conscious of a sexual attraction to someone of the opposite sex? Did you feel you were in love with them, or was the feeling a purely physical one?

9. Did you read magazines or books about sex as a teenager? Did you read them to get information, to excite yourself, or both? Did you share this material with others, or keep it to yourself?

10. When did you first kiss someone of the opposite sex? Was it in

a private setting or a public one (party, dance)? Who initiated it?

11. When did you first engage in "necking" or prolonged, repeated kissing with someone? What were your feelings like before, during, and afterward?

12. When, if ever, did you engage in "petting" or manually exploring and stimulating the body of someone of the opposite sex? Did your first experience involve touching through clothing, underneath clothing, or removal of clothing? Were the genitals involved, or only breasts? What were subsequent experiences like? Did you ever have orgasms during "petting"?

13. As a teenager, did you engage in physical contact with many partners, or relatively few? Did you limit sexual activity (with or without intercourse) to "steady" boyfriends or girlfriends, or did you engage in such activity even with those to whom you had no particular commitment?

14. Did you engage in sexual activity despite some misgivings, either because someone pressured you into it or because you thought it would enhance your popularity? Did you feel people would reject you if you did not engage in some type of sexual activity?

15. Did you discuss your sexual experiences with friends? Did you ever lie or exaggerate? Did you want your friends to think you were more or less experienced than you actually were?

16. Did your parents ever ask you about your sexual activities? Did you ever volunteer information to them?

17. Did either or both of your parents discuss sexual matters with you? If they did, was the discussion limited to body aspects, such as menstruation and changes in the genitals, or did they discuss sex acts specifically? Did they advise or prohibit certain sexual conducts?

18. If you are a woman, did your mother tell you about menstruation before your first period? If not, did you learn about it through sex education lectures, booklets, friends? What was your reaction to menstruation when it began? If you are a man, where and when did you first learn about menstruation? What was your reaction?

19. Did your parents ever give you books or other reading material to educate you about sex? Was it helpful?

20. Where did you pick up your first information about sex? From friends, brothers and sisters, parents, books? Did you actively

seek information, or did others volunteer it? Did you try to verify the information you got, or did you generally accept anything you heard as true?

21. As a teenager, were you generally happy or unhappy with your body? How did you think your body compared with those of your peers? Were you happy with the size and shape of your "sexual parts" (breasts, penis, testicles, buttocks)? What about nonsexual aspects of your body (skin, hair, weight, height)? Did you do anything specific to change your body (exercise, diet, hair coloring, skin treatments)?

22. Did you consider yourself popular or unpopular with the opposite sex as a teenager? Did you feel your looks or your personality was your strongest asset?

23. When did you first date someone? Was your first experience with a group or was it a "single" date? Was the first person or persons you dated people you were strongly attracted to, or did you date them primarily for other reasons (to have a dance partner, to be part of the crowd, to avoid refusing their invitation, etc.)?

24. Were you ever in love as a teenager? How many times did you fall in love? Were the feelings reciprocated? Did you tend to have more physical involvement with those whom you loved?

25. Were you deeply upset by the breakup of a love affair as a teenager? Did this happen more than once? Was it you or the other person who usually ended it?

26. Did you drink or use drugs as a teenager? Did the use of these substances affect your sexual behavior?

27. Did you and your parents have conflicts over your dates, relationships with members of the opposite sex, or hours spent outside the home?

28. If you and your parents had a disagreement about your dating activities, did you usually give in to them, continue what you were doing and try to keep it secret, or openly defy them?

29. Did you have any particularly traumatic experiences as an adolescent, such as being sexually molested, fear of or actual unwanted pregnancy, being discovered by parents or other adults while engaged in a sexual act, being seduced and abandoned, etc.?

30. Did you engage in intercourse as an adolescent? Did this involve one, a few, or many episodes? Did you have one, several, or many partners? Were your partners generally peo-

ple you cared deeply about or did you just want the experience?

31. Did your erotic fantasies as a teenager deal mostly with impersonal objects (pictures of attractive people or thoughts of
screen celebrities), remote persons (classmates, acquain-
tances you found attractive but were not really involved with),
or real objects (people you dated or had friendships with)?
Were your fantasies chiefly about intercourse, sexual activities
unrelated to intercourse (nude bodies, caressing, oral sex), or
nonsexual romantic activities (dancing, walking together, exchanging confidences, kissing)? Did you have some fantasies
specifically for the purpose of sexual arousal and masturbation, different from your other erotic or romantic daydreams?
Did you enjoy romantic or erotic fantasies more?

32. Was there a period during your adolescence when you wanted
to live a celibate existence and stay away from the opposite
sex as much as possible? What brought this about?

33. Did you have friends of the opposite sex whom you genuinely
liked but would never consider getting involved with romanti-
cally or sexually?

34. Did you at some point imagine what the perfect lover and
spouse would be like? Did you ever find yourself comparing
prospective partners with that ideal?

35. Did you consider yourself oversexed, undersexed, or about
average for a teenager?

Adulthood

1. Are you currently married or living with someone of the opposite sex? Are you having intercourse or other sexual activity
on a fairly regular basis, even if it is not as often as you or your
partner would like? If you are living alone, do you have an
active sex life with one or more partners?

2. How satisfied are you with your sex life? How would you want
it to be improved?

3. Comparing your present sexual relationship with what it was
like when you and your partner first became involved sexually,
are things now better, worse, or approximately the same? If
different, in what way?

4. During the time you and your partner have been together,
have your sexual relations become more frequent, less fre-

quent, or stayed the same? If there has been a change, are either of you dissatisfied with the frequency? To what do you attribute the change? (If you have no regular partner, are you having sex more or less frequently than at other times in your life when you were single? Has your sex life gotten better or worse over the years?)

5. What is your favorite sexual activity (intercourse, oral sex, caressing and kissing, masturbation)? What is your partner's? Is there a significant difference between what you and what your partner like to do? If so, how do you deal with this difference?

6. Do you have difficulty getting sexually aroused at times? If you are a man, do you sometimes have difficulty getting or keeping an erection? If you are a woman, do you have problems with vaginal lubrication or with relaxing, so that intercourse is uncomfortable? Does this difficulty occur only when you are not really in the mood to have sex, or does it also occur when you really feel a desire to have sex?

7. Are there certain days or times when you and your partner always have sex, such as Friday or Saturday night, after an evening out, every other night, etc.? How do you feel about having sex at specific times, on a regular basis? Is sexual activity limited to such times, or do you have sex at other times, too, depending on your moods?

8. Who usually initiates sex? Do you, your partner, or do both of you initiate about equally?

9. Is the frequency of your sexual activity fairly constant, or are there periods of frequent sexual involvement that alternate with periods of relatively little sexual contact? If there is a variation, is it due to unavoidable circumstances (periods away from one another because of work), physical factors (menstrual discomfort, flare-ups of chronic physical illness), prolonged quarrels, work loads, or erratic desire on the part of either partner?

10. Do either you or your partner feel uncomfortable about going without sex for an extended length of time? Does either one of you initiate sex just for the sake of reactivating your sex life? How long can you go without sex before feeling uncomfortable or unnatural about it?

11. What is the longest period of time you have gone without sex since getting married or being involved in your current rela-

tionship? What is the longest period of time you have gone
without having sex since becoming a sexually active adult?
What was the cause of this inactivity (lack of a partner, lack of
desire, illness, depression, excessive work demands, other
preoccupations)? How did you feel about being sexually inac-
tive?

12. Do you ever masturbate? Do you do it because it offers you an
experience that is better or different from sex with a partner
or only because your partner is unavailable, not in the mood,
or quarreling with you? Are your masturbatory fantasies usually about your partner, about a previous lover, about someone you know, or about people you don't know? When you
masturbate, do you think about intercourse or about some
other type of sexual or nonsexual activity? How often do you
masturbate? Does your partner know about it? What are your
feelings about masturbation?

13. Do you have orgasms during sex? All the time, usually, or only
occasionally? If you do not have an orgasm, do you feel dissatisfied? If your partner doesn't have an orgasm, do you feel
bad? Are you less likely to have an orgasm if your partner
initiates sex when you are not in the mood? If you do not have
an orgasm through intercourse, does your partner help you
reach one by oral or manual means? Do you help your partner
to have an orgasm by manual or oral means if one does not
occur during intercourse?

14. If you are married, was your sexual desire greater or less
before marriage? If it has changed, how soon after you got
married did it begin to change? What do you think is the
reason for the change?

15. How do you feel about your present relationship, outside of
its sexual aspects? What's good about it and what are the
negative elements? How would you like to change it?

16. Does your partner show affection outside of sexual encounters? Do you show physical affection outside of sexual
encounters?

17. Do you and your partner show affection for one another in
nonphysical ways, such as telephoning one another during
the day, buying small gifts, helping with each other's chores,
etc.?

18. What do you and your partner quarrel most about? Do you
ever quarrel about sex?

19. After a quarrel, do you like to make up by having sex, or do you tend to avoid having sex for a while? How does your partner feel about having sex following a quarrel? What is the longest period you have gone without having sex as the direct result of a quarrel?

20. Do you and your partner discuss your sexual preferences and things that please you while engaged in lovemaking? If you don't, is it because you are both satisfied with things as they are, or because you feel uneasy talking about it?

21. Do you and your partner have talks about your sexual activities at times other than when you are actually involved in sex?

22. Do you ever share your sexual fantasies with your partner? Have the two of you ever acted out a sexual fantasy or done things to make your sexual activity more closely approximate a favorite fantasy?

23. Are there things you would like to try, but would not suggest to your partner for fear you would be thought strange, perverted, or dirty-minded?

24. Has birth control had a negative effect on your sex life, either because of fear of pregnancy with or without contraception or because the methods of birth control you use detract from the pleasure?

25. If you have had experience with partners other than your present one, were any of them more satisfying as lovers? Why?

26. If you are married or committed to one partner, have you ever had sex with someone else after becoming involved with your current partner? Are you still involved in such a relationship? What was your reason for getting involved? Was the sex better or worse with the person or persons with whom you got involved?

27. Have you ever purchased a book with the specific aim of learning something that would better your sex life?

28. Have you ever considered seeing a therapist in order to improve your sex life? Have you ever actually done so? Would your partner be willing to accompany you for therapy if you thought there was a problem in your sexual relationship?

29. Do you have children? Do you feel they have had an effect on your sex life? What effect have they had?

30. Do you usually have more than two alcoholic drinks (this includes more than two cans of beer or two glasses of wine)

per day? Do you generally drink heavily on weekends? Have you ever felt that alcohol was interfering with your ability to enjoy sex?

31. Have you had medical problems involving the pelvic area, such as venereal disease, cystitis, very irregular menstrual periods, prostate condition, uterine or ovarian tumors or cysts, etc.? Have there been times when you had to abstain from sex because of these conditions?

32. Have you had any nongenital medical problems that have sometimes interfered with your ability to have sex?

33. If you are a woman, have you ever had a spontaneous miscarriage or a planned abortion? Did it occur before or after marriage? If you are a man, has your wife or partner ever had a spontaneous miscarriage or a planned abortion?

34. If you are a woman, have you had difficulties with childbirth and pregnancy, such as a prolonged labor, a cesarean section, or postnatal complications? If you are a man, has your wife had difficulties with pregnancy and delivery?

35. Have you had difficulty conceiving a child? Have you consulted a physician about this, undergone fertility tests, or explored the possibility of adoption?

If you have attempted to respond to the sexual inventory in personal terms, you have just seen your entire sex life flash—or plod along—before your eyes. You've done something that most people never really do—taken stock of the activities and influences that add up to what you might call your sexual nature. Some of the questions about parents and family might seem to have little bearing on sex, but for certain people they might have had profound influences. For example, children whose parents were in their forties when they were born might view their parents as less sexual than younger parents. Having an older brother might make a girl less uneasy about dating when she reaches adolescence. A huge family might turn a person off to family life and even induce them to become "loners" to avoid any prospect of marriage.

How does your sexual inventory affect desire? The more satisfying your past and present sexual experiences, the more you would want to repeat those experiences. You will want to do what has been pleasant and avoid whatever has proved unpleasant. Some people may have sex for reasons other than pleasure—such as maintaining a relationship—but continually engaging in sex without much enjoyment can hardly be considered having "desire" for it.

PERSONALITY TYPE ASSESSMENT

The average person's personality is composed of a blend of traits, so we usually do not characterize ourselves as belonging to one type or another. Some people's personalities, however, are dominated by certain traits and they lack the flexibility to use a variety of healthy psychological defenses against stress.

Psychiatrists often treat patients with personality disorders, people who predictably react to life situations with a psychological attitude that limits their range of adaptive behavior. The goal in therapy is to decrease the patient's reliance on one type of behavior and develop complementary traits to become a more well-rounded individual. No matter how well adjusted we are, we all have certain traits that predominate over others in our personalities.

Psychiatrists envision personality types as lying along a linear spectrum; at one end are the *compulsives,* who are rigid, scrupulously introspective, and devoid of emotional display, while at the other extreme are the *histrionics* (formerly called hysterics), who are impulsive, erratic, and overly emotional. These are the "head" and the "heart" people of the world, one set governed by cold brainpower and the other by inflammable emotion. At the compulsives' end of the spectrum are the *paranoids,* who are untrusting, guarded, and emotionally independent. Also down at that end are the *schizoids,* the loners who have such difficulty relating intimately to anyone that they lose the conscious awareness of loneliness, and the *avoidants,* who desperately want to be liked but are crushed by the slightest indication of disapproval or rejection.

In the middle ranges of the spectrum, we find those who are continually interacting with others, but in counterproductive or abrasive ways. The *aggressives* are self-centered bullies who demand their way through behaviors that range from shouting to physical coercion. The *passive-aggressives* try to get their own way through procrastination, pleading illness or incapacitation, and a variety of nonviolent but infuriating obstructive maneuvers. Moving farther along the scale toward the more emotional types, we encounter the *dependents,* the clinging vines who exert an emotional stranglehold on their loved ones, and who are incapable of making a decision, much less a move, on their own.

The most emotional types are the narcissists and the histrionics. Whereas the compulsive thinks things through (and through and *through*) before acting, the histrionic runs on gut reaction, making impulsive decisions. The histrionics' love affairs are impetuous, stormy, erratic, and generally ephemeral, since they fall in love not with real people but with phantoms constructed from their own inner needs and romantic fantasies at a particular moment. Narcissists are so self-centered that they have difficulty understanding why anyone with whom they are involved would not readily accede to their every whim and make them the center of the universe.

In moderation, these personality traits help us make our way along life's challenging roads. Compulsive traits help us finish work assignments on time and keep our tempers and passions under control. Paranoid traits protect us against unscrupulous people who would con us out of our money or manipulate us for their own ends. Passive-aggressive traits help us hold our own against people with authority over us while avoiding frank confrontations. Histrionic traits allow us to let our hair down, to be spontaneous, and recapture some of the joys of childhood and passions of adolescence.

Our personalities rarely fall into one exclusive category, but our predominant traits will place us somewhere along the head-heart spectrum, leaning either to the intellectual or emotional end. Your personality will affect the intensity of your sexual desire, its mode of expression, and what is likely to interfere with it. By answering the assessment questions below, you can determine to which personality group you belong and the implications with regard to your sexual desire. The groups do not correspond to specific types, but each blends traits of two or more personality types that lie along the spectrum we have described.

Check off each statement with which you agree or which describes your feelings or actions.

Group A

1. Sexual performance requires effort and concentration and it can usually be improved.
2. I vividly recall details of my past sexual experiences.
3. I like to read books and articles about how to improve my sex life.
4. My mind often wanders onto nonsexual concerns during sex.
5. I often just don't have time for sex.
6. I like to have sex at definite times on specific days.
7. I sometimes feel that my partner is not enjoying sex as much as he or she claims to be.
8. I sometimes worry that my partner will leave me for someone who is a more attractive or proficient lover.
9. I rarely discuss sex with my partner.
10. I would not like to reveal my sexual fantasies to anyone, including my partner.

Group B

1. I often decline sex because of headaches, stomach upsets, fatigue, or other physical symptoms.
2. I strongly dislike arguments and will always try to avoid them.
3. My sex life would be better if my partner knew how to turn me on.
4. I do most of my reading and television watching after 10 P.M.
5. I like to have sex as a way of making up after a fight.
6. I have to be in the right mood to have sex, and if I'm not, nothing is going to change it.
7. Masturbation can often be far more satisfying than sex with a partner.
8. I fantasize about sex a lot.
9. I feel uncomfortable around people of the opposite sex who are very attractive or accomplished.
10. When having sex, I often feel my partner would rather be doing something else.

Group C

1. I really dislike being alone.
2. Sex is best when it is spontaneous and out of the ordinary.
3. Sex with just about any partner is more satisfying than masturbation.
4. I often feel taken for granted by my partner.
5. I think that clothing is one of the major factors in sex appeal.
6. My mood can change very abruptly during sex.
7. I can usually get people to do whatever I want.
8. Sex usually doesn't live up to my expectations.
9. There is not enough romance in today's world.
10. I often agree to have sex when I don't want to so that the other person will not be angry and reject me.

Give yourself one point for each answer you've checked off. A score of 5 or more qualifies you for inclusion in that personality group. If you score 5 or more in two or all three groups, it indicates a personality with a wide range of adaptive patterns. Look for a group score that is significantly higher than the others; a 9 or 10 for Group A and 5 or 6 in the other groups would indicate your personality is compatible with the first group. Scores under 5 in all three groups indicates that you are probably very wary about committing yourself to anything and dislike making flat statements; despite the overall low scores, you probably belong in Group A.

Group A personalities are the mind-over-physical-matter types. They are methodical and rarely impulsive. If they constantly defer to the pressures of work and household chores, their sex lives may be almost nonexistent. If they apply the philosophy "anything worth doing is worth doing well" to their sexual activity, their sex lives may be rather active. The best of this group really try hard to please their partners and, having succeeded, take pleasure in their accomplishment.

One could argue that sex should be carefree, spontaneous fun, not a task to be carried out, but there is not much that's spontaneous about these organizers. They tend to be faithful to their mates;

having once established a routine that meets their scrupulous specifications, why jeopardize things with an uninitiated newcomer? Besides fidelity, their other strong points are evenness of temper, consistency, and a tendency to perform effectively, though not with much originality or range.

When desire problems develop in a Group A person, they should check first for causes outside the bedroom. Difficulties on the job or with the children will intrude on sexual pleasure, since A has difficulty switching gears and laying other concerns aside. Reassurance and assistance from a partner may help, because A will not freely verbalize conflicts. When stress occurs, A will think in the circular pathway of the worrier, not the linear course of the problem solver. He or she should not obsess about the way things are, but rather imagine how he or she would like them to be. A new negligee or a romantic weekend away from home will not help if A is more threatened than turned on by anything new. Rather than struggle to dam up an unexpected surge of emotion, A should try to go with the flow.

Group B personalities have difficulty in negotiating interpersonal relationships. To their credit, they usually make a genuine attempt to interact with their partner, rather than walling off their emotions like the compulsive, or focusing only on themselves like the histrionic or narcissist. Most B's adopt a passive-aggressive method of coping, rarely confronting a difference of opinion or desire head on. They give in to distractions or talk themselves into headaches or stomachaches to avoid a sexual or personal encounter that they fear will be problematic. They are logical and rarely given to mood extremes or impulsive action, making them secure choices as partners.

When lack of desire strikes a Group B person, he or she should look to the relationship. B tends to view relationships as ongoing power struggles and strives to maintain control. When B feels he or she is losing the battle, desire will evaporate. B's neglected partner, unaware of B's conflicts, may have missed the entire war. It is important for B to resist the temptation to withdraw from the field entirely, whether the customary fall-back position is in front of a TV, the land of Nod, or Fantasyland. B's emotional resources are generally in good enough supply for him to come effectively to terms with his partner, provided B continues the sort of face-to-face discussion that can lead to body-to-body merging.

Group C personalities are highly emotional. They do not analyze things in detail and their first impressions of people rarely change with time. They tend to have a romantic, sentimental view of life, and often act impulsively. They can be very passionate and exciting lovers, devoted spouses who tend to overlook their partner's flaws, and creative souls who are always seeking and usually finding some new delight in life. When they are upset, however, they can be explosive.

When C suffers from a desire problem, don't look for logical explanations. They have a very subjective view of circumstances and their vulnerable egos are easy prey to feelings of rejection or disappointment, even where no slight was intended by their partners.

They require a lot of attention from partners. A small gift or heartfelt compliment may do more to restore C's desire than the most earnest attempt at soul-searching dialogue. C's can restore their own desire by pursuing whatever makes them *feel* sexy and desirable, whether that means buying something attractive to wear, reading a favorite romantic novel, listening to music conducive to lovemaking, or recalling a past sexual experience and embellishing on the fantasy.

ATTITUDE SCALE

If you were asked to characterize a person's attitude toward sex as basically conservative, moderate, or liberal, you would probably want to know as much as possible about his or her sexual activities. Someone who participated in a variety of activities, had several partners, and wore revealing clothes would undoubtedly be designated "liberal," while someone who engaged in sex infrequently and limited activity to one partner, while always wearing clothing typical of the proverbial schoolteacher, would be pigeon-holed as "conservative."

The trouble with this approach is that it does not take into account those people whose mental attitudes vary considerably from their behavior. Take, for example, a passionate woman married to a compulsive, work-oriented man who has rigid ideas about traditional male-female roles and who rates sex as a low priority among the activities of daily living. The wife's sex life might be characterized by low frequency and little variety, and her demeanor might be very decorous and circumspect, but her actions would be controlled not by her own attitudes and values but by those of her spouse.

Consider an unmarried woman who is now involved in her fifth relationship this year and has experimented with group sex, swum nude with boyfriends, and whose wardrobe seems specifically designed to attract male attention. She may actually be a guilt-ridden individual, one who complacently acquiesces to any activity that is suggested by her partner, despite her personal embarrassment and repugnance, because she feels this is the only way she can attract and hold a man. She really longs for a marriage and family life.

It would be an oversimplification to say that people with liberal attitudes have high desire levels, while conservatives have low levels. Rather, liberals feel desire in a wider range of situations, while conservatives tend to get turned on only in conventional situations where they feel confident and secure. Often, people's sexual activities are dictated not by their own attitudes, but by the partners' wishes, parents' prohibitions, or the current norms of society. With a different spouse or partner, their sex lives might be quite different, just as there might be a great difference if they followed their own inclinations instead of deferring to the expressed wishes or perceived values of others.

Unless you take particular delight in philosophical discussions or heated debates about sexual standards—and meaningful talk about sex still seems rarer than quick physical involvement in our verbally squeamish society—you have probably never really taken stock of your sexual attitudes, which have a major influence on sexual desire. Therapists frequently hear patients say, in response to questions about their attitudes, "I never really thought about it before." This admission is the first step toward self-awareness and self-improvement.

For each question below, choose the statement closest to your own thoughts on the subject; if you disagree with all the statements, choose the one with which you disagree *least.*

1a. Sex education should not be taught in school.
  b. Sex education should begin in junior high.
  c. Sex education should be given in elementary schools, as well as high schools.
2a. There is an age at which, for most married couples, sexual activity normally ceases.
  b. While most married people continue to have sex throughout life, they become less passionate and more conservative as they age.
  c. Married people should retain a strong interest in sex and continue to have sexual activities as they age.
3a. I cannot imagine my parents ever being interested in sex.
  b. I imagine my parents' sex life has been very conservative and limited.
  c. I imagine my parents to have had an active, full sex life.
4a. I am still embarrassed by my own or another's nudity.
  b. I am comfortable with nudity only with my spouse or long-term partner.
  c. I would be comfortable with nudity at a nudist camp, nude beach, or private swimming-pool party.
5a. I feel that people who are homosexual or bisexual have serious mental problems.
  b. I feel that homosexuality and bisexuality are morally unacceptable.
  c. I feel that there is nothing inherently wrong or unhealthy about homosexuality or bisexuality for those who want it.
6a. Sex can never be a satisfying or positive experience if you do not have strong affection for your partner.
  b. Sex is much more satisfying if you love your partner, although sex without strong affection is also frequently pleasurable.
  c. Sex is a highly pleasurable activity, independent of any emotional feelings toward your partner.
7a. Laws against prostitution should be strictly enforced for the good of society.

   b. Laws about prostitution should restrict it to certain areas and eliminate health hazards.

   c. Prostitution should be legal, with no government interference.

 8a. I do not feel that sex is a strong indicator of marital compatibility.

   b. Sex can significantly improve a married couple's overall compatibility.

   c. Lack of a good sex life should be grounds for divorce.

 9a. The quality of sex depends chiefly on the love expressed and felt between partners; technique has little bearing.

   b. Sexual knowledge and lovemaking technique are as important as expression of affection for good sex.

   c. Techniques and proficiency are the most important ingredients for good sex.

10a. Sex should be regarded as a beautiful and almost sacred expression of love.

   b. Sex is strictly a physical pleasure and should be thought of as fun.

   c. Sex is most exciting when it's thought of as somewhat dirty and forbidden.

11a. Wearing exotic lingerie to bed is degrading.

   b. Wearing exotic lingerie is fine for those who like it, but is really unnecessary.

   c. Wearing exotic lingerie can strongly enhance sexual excitement and pleasure.

12a. Couples who engage in bondage, spanking, or similar sadomasochistic activities are mentally disturbed.

   b. Sadomasochistic activities are not psychologically harmful, but have little appeal for the average person.

   c. Sadomasochistic activities can strongly enhance sexual excitement and pleasure between mutually consenting adults.

13a. Pornographic material, whose sole object is sexual arousal, should be illegal.

   b. Pornography is undesirable, but should be available to those who want it.

   c. Pornography is not harmful and can enrich the sex lives of many people.

14a. Having a sexual fantasy about someone other than your spouse or loved one is tantamount to infidelity.

b. Fantasies about others are acceptable, but not during actual sexual relations with a spouse or loved one.

c. Any type of sexual fantasy that enhances pleasure and arousal should be encouraged at any time.

15a. I feel most comfortable having sex in the dark.

b. I feel most comfortable having sex in a room with the lights dimmed.

c. I like sex best with the room fully lighted.

16a. I feel comfortable having sex only in my bedroom.

b. I feel comfortable having sex anywhere in the house and I like a little variety.

c. I enjoy sex in unconventional places, such as outdoors or in cars or offices.

17a. I feel comfortable having sex only in the male-superior position.

b. I don't mind experimenting, but I have sex in one position nearly all the time.

c. I enjoy a variety of sexual positions.

18a. I feel very uncomfortable talking to my partner about what we do sexually.

b. I would like to talk to my partner more about sex, although we do so infrequently.

c. I talk freely with my partner about our sexual activities.

19a. I would find sexual relations during the menstrual period repugnant.

b. I would have sex during the menstrual period, but feel a little uneasy.

c. I would enjoy sex during the menstrual period as much as at other times.

20a. I believe that masturbation is immature and should not be practiced by adults, especially those with partners.

b. I believe that masturbation is acceptable, but a poor substitute for intercourse.

c. I believe masturbation is a sexual pleasure anyone should freely engage in whenever he or she wants to.

21a. I believe oral sex is unnatural and feel uncomfortable with or repelled by the idea.

b. Oral sex is acceptable as foreplay prior to intercourse.

c. Oral sex is a pleasurable activity that can sometimes be a substitute for intercourse.

22a. I believe that anal stimulation should not be a part of sexual activity.

  b. I believe anal stimulation is acceptable, but not anal intercourse.

  c. I believe in any form of pleasurable anal sexual activity, including anal intercourse.

23a. I believe people should not have intercourse until they are married.

  b. I believe people should have sex only if they are committed to marry one another.

  c. I believe any adult couple that wants to should have intercourse, regardless of marital intentions.

24a. I believe men should always initiate and take the lead in sexual relations.

  b. I believe women can occasionally initiate sex, but men should chiefly control a couple's sex life.

  c. I believe either men or women should initiate sex whenever they desire.

25a. I do not feel that orgasms are necessarily important for sexual satisfaction.

  b. People should try to have orgasms as often as possible during intercourse.

  c. People should always try to have orgasms either during intercourse, or afterward, through oral or manual means.

To score this inventory of attitudes, give yourself one point for each "a" response, two points for each "b" response, and three points for each "c" response.

If you scored 25 to 37, consider yourself *conservative.* A score from 38 to 62 rates you as a *moderate.* A score of 63 to 75 designates you as a *liberal.*

Conservatives, early in life, are more apt to have low sexual desire. There are too many potential turn-offs for them to be able to maintain a predictable and reasonably high level of desire. On the other hand, once they find a suitable partner, they may be less susceptible to desire problems than others, because they know exactly what they want and are unlikely to be disappointed once they have settled on a partner. Since they are not tempted to seek new thrills, they tend to be content with their established routine.

The idea of expanding their repertoire is more threatening than the prospect of years of sameness.

Boredom, however, can be a powerful deterrent to desire, so an established routine can become much less satisfying with time. Some conservatives, married to spouses of similar personality, may become more liberal as years pass; if their partners do not keep pace with this change in attitude, compatible marriages can become troubled relationships. Since conservatives tend to invest their sexual feelings with more moral significance than liberal people, any temptation to experiment with practices previously avoided will arouse pangs of conscience; lack of desire may result from an inability to choose between intolerable boredom and unacceptable temptation. By confronting the conflict between evolving attitudes and stagnant internal values, the conservative may be able to make some compromises and revitalize desire.

A *moderate* tends to be middle-of-the-road. Gravitating toward the mean is no mean spot to be in, and we might expect desire problems in this group to be infrequent. Sometimes, however, the apparent moderate may really be a closet conservative or liberal who doesn't quite have the guts to follow his or her inclinations all the way. Someone who would be a natural liberal but whose parents are very conservative may take a moderate approach. Or someone who deep down espouses very conservative beliefs may feel so out of step with liberal peers that he or she shifts into a set of professed moderate attitudes. The less flexible people at either end of the conservative-liberal attitude scale may not get along with as many people, but they may be more at peace with their own viewpoints.

The moderate values both the spiritual elements of a relationship and the purely sensual pleasures, though maintaining the balance can be tricky.

The *liberal* enjoys a wide range of sexual activity but this does not guarantee a consistently high desire level. A taste for new experiences can often land you in distasteful situations; obviously not every sexual experiment is going to work out well. A desire for new experiences generally extends to having new partners, so the liberal might have difficulty maintaining a high level of desire toward a single partner.

Liberals acknowledge the pleasure of sex of its own sake; they may be a little weak in the area of developing intimate personal relationships, leaving them vulnerable to marital conflicts that lessen desire. When desire problems resulting from marital friction occur, the liberal will have to limit his or her free-ranging quest for adventure and concentrate on reconstructing the homestead.

SENSUALITY SCALE

Is sex primarily a mental or physical process? It has been truly observed that the mind is an erogenous zone and that the human brain is the most important sex organ. Yet, the modern euphemism "Let's get physical" points out that until the body gets involved, sex is a blueprint that never got off the drawing board. Without that blueprint that we call desire, however, sex can be a heap of malfunctioning rubble.

Think "physical" and you think in terms of *action*. Yet, for every motor nerve that propels a muscle or organ into action, there is usually an accompanying sensory nerve providing feedback to the brain. Since desire is mental, it can occur in the complete absence of any physical stimuli. Yet, desire generally depends on images or memories of past experiences that had a distinctly physical component. Even fantasies draw on something from the physical realm to put our brains in a sensual mode.

Sensual is not the same thing as *sexual*. *Sensual* refers to what is experienced through the five senses, usually perceived as pleasurable. *Sensuous* is used by some to describe people who are particularly sensitive to the erotic effects of pleasurable sensations, although most dictionaries have made *sensual* and *sensuous* synonymous.

Any type of pleasurable sensual stimulus can contribute to desire, even if the stimulus itself is not specifically sexual. In some individuals, stimuli that most would consider unpleasant—such as pain, restraint, and verbal abuse—can produce desire. The sexual implications of any sensation must ultimately lie in the eye, ear, nose, tongue, or touch of the beholder.

Sensory experiences contributing to desire may be sensual, erotic, or romantic. Sensual experiences give pleasure to the body, but do not necessarily involve a partner. Erotic experiences occur in specifically sexual situations. Romantic experiences arise in the context of a relationship, in a caring, but not frankly sexual, situation.

Being sensitive to the perceptions of our five senses can augment desire. Knowing which type of experience increases our desire the most will enable us to incorporate these pleasurable sensations into our lovemaking on a regular basis. A lack of our favorite experience will cause desire to diminish.

Some individuals are equally responsive to sensual, romantic, and erotic stimuli. Others may respond more strongly to one type of stimuli than to the others.

How sensuous are you? More importantly, how is this sensuousness best elicited?

Rate each of the activities described from 0 to 3, depending on whether you would find such an experience unenjoyable or unpleasant (0), mildly enjoyable (1), moderately enjoyable (2), or very enjoyable (3).

Sensual

1. Dancing by yourself.
2. Engaging in a short period of vigorous exercise.
3. Taking a long warm bath or shower.
4. Listening to music.
5. Putting on perfume or cologne, even if you're going to be alone all day.
6. Walking in a summer drizzle.
7. Hugging a friend.
8. Watching the waves and listening to the sound of the ocean.
9. Picking out an object in your favorite color.
10. Riding in the country to see the autumn foliage.

Erotic

1. Putting on special lingerie or nightclothes before going to bed with a partner.
2. Putting music on in the bedroom.
3. Reading erotic material with a partner.
4. Watching an erotic video cassette with a partner.
5. Having your partner give you a massage.
6. Dancing with someone you care about.
7. Taking a bath or shower with a partner.
8. Smelling your partner's perfume or cologne.

9. Talking with your partner in bed.
10. Cuddling in bed with your partner.

Romantic

1. Receiving flowers from or sending flowers to someone you care about.
2. Writing a poem or a letter to someone you love.
3. Having someone you love pay you a compliment.
4. Sharing a problem with someone you love.
5. Talking to someone you love on the telephone during your lunch hour.
6. Picking out a gift for someone you love.
7. Calling someone you love by a special name used only by you.
8. Sharing a task with someone you love.
9. Dressing up especially for someone you care about.
10. Hearing someone you love tell you, "I love you."

For each of the three areas, the maximum possible score is 30. Consider a score over 15 as "high" and 15 or under "low." You should now have either a "high" or "low" rating for the sensual, erotic, and romantic areas, which we will designate below as S, E, and R, respectively.

PROFILE 1 *High S, High E, High R.*

You enjoy sex and give it high priority in your life. If you run into desire problems, it's probably because you have high expectations and feel disappointed when even one element in your sexual relationship seems lacking. You might perceive your partner as romantic and caring, but just not "physical" enough. Or perhaps your partner is a good lover as far as technique goes, but leaves out a few of the romantic preliminaries. The best remedy for restoring desire is for you to figure out what element is missing from your love life and to help your partner supply it. The second-best remedy is to realize that you can't always have everything all the time, so you must fill in the missing gaps through pleasurable social and recreational activities and appreciating your sex life for the many delights it *can* supply.

PROFILE 2 *High S, High E, Low R.*

You enjoy physical pleasures and a creative sex life, but have difficulty showing affection through nonphysical means. If you have desire problems, chances are your partner is pressuring you to show affection outside the bedroom. "You Don't Bring Me Flowers" is probably the prevailing refrain at home, with a chorus of "All You Want from Me Is Sex!" You may never write a love note, but you can at least resolve to start inviting your partner out for a night of dancing or a walk on the beach, which might prove even more romantic than the written word.

PROFILE 3 *High S, Low E, High R.*

You generally make your partner feel loved and you are capable of physical pleasure, but you may be rather uptight and perfunctory in the bedroom. If there is a desire problem, listen for the echo of some puritanical prohibition against sex first heard in childhood or adolescence. You might not even be conscious of some old guilt that is interfering. To increase desire, carry some of that romance in your nature from the parlor to the bedroom, emphasizing that love and sex make compatible bedfellows.

PROFILE 4 *High S, Low E, Low R.*

You enjoy physical pleasures, but sometimes have difficulty sharing them. Low desire may stem from anxiety over intimacy. When by yourself, you enjoy the sensual pleasures the world around you offers, but the presence of a partner seems to interfere with your receptive powers. The solution lies in including your partner in some of those physical delights you experience *outside* the bedroom, getting used to the idea that shared pleasure doesn't mean *less* pleasure for you.

PROFILE 5 *Low S, High E, High R.*

You usually have a high sex drive, placing emphasis on the relationship, both sexual and personal, rather than on the simple bodily pleasures sex can afford. This is fine until some conflict develops in your relationship. Then, "drive" alone cannot be counted upon to keep the sexual activity on schedule, and desire problems may arise. You may be overly concerned with your partner's satisfaction. Focusing on your own sensations and preferences during sex might benefit the relationship for both of you.

PROFILE 6 *Low S, High E, Low R.*

You are probably a "no frills" lovemaker. You are interested in getting down to sex without wasting much time on preliminaries. Men of this type are prone to desire loss as they get older, because when the instant erection hits a time warp, panic ensues. Sensate focus exercises, Masters and Johnson's technique for giving one another pleasure without the performance demands of intercourse, may help if you can accept *less* emphasis on intercourse not only from your own partner but also from your own ego. Equating sexual pleasure exclusively with intercourse is like putting all your eggs in one basket. Who wants their sex life to be a basket case?

PROFILE 7 *Low S, Low E, High R.*

When they said, "It's the thought that counts," they had your sentiments in mind. If your spouse criticizes you for lacking passion, you might vehemently retort that you are brimming with hot-blooded romantic feelings, only a certain critical party is remarkably inept at flame fanning. Connecting romantic to erotic energy is not simple. The likeliest route to success is R through S through E —in other words, awaken your body's ability to enjoy simple sensual pleasures, preferably in a romantic atmosphere, before proceeding to frankly sexual activities.

PROFILE 8 *Low S, Low E, Low R.*

"It's all in your mind" might well apply to your entire sexuality. The turn-on begins for you—and ends—somewhere north of your eyebrows. You may be out of touch with touch—and the other four senses as well. You probably feel sex is something you *should* do, from a rational, intellectual viewpoint. You may be doing it to please a partner or because it reassures you that you are normal or because you want to cement a relationship. You rarely do it simply because it feels good. If your desire is based on believing you *should* have sex, a lack of desire will probably stem from an equally strong counterconviction that you should *not.* Likely, a turn-off of desire will relate to anger or dissatisfaction with your partner. Working through the conflict will help, but a trip to an art gallery, concert hall, or botanical garden might lay the groundwork for relating cerebral aesthetic pleasure to the tangible physical world. Letting your partner stimulate you while you relax may reduce some of your concern about performing well and allow you to focus your attention on enjoyable sensory experiences.

The strong, somewhat irrational longings that underlie desire are based to a large extent on how pleasurable certain elements of sexual activities have been in the past. Recognizing which of these aspects—sensual, erotic, and romantic—have been most important to you in the past will help you, if desire ever wanes, to identify more accurately the source of the problem and go on to correct it.

SUMMING UP: YOUR DESIRE POTENTIAL

Your sexual history, your personality type, your attitudes, and your sensuality all contribute, positively or negatively, to your desire level. Good past experiences, a lack of inhibitions, a taste for variety, and flexibility tend to add up to a high desire level; that is, the wish for frequent sex, making sex a high priority, and more intense enjoyment of sexual experience. People with a low desire level can, nevertheless, be very happy with their sex lives. A good sex life depends not so much on fulfilling a strong level of desire, but on fulfilling *your* level of desire.

A loss of desire can affect people with high potential, as well as those in the lower range, and may be more traumatic for those who are accustomed to strong desire. People at any desire level can be adversely affected by personal problems, unhappy situations, or conflicted relationships, but there are specifically vulnerable areas for high, medium, and low levels.

If you usually have a high level of desire, a decrease can usually be best overcome by working on nonsexual methods of gratification and communication. Learning to enjoy simple touching through sensate focus exercises, getting accustomed to putting your feelings into words instead of sexual actions, and acquiring a better understanding of your partner's sexual needs can add dimensions of experience to your sexuality that transcend the purely physical aspects.

If you have a medium desire potential, seek help for desire loss by improving the interpersonal aspects of your relationship. Exercises in switching roles and learning how to cope with the times when your partner declines sex, as well as mastering fair-fight techniques, can swing your equilibrium back to a higher level of desire.

If you have a low potential and feel it's getting lower, you will probably want to concentrate on methods that increase your personal range of fantasies and sensual experiences. Hypnotic imagery fantasy breaks, self-dialoguing, and other methods of self-help described in Part IV will raise your potential and enable you to share your new interest with your partner.

Self-evaluation is crucial to success in improving sexual desire. Before you can fix something, you have to understand how it works, whether you're a doctor healing a body, a mechanic repairing an auto, or a psychiatrist treating a troubled psyche. Once you understand where you are and how you arrived there, it is far easier to find the road that will take you to where you want to be.

❧ *IV* ❧

THERAPY AND SELF-HELP

❧ 9 ❧

The Full Treatment

Types of Therapy for Desire Disorder

Desire is the beginning of a journey to sexual gratification, proceeding through arousal, up to and beyond orgasm. As we have seen, loss of sexual desire can result from many different causes, often from a combination of influences, so treatment must be tailored to the individual.

"Basically, I will do anything," Dr. Bernie Zilbergeld says. While practitioners who treat desire disorders may occasionally be able to draw on some of the principles of sex therapy as developed by Masters and Johnson, they cannot rely on a stepwise, one-fits-all formula, such as those used to treat performance problems. Yet, the seeming complexity of desire disorders should not be cause for discouragement. Practically everyone has *some* sexual desire to work with and can usually tell fairly quickly what techniques are helping to improve desire and which are not.

Treatment is understandably the main concern for anyone who has a problem or is affected by the problem in a partner. In this section, we will discuss *specific* treatment approaches, both as used by experts in their practice and as self-help methods that you can apply without a therapist. At the end of the description of each type of treatment, you will find a self-help section headed "On Your Own." Desire disorder is, fortunately, a problem that is particularly amenable to self-help because it is a mental process. You don't need a blood test or an X-ray to tell you how you are progressing.

Nobody can monitor better what goes on in your mind than you yourself.

We can simplify the formidable number of variations in treatment methods by categorizing them as either *behavioral, cognitive,* or *experiential.* Most therapists will employ more than one type of treatment, depending on the individual patient.

The theory behind *behavioral* therapy is that behavior is the product of what we learn and, therefore, much of abnormal or unhealthy behavior results from faulty or inadequate learning. The therapist's task is basically to reeducate the patients by guiding them into specific, more effective coping mechanisms. Dependency on the therapist is minimized by teaching the patient self-management techniques, with assignments to be practiced at home between office appointments.

When sex therapists began to focus on desire disorder as an entity separate from arousal problems, they often employed methods that concentrated on what was going on in their patients' minds rather than the physical activities and sensations involved in sex. Thus, *cognitive* therapy was increasingly utilized to augment or supplant behavioral techniques. Cognitive therapy may involve more verbal dialogue between patient and therapist than classical behavioral therapy, but again, the therapist can give the patient specific assignments to work on between sessions.

Early in life we are taught, either by spoken precepts or by example, certain ideas and values that we carry into adult life. Unfortunately, they are not always accurate. If, for instance, a woman learned from her mother that sex was an unpleasant duty, she would probably develop the cognition, "I'm not supposed to be orgasmic." Conversely, if she immersed herself in books written by overly zealous "experts," she might instead hold the equally erroneous notion, "I'm supposed to be orgasmic all the time." Either attitude can interfere with her sexual desire, sexual functioning, and general level of well-being.

There is a final dimension of therapy for desire disorder, one that depends on emotional experiences, which we shall classify as *experiential.* The cultivation of fantasies and ideas can rekindle desire by taking advantage of the individual's own unique experiences, preferences, and conceptions about what good sex should be. This is an area of treatment that, more than any other, requires an active effort on the part of the patient; here, the therapist can direct and suggest, but cannot supply step-by-step instructions identical for each individual. Experiential techniques call upon the powers of creativity and fantasy, which evoke the strengths and foibles of human individuality and reawaken sensual awareness not only in the area of sex, but across the spectrum of interpersonal relationships and self-awareness.

Since sexual desire takes place entirely in the mind, any form of treatment has a cognitive component. People can learn to hate, to feel anger, or to love, just as they can learn mathematics and art appreciation; likewise, they can learn to desire by removing inhibitions and replacing them with positive responses. Even if the problem lies chiefly with stressful circumstances or an incompatible partner, the final step, after all external adjustments have been made, is what *you* feel after carefully reassessing the situation.

We will begin with experiential therapies because they put you in touch with those aspects of sexual desire that are personal and uniquely yours. They are the energizers and mood creators, reacquainting you with neglected, half-forgotten positive memories and fantasies and reawakening dormant drives. The experiential therapies, by stimulating desire on the most personal and intimate level, establish a receptive mental climate for the more intellectual cognitive and pragmatic behavioral therapies that follow.

Depending on You

Experiential Therapies

"We're number one!"

At the close of any championship sports contest, the television cameras pan across hoardes of deliriously happy fans thrusting their forefingers heavenward to proclaim their numerical rank.

But we *all* consider ourselves number one and not because we are egocentric or selfish. Whatever we see or experience in this world must filter through a personal interpretation that is based on what we have done and learned in the past. It is this unique perspective that makes desire a truly human experience. Other creatures can be subject to sexual arousal and orgasm, not very different physiologically from our own responses, but desire is interpersonal, and if there is a specific object of desire, there must be a concept of *subject*—"I"—as well. So, while various forces in our environment and our actual and potential sex partners may profoundly influence our desire level, desire ultimately becomes a highly personal experience which no two individuals could appreciate in exactly the same way.

In the experiential therapies, patients respond, through their imaginations, in highly subjective, individualistic ways, whether in the form of fantasies, scenarios, communications, or practices. A therapist using the tools of fantasy, hypnotic imagery, internal dialogue, and role playing will be following in the footsteps of Robert Frost, who, when asked why he wrote so many poems, replied, "To see if I can make them all different."

YOU ARE GETTING SLEEPIER, SLEEPIER, SEXIER . . .
Hypnotic Imagery

Many people think hypnosis requires a charismatic, formally attired foreigner swinging a watch fob; they would be surprised to learn that their bedrooms offer the best entries into the hypnotic state.

Dr. Bernie Zilbergeld says that the best example of what is called a "hypnotic trance" is good sex, because you are focused so intensely on what is happening to you and your partner. An orgasm is the ultimate trance. "I think that's the one time in life," he says, "where you are so captivated by feelings in your body that you cannot possibly think of anything else."

Hypnosis does not require entering a deep trance state where you become totally oblivious to everything but the hypnotist's suggestions; probably no more than 10 percent of the population would be capable of reaching this depth of hypnosis. But this extreme degree of selective focus is not really necessary to benefit from hypnotic techniques.

The essence of hypnosis, whether self-induced or directed by a therapist, is achieving a state of relaxation and focused attention on mental images. "People often get into that state when they are at a play or a movie," Dr. Zilbergeld points out. "They are so involved that they don't realize the person they came with got up and went to the bathroom."

If hypnosis worked in real life the way it does in movies, the therapist would put a woman with low desire into a deep trance and tell her, "Each time your husband walks in the door, you will be filled with an intense desire to have sex with him and will be very excited throughout your sexual activity, which you will enjoy immensely." Unfortunately, the hypnotist cannot "command" the subject to have desire anymore than he can instruct a man with erectile failure to get an automatic erection each time he attempts intercourse. Hypnosis can help some people to eat less and smoke less, but it is far from foolproof.

Relaxation and the production of vivid mental images are the usual goals when hypnosis is used to improve desire. We are capable of relaxing and fantasizing on our own, but a hypnotherapist can facilitate these mental processes. Dr. Zilbergeld explains, "In the office, I might have a woman imagine: 'You are in bed now, imagine yourself being in bed with Tom and focusing only on what is happening. His hand is on your leg, your lips on his.' I go through the whole sexual experience, but don't say, 'You are *not* going to worry about the kids.' You just tell them to concern themselves only with how good it is feeling and how to make it feel better. Then, the posthypnotic suggestion would be that what we just went through in your imagination can be the way it will be the next time you go to bed with Tom—only focus on *how it feels* for you, with his hands on you and your hands on him, etc. So there, by using imagery and direct command, you can create that state."

The new hypnotic techniques used in the treatment of desire disorder are as much experiential as behavioral, since they often center on helping the patients to conjure up vivid mental images that have particular relevance to themselves. The images may consist of objects that the patient contemplates to get in touch with sexual or other emotional feelings, or they may involve complex scenes which the patient actually enters to interact with significant people in the present or past.

Through the methods we will be describing, people can use images to enhance positive feelings about sex or to discharge pent-up negative feelings. Under hypnosis, past memories become more vivid and people can either recapture exciting experiences from a time when their desire was stronger or understand what negative past influences undermined their interest. People can replace patterns of thought and behavior that inhibit sexual desire with more constructive attitudes once they have been able to experience new feelings under hypnosis.

Hypnosis can make us more aware of our bodies and the sexual feelings that emanate not only from the genitals but from all sensual areas. And while hypnosis can allow us to relax and get in touch with physical sensations on a passive level, it can also, through structured fantasizing, allow us to gain an unprecedented sense of mastery over situations that made us anxious because we felt we lacked a sense of control. Hypnosis can, therefore, reinforce past and present experiences to promote desire, as well as overcome the obstacles in life that inhibit desire.

RESURRECTING DESIRE
Dr. Lazarus's Multi-Modal Therapy

"The power of imagery, I like to say, is the only force that goes faster than the speed of light; through mental imagery you can be on the planet Mars in milliseconds and then go to the end of the universe milliseconds later," says Dr. Arnold J. Lazarus.

Dr. Lazarus is a clinical psychologist with a private practice in Princeton, New Jersey, specializing in marital therapy. A distinguished professor at Rutgers University's Graduate School of Applied and Professional Psychology, he is one of the leading experts in the field of imagery and the author of *In the Mind's Eye.*

Although he relies heavily on techniques of imagery and behavioral modification, Dr. Lazarus does not depend on them exclusively. Because of the complexity of desire disorder and other sexual problems, he utilizes as wide a spectrum of assessment and treatment methods as possible. A comprehensive evaluation will indicate which of the many influences on sexual desire are problematic and influence the course of therapy. Dr. Lazarus calls his approach "multi-modal therapy" because of his appreciation and use of many individual factors that influence the psyche in any area of its sexual functioning.

Imagery is one of the seven modalities covered in his approach, which he has labeled with the acronym "BASIC I.D.," standing for:

B **ehavior:** What actually goes on, what people do sexually alone or together.

A **ffect:** The psychological term for emotions. Guilt, anger, anxiety, shame, apathy, and whatever else impairs desire.

S **ensation:** Physical perceptions, what a person finds pleasing or displeasing that is modulated by the five senses.

I **magery:** Fantasy and mental pictures, positive or negative, that enhance or inhibit desire.

C **ognitions:** Beliefs, attitudes, values, prohibitions, taboos; the "shoulds," "oughts," and "musts" regarding sex.

I **nterpersonal relationships:** Lack of attraction for a specific partner, power conflicts, quarrels.

D **rugs:** Actually, not only the possible effect of medication on desire, but interference from any sort of medical condition.

Dr. Lazarus explores each of these areas in detail and proceeds with treatment according to the aspect most requiring some sort of intervention. Not all of his patients have their primary difficulty in the area of imagery, but many do, including some who are troubled by intrusive thoughts of unpleasant images whenever they start to experience desire.

Images often are those of parents or religious authorities (priests, rabbis, nuns) who openly or tacitly disapproved of sexual activity in the patient's past. They have the disconcerting tendency to pop into consciousness only when their victim is actively engaged in sex or its preliminaries. Since the person is least capable of coping with the images at such times, Dr. Lazarus advocates deliberately conjuring up the disapproving image voluntarily many times during the day and disputing it or possibly replacing it with a permission-giving image, such as a favorite teacher with a liberal attitude. Deliberately summoning the image gives the person control over it and will ultimately change an involuntary phenomenon into a voluntary one.

A refinement of this technique is developing the capacity not only to switch off the negative image but to replace it with an erotic one or with a series of erotic images, almost like a slide show. Dr. Lazarus tells his patients to say "stop" or "switch off" to the disturbing image and then switch on the sexy image. If one particular image does it best, such as imagining a passionate kiss from Tom Selleck, then that becomes the woman's "flash-on image."

Guilt often gets in the way of erotic fantasies, and often Dr. Lazarus finds he has to "give permission" to people to have whatever fantasies turn them on. Sometimes the guilt arises from having a fantasy that people consider perverse or demeaning, such as forcing someone or being forced to have sex. In other cases, people who are married or committed to a lover will feel guilty about fantasies that involve outside partners.

Dr. Lazarus feels that it's a "big mistake" for people to think they should have images or fantasies only of their mates. Another mistake, he believes, is seeking permission from a spouse to have such fantasies. "Your fantasies are your business and no one else's; you are not cheating," he emphasizes.

Dr. Lazarus views desire disorder as symptomatic of many people's preoccupation with work and success. "One of the things that people are *not* into today," he laments, "is fun and joy."

To develop the ability to focus on erotic imagery in bed instead of letting one's mind wander to nonsexual preoccupations, Dr. Lazarus advocates rehearsing a lot of fantasies beforehand, rather than trying to improvise in bed. As with anything one wants to do well, some practice is required.

"I'm not suggesting that people make it a vocation," he says, "but that they really put *some* effort into it. What are we talking about? We are talking about twenty minutes a day of imagery exercises for those people who are having a problem. Putting in fifteen or twenty minutes a day would make a big difference, until they find that they can switch on 'automatic pilot' in the bedroom."

PICTURE THIS
Self-hypnotic Techniques

"I don't believe in hypnotizing; I believe what I do is guide people so that *they* get into that hypnotizing," says Dr. Daniel L. Araoz, professor of community mental health counseling at C. W. Post Center of Long Island University and past president of the Academy of Psychologists in Marital, Sex and Family Therapy. "What we really have to do is capture the person so that she can get into her inner imagery and inner self, and become aware of what is going on in her mind at this particular moment. That is hypnosis, because once she focuses on that, she detaches herself from the things around her. She becomes oblivious to things like time and temperature."

Dr. Araoz, who is the author of *The New Hypnosis* and *Hypnosis and Sex Therapy* and co-author of *Hypnosex: Sexual Joy Through Self-Hypnosis,* tries to help people get in touch with their mental images and then revise or replace them with more positive ones. An image might not be so much a vivid picture, but a self-concept. Unfortunately, many people, as they get older, see themselves becoming asexual because of aging.

In dealing with diminished sexual desire, Dr. Araoz encourages his patients to develop more positive and optimistic self-concepts through imagery. He asks them questions such as, "Where do you think the desire resides in your body?" Very few people, he finds, talk about the sexual organs, usually pointing instead to the brain or the heart. He asks them to visualize this central control place.

Many see an image of a dial or a meter set very low, so Dr. Araoz will ask them to imagine turning it up a bit, like the volume on a radio, and to think about how they would react sexually as their desire goes up.

He then encourages the patients to develop a picture, like a film sequence, in which they see themselves enjoying sex in a very free and uninhibited way with the partner of their choice. This may not be easy, because by the time such people come into therapy, they have allowed negative imagery to persist for many years.

Dr. Araoz reinforces the mental imagery experienced in his office by asking his patients to repeat the fantasies at home. He also gives them audio tapes of the therapist's voice guiding them. He has found that while video tapes are better for instructing patients in certain areas, audio tapes (which allow you to close your eyes) are better for repetitious self-practice. When we close our eyes, the brain can produce alpha waves that are associated with a relaxation state.

"I work with them on the idea that in order to undo the negative patterns that they have developed through the years, they have to establish a new pathway or circuitry in the brain," Dr. Araoz explains. "To do this, they have to repeat exercises over and over, as with the development of any skill that requires repetition." Sometimes the patients do not practice as instructed, which alerts Dr. Araoz to some underlying resistance. Such people may come into therapy to please a partner or to get the partner to stop nagging, but they are not convinced that they should desire and enjoy sex more than they do.

With resistant patients, Dr. Araoz incorporates psychoanalytic techniques with imagery, delving into the past for images that may be auditory as well as visual. "I have found that in many, many cases," he relates, "the first reaction is 'Oh, no, I want to have sex and I enjoy it!' but when they concentrate, they pick up something that someone is saying, such as 'You are too old' or 'You should be ashamed, you shouldn't be with this person.' These are all usually voices from the past."

With the patient in a state of hypnotic relaxation, Dr. Araoz tries to help the person identify the voices as they come up. Even people who have not practiced their religion for years may be recalling prohibitions from early religious training, or the voice may be that of an admonishing parent.

Having identified the source of the voice, the next step is to locate that source in time and place. Invariably, memories of childhood experiences emerge, associated with negative feelings, emotions of sadness, disappointment, anger, or fear of being rejected or unloved. "The reason I call it 'hypnotic,' " Dr. Araoz explains, "is because I am not trying to make sense out of these things, or interpret them or put them logically together, but just help them get in touch with these things that happened. At times, images that flash back from the past come up in very confused ways; there is no sequence."

Dr. Araoz described one patient who experienced conflicting auditory and visual images. First, he recalled words from a priest that seemed to have some sort of negative connotations about sexuality and the human body, then he became conscious of a visual image of being in a bathtub with his mother. He visualized his mother's body as big and, since she was not in reality a big woman, he realized, by focusing a little more, that he could not be older than three or four. At that age, he was aware of her nakedness and curious about her body, but had conflicting feelings, both wanting to touch her and ask questions, and being aware that doing so might be dangerous and incur her disapproval.

Most of the voices from the past that emerge during hypnotherapy are prohibitive and convey messages that sexual desire and sexual functioning are sinful or harmful, but occasionally even an encouraging voice can prove troublesome. One male patient recalled a female voice, encouraging him to do something that was not permissible according to his childhood moral standards. The voice was identified as belonging to a long-deceased aunt, the black ewe of the family, who had been a liberated young woman two-score years earlier when the patient was ten. Even as a child, he had found the aunt attractive and seductive, but his parents had warned him against her crazy ideas, setting up a conflict that was reactivated when he was a mature adult.

A BRIDGE TO SPAN THE YEARS
Recapturing Memories Through the Somatic Bridge

One might think that the more you try to delve into the unconscious depths of your mind, the less you would want to be conscious of your body. Dr. Araoz, however, has found that awareness of the body can often provide cues that recall suppressed memories that have an effect on sexual feelings. Dr. Araoz refers to physical sensations that facilitate a mental return to the past as a "somatic (bodily) bridge," reaching across the years to reunite us with distant images lost in memory's recesses.

Each time the patient reports an image that comes to mind when asked to think of sex, Dr. Araoz says, "Check your body. What's happening now? Is there any tension?" If the reaction to sexual thoughts is negative, there is usually tension someplace. "Where is it?" he asks the patient. "In your stomach, in your chest, your shoulders? Where does it go *to?*

"I ask them to think about their body, to monitor it all the time, to see what's happening right now. My interest is not so much in their description as in their awareness. Once they say, 'There is some tension in my chest,' I say, 'Well, see if you can stay with that tension. Allow it to guide you further. Where does it lead? Does it go to any scene of the past, any connection with the past?' It's almost as though I were establishing a somatic bridge between the current tension and something that happened long ago to produce that tension."

You don't get in touch with a person's feelings by asking, "How do you feel?" The moment you ask them that, they stop feeling and start thinking. By asking them simply to feel, to see where it leads, to follow any tension and focus on any discomfort, a bridge may be established between the present and a previous instance in which they felt similar.

Dr. Araoz advises someone not in formal therapy who wishes to try some of these techniques at home "to start getting in touch with your body. Stay still, relax, try to breathe gently and become aware of your body. What comes first? It may be your hands, it may be your buttocks, it may be your neck. Then concentrate on that and see where it leads you. What associations do you make with this area of your body to other things that are uniquely yours? Body awareness may trigger memories, thoughts, feelings, sensations, and so on."

In another exercise he calls *subjective biofeedback*, Dr. Araoz encourages the replacement of ideas that produce guilt and discomfort with more mature and healthy attitudes. If someone becomes aware that he is being influenced by negative messages, the source of the message is identified. The person is then asked to draw on his own wisdom, values, and common sense to replace the prohibitive message with a more positive one.

Dr. Araoz has found that even though we expect people to be sexually uninhibited and liberated, there are still many people who connect sex with ideas of evil and punishment. In the last few years, with the increase in AIDS, herpes, and other sexually transmitted diseases, people often think, "Well, this is God's punishment," although they may intellectually deny it.

Interestingly, most of the positive messages formulated by Dr. Araoz's patients are rather discreet and conservative in tone, such as, "Sex is okay and can be enjoyed under certain circumstances," rather than "Any form of sex goes."

On Your Own

In his book, *Hypnosis and Sex Therapy,* Dr. Araoz has described several hypnotic techniques that have proved effective in the treatment of sexual desire disorder. These involve mental images, often a complex scene in which the patient imagines he is taking part. Some of these techniques can be adapted as self-help exercises to overcome inhibitions that diminish desire and to promote desire directly. You don't have to achieve a trance state; a quiet room free from distractions and a relaxed attitude are all it takes.

Revivification: Think about a very positive experience from your past. Visualize it as it actually happened and try to concentrate on the sensations it recaptures. If you have never had such a pleasurable experience, construct a fantasy you would find most desirable. If you reexperience the warm or stimulating feelings you associate with the memory, tell yourself that you will remember them during your next sexual experience.

If you feel uneasy about imagining yourself in a sexual scene, substitute a favorite celebrity of yours in the fantasy. If watching your understudy stimulates your desire, take over the role yourself, but instead of pretending you are in the middle of the action, observe as though you were watching a film with you as the star. If you find the picture exciting and inviting, *then* you may "step into the movie" and imagine your fantasy as though it were actually happening.

Pleasure hierarchy: If you find that foreplay gives you the most enjoyment, and are more anxious or less enthusiastic about later aspects of sexual activity, set up your own pleasure hierarchy by listing in order all the involved activities from the most to the least pleasurable. If being held in a naked embrace is the most positive aspect for you, concentrate on that first, trying to recapture those sensations that you have felt in the past as vividly as possible. While still immersed in these good feelings, proceed to the next item on the hierarchy, adding its positive input to what you're already experiencing. By the time you work your way down to the least pleasurable part, you will be able, after a time, to regard the total sexual experience in unequivocally positive terms.

Rerun your entire hierarchy through your imagination several times before your next sexual encounter. When it's time to put your fantasies into practice, take a preliminary minute to review mentally the chain of anticipated events and reexperience the feelings you've been evoking through the fantasies. Sharing your hierarchy with your partner may help him or her to understand what turns you on the most and the sequences that will maximize your arousal and enthusiasm. Several weeks of practicing the mental exercises can result in a marked increase in desire for and enjoyment of sex.

Negative processing: Unfavorable responses to an ordinarily pleasant sexual experience may be caused by guilt, anger, or anxiety. For example, a woman might feel little desire for sex because her mother had led her to believe that sex is animalistic and she, therefore, subsequently had inhibitions about experiencing orgasm. Her conflicts about it might be unconscious, and on strictly an intellectual level, she might readily say that sex is a natural, beautiful thing and she certainly does not feel it is dirty.

If you find you can tell yourself how healthy and enjoyable sex is, but it just doesn't translate into desire, think of someone, living or dead, whose opinions you would respect and would regard as totally credible. It may be an author, a medical expert, a psychologist, a teacher, or a clergyman. Then, imagine that person giving you a friendly lecture about the healthy and natural attitudes you should have about sex. The woman in the example above might not be able to weigh her own good advice against the negative opinions of her mother, but the added weight of an "expert" who approved of lusty, uninhibited sexual enjoyment could enable her to increase her sexual desire. If your parents or other authority figures in the past have made you feel guilty or negatively about sex, picture them in the audience along with you, listening to the same lecture.

Poetic images: Some men and women have developed a negative attitude toward specific parts of the body, especially the genital areas. If you enjoy the closeness of sex, but are shy or squeamish about your partner's private parts, try to imagine them as aesthetically attractive objects. A man can try to visualize the woman's labia as the petals of a flower or the convolutions of a sea shell. A woman might imagine a penis as an ivory pillar or a spiral horn. Positive images will come to replace the previously established negative imagery associated with sexual themes.

Violent imagery: If you find yourself resenting your partner or feeling overt anger over past differences whenever you start to get sexually involved, form a vivid mental image of your anger as a volcano, fire, or earthquake, and let it run its course with full force and fury. Then try to picture sexual activity without anger, and appreciate the peace, quiet, and harmony that prevail after the disruptive forces have been eliminated from the scene.

Movie director: If you feel anxious in sexual situations, imagine a situation in which you would feel most uncomfortable. It might be the first time in bed with someone, sex in a strange place, or being asked to have sex when you are upset after a very trying day. Having set your imagined self in the least desirable of situations, step in as "director" and assume full control over the situation. The feeling that you can control your sex life and are not helpless will reduce the anxiety that impedes sexual desire.

While the techniques such as revivification, pleasure hierarchy, and poetic imagery emphasize the positive aspects of sex, dealing with negative emotions, such as guilt, anger, or anxiety, that inhibit desire will also raise the desire level. Developing the appropriate imagery just requires some privacy and quiet; the desire will follow once you get the picture.

❧ 11 ❧

Fantasyland

Taking a Fantasy Break

In 1907, Sigmund Freud wrote about a surprising discovery he had made, something his patients were confiding to him that no one had ever dared confess before: adults have daydreams and fantasies. This is hardly shocking news today, but at the turn of the century, adults would no more admit to fantasizing than they would to masturbating.

Why not? As Freud explained it, people expected children to daydream, because their fantasies were always about the commendable things they would do if they were adults. Adults, on the other hand, had daydreams that were childish in nature, regressive fantasies that were irresponsible and focused on nonconstructive pleasure—in short, shameful.

Today, in our work-oriented society, therapists often have to teach people to put the fun back into sex, and just as some people with sexual dysfunction are taught to masturbate, others with desire disorder have to be guided in learning the art of fantasy. Imaginative creativity *can* be taught. People do, after all, learn it in writing classes, art workshops, and music lessons. True, you cannot acquire artistic genius in a classroom, but you can develop enough talent to produce something that expresses your inner spirit and pleases you. The ability to fantasize may not enable you to write the next *Tropic of Cancer,* but if it turns *you* on and ignites *your* desire, the effort will be amply awarded.

Dr. Jerry M. Friedman, who practices sex therapy at Stony

Brook, New York, explains how he incorporates the *fantasy break* into his treatment approach for low sexual desire.

The fantasy break involves the patient's taking a few moments to think about sex each day, perhaps even scheduling a specific time for it. Dr. Friedman uses it particularly for people who say, when asked about their desire for sex, "I don't know—it just never occurs to me." He then says to them, "Well, what happens when I ask it to occur to you? What do you *choose* to think about if you were to think about sex?"

Dr. Friedman uses the patterns of the fantasies that are produced as well as their actual content to understand the basis of decreased desire. If a patient thinks about sex when no one is available but never thinks about it when someone is around, he may be anxious about actually engaging in the sex act and will allow himself to think about it only when it's impossible for anything to occur. Some people never allow themselves to think about sex at all, despite their seeming willingness to follow the therapist's prescriptions. Avoidance of this sort may indicate performance anxiety or fear of vulnerability if they become intimate.

According to Dr. Arnold Lazarus, clinical psychologist and distinguished professor at Rutgers University, if you can't imagine what it is you are going to do, if you don't have the cognitive pathways laid down in your mind, you are never going to do it.

Or as Rodgers and Hammerstein's "Bloody Mary" noted more simply, you've got to have a dream to have a dream come true.

JUST IMAGINE
Using Fantasies in Therapy

Dealing with dreams may be old hat for psychotherapists, but fantasy is a newer type of headgear. Fantasies are similar to dreams in some respects, except the fantasizer has a lot more control than the dreamer.

The fantasizer does not have total control, however, since the unconscious supplies many of the building blocks from which fantasies are constructed and the final product may surprise the architect. Fantasy is one of the most potent stimulators of dormant

desire and therapists have developed techniques for helping patients work with their imaginations in the service of desire.

Let's follow Glenda, the thirty-two-year-old "Sleeping Beauty"
we first encountered in Chapter 2 through several therapy sessions.
Glenda, you may recall, had reached a point in her life where she
could have had it all: a career move from routine clerical duties to
creative advertising campaigns, a caring and supportive husband,
and a seven-year-old daughter. Inexplicably, she had suddenly lost
all sexual desire, and after months of frantic, fruitless attempts by
her spouse to revive her desire, Glenda had reluctantly decided that
a trial separation was the best course to take while she gave herself
some time and space to explore the troubled situation in which she
was mired.

Therapy was part of that exploration. While her keen imagination had served her well in the realm of advertising, Glenda had
never made fantasy part of her sex life. The therapist had prescribed fantasizing as a between-sessions assignment and asked her
to share one of her newly created daydreams with him. When
Glenda protested that since lack of interest in sex was her problem
she was unlikely to be able to produce sexy fantasies, the therapist
told her to come up with whatever occurred to her and not worry
about how erotic it was. So she did.

"The bunkhouse is pretty dark," Glenda says, her voice barely
audible, "but with the light of my lantern I can see Lem and Zeke
tied up on the floor, which is spattered with little drops of blood. I
suspect there's something wrong. A mean voice behind me says,
'Okay, lady, turn around real slow!' That was a mistake, because as I
turn slow, I think fast. I'm swinging the lantern as I turn; I let go of
the handle and it sails into his face. The lantern hits him in the jaw
and he's momentarily blinded by the light. With my left hand, I
grab his wrist and bring my right hand across his forearm in a karate
chop. I hear the gun hit the floor, and I'm already bringing my knee
up hard into his groin.

"By the way, Doc," she interrupts, again lowering her voice,
which had risen steadily, "I hope you don't think there's too much
violence and not enough sex in this fantasy. There are some kind-
of-sexy parts in it later, and you *did* say the fantasy-break fantasies
didn't have to be all that sexy if I didn't feel like it, right?"

"It's *your* fantasy," the therapist says.

"Well," she continues eagerly, "this bozo doesn't know what hit
him, because, I mean, who knew about karate back then in

Amarillo? He crumples on the floor as I pick up the gun. Just then, another guy yells, 'What's going on in there, Blackie?' This huge guy, about six-five, lunges into the bunkhouse, gun drawn.

"Then, I let him have it!" Glenda exults.

"With another karate chop?" the therapist clarifies.

Glenda looks at him with a perplexed expression. "No!" she protests. "I have Blackie's gun, remember?"

"I'm about to untie Lem and Zeke, when I hear hoofbeats outside. Picking up the big guy's gun, so that I've got one in each hand, I turn outside, ready to make a final stand to save my ranch, and my life, and my honor. But it's not more bad guys! It's a man with a white hat and a black mask riding a big white horse, and behind him is an Indian on a smaller, brown-and-white horse.

"The masked man gets off his horse, tips his hat, and says, 'Having some trouble, ma'am?' I give my right-hand gun a little casual wave and say, 'Thanks, but nothing I couldn't handle.' He's impressed, I can tell. He's not used to having women handle things on their own, but I can't gush with gratitude like he expects, because he hasn't done anything for me. Just to throw something his way, I say, 'Why don't you go into the bunkhouse and untie my hands—hired hands, that is.' "

Glenda smiles mischievously. "He scowls and moseys off, as I walk right past him to Tonto, who's just standing there like a wooden Indian, the way he always does when women are fawning over his *kemo sabe*. He's just as tall as the masked man and I realize that he's really gorgeous. His skin is flawless bronze and his brown eyes have this funny, soft expression that looks as if they're going to just dissolve. 'Hi, I'm Glenda,' I say.

"He looks at me and turns on this real warm smile that says, 'Well, you know my name, but there's a lot more that you don't know.' After we've been staring into each other's eyes for a while, he says, 'I guess you know your way around a gun.'

" 'Not much choice, being out here alone,' I say.

" 'You're a widow,' he says, with such gentle compassion that I feel a lump in my throat. I give him a sad little nod." Glenda breaks off her narrative to add, with a trace of guilt, "Well, I really didn't want to get into living separately from my husband, especially since we're not *legally* separated. I suppose squaws never set up separate teepees. '*You* know what it's like being alone,' I say. The Indian takes both my hands in his. His hands feel so strong, yet soft. I look straight into his eyes.

" 'So he saved your life once. You owe him gratitude for that, but not the life he saved. You can't ride forever five horse-lengths behind him on that—pony! He rides off gazing into a beautiful sunset and you're staring at his horse's rear end!'

" 'I know, Golden One,' he says to me, still holding my hands. 'I have paid my debt to the masked man. Now I will go where my own heart leads me. Or I will stay where it keeps me.' The masked man, looking kind of ticked off, gets up on his horse without even a goodbye or a haughty 'Hi-yo, Silver,' and rides off into the darkness.

" 'Who was that masked man, anyway?' one of the hired hands asked. 'Is he the Lone Ranger?' asks the other one.

" 'He is *now!*' I say, putting my arms around Tonto.

Glenda heaves a sigh and swings her crossed leg nervously. "I'm sorry," she says, only half-regretfully, after a silence. "I know you gave me an assignment to have a fantasy and I was determined to come in here with a doozy, not some hokey tall, dark stranger on a moonlit beach, like you probably expected. If I'd followed the usual script, I would have been tied up, the Lone Ranger would have saved me, and with luck, I might have seduced him, instead of him just dumping me and riding off. I rejected *him*. I was a hostile bitch."

"Not to Tonto," the therapist notes. "You two seemed to be quite compatible."

Glenda wrinkles her nose derisively. "Blond, trim, Christian advertising exec seeks single Indian brave, 30–45, no smoke-em peace pipes, no loco weed or firewater. . . ."

"You both seemed to understand perfectly what it's like to ride silently behind another man, even a man you really cared about," the therapist observes.

Glenda looks stunned. "Oh no, Doc, you don't think *I* felt that way. I told you in our very first session that there were no conflicts between Victor and me. He's never stood in the way of my career. He's respected me even more since I went from being a Gal Friday to my present job, where I can do something creative and make some decisions."

"Did he ever call you 'Golden One'?"

"What?" she exclaims. Then, she says, "Oh, what Tonto called me. No, that just seemed like something a stereotype Indian would say to a paleface." She pauses. "Vic used to call me 'Golden Girl.' "

"Used to?"

"Yeah, when we were young." She corrects herself. "I mean, we're *still* young. Just . . . when you get older, some of these pet names seem silly. He just stopped."

"You didn't ask him to?"

She shakes her head emphatically. "I liked it. Why would I ask him to stop?"

"Just a hunch," the therapist answers. "Some women in recent years have taken exception to being called 'girls.' "

Glenda sits in thoughtful silence. "Yeah, a couple of times I did tell him not to call my friends 'girls.' I mean, it wasn't a big fight or anything. I was just trying to raise his consciousness a little. Do you think that's why he stopped calling me 'Golden Girl'?"

"I don't think it was because you got old. You said that Vic respected you more. Do you feel he liked you more? Does he like you as much?"

"Doc," she interrupts, "I thought these fantasies were supposed to get my desire back. Now we're moving into some heavy stuff and I'm not sure it's relevant. I could as easily have had a fantasy about Tom Cruise or Camelot or Popeye—I just tried to come up with any far-out fantasy."

"But you picked *that* one," the therapist points out. "And how did you get interested in the Lone Ranger?"

"Victor's the Ranger freak," she admits. "He bought cassettes of some of the old TV shows and even has tapes of the old radio shows: 'A fiery horse with the speed of light, a cloud of dust . . .' No, I never really liked that macho do-gooder, always hiding behind a mask, running away from potential relationships. But Vic can tell you the name of his nephew, every actor who's played him, and he can play the 'William Tell Overture' by blowing into an empty beer bottle. *Those* two must have something in common."

"Getting back to desire," the therapist says, "I couldn't help feeling that you *were* somewhat attracted to Tonto. How far would he have gotten with you?"

Glenda's body visibly relaxes in the chair and she smiles dreamily. "Gee, it's hard to say, but I do know there's just no way you can sleep three men in that little bunkhouse!"

Fantasies not only can turn us on, but can help us get in touch with attitudes and inner feelings that we might be uncomfortable about expressing directly. Glenda could have derived her fantasy from an infinite variety of sources, but out of all the comic strips, movies, and television shows in the world, she chose that particular one. The Tonto fantasy did turn Glenda on a bit and that alone made it worthwhile; however, it also enabled the therapist and ultimately his patient to understand more about Glenda and her situation.

Glenda's fantasy lover was a doubly safe choice: he was a man of a different race and culture, the type she would be unlikely to meet, much less get involved with in real life, and his being a comic-strip character established the liaison as totally make-believe. Fantasizing about someone you actually know, such as the next-door neighbor or a co-worker, tends to provoke guilt, which, like any uncomfortable feeling, inhibits desire. Despite her marital problems, Glenda was too conservative to consider an extramarital adventure, even in fantasy, unless it was completely implausible.

There was a distinctly aggressive component to Glenda's fantasy, one that initially outweighed the erotic elements. By showing her husband's macho hero how independent she was and by luring Tonto from his side, she was rebelling against her husband and lover. If her husband was truly supportive of her career changes, why did Glenda have to rebel? It was a little too early in therapy to be certain, but the therapist had some inklings. What had happened when Glenda's desire waned? Vic had taken charge of *her* desire, determined to raise it to its previous level through his own efforts rather than trying to understand what was going on.

Another potential difficulty lay in the difference between intellectual approval and gut feeling. For centuries, many men have acquired increased respect and admiration for their wives when they become mothers, only to lose physical passion toward them (the prostitute-madonna split). Now, there are men who have a genuine regard for women who show intelligence and authority in business, but cannot feel tenderness or sexual attraction the way they experience it toward females perceived as helpless and dependent.

Women are, likewise, prey to these splits. A woman who has given birth may feel that she has changed sexually, that she can no longer engage in sex with the carefree abandon of her earlier years because it is not the proper thing to do. A woman with a new awareness of her potential and intellectual growth may subconsciously feel that her old sexual behavior reduced her to sex-object status and reinforced stereotyped roles in her love relationship. We cannot change and expect our sex lives to continue unchanged; not as long as sex involves relationships and relationships involve people. If sex seems to go on as usual, it's probably because the parties have reassessed the situation and decided that there was no reason to change the way they relate to one another, regardless of how they now relate to the outside world.

Glenda had become more assertive, Vic had become less intimate. Glenda had decided to put her libido on hold, Vic intensified his efforts to reinvolve her. Glenda retreated, Vic pursued. Glenda became the patient, Vic became the therapist, and the old dominance-submission marital relationship was reestablished. Subtle, but it was there.

So, if Glenda was angry at Vic, why didn't she turn her desire toward other men, at least in fantasy? First, she wasn't even aware that she was angry at such a supportive, concerned husband. Second, she would have been too threatened by the notion of adultery, even in fantasy. Loss of desire for Vic generalized to loss of desire. The Tonto fantasy was the first indication in a long time that she did have a spark of desire still glowing.

Glenda, like most patients, does not relish being in therapy. At a time when she is struggling to develop an identity independent of those of wife and mother, she finds herself in the dependent role of patient with a male therapist. Her quick wit and her bantering lets her offer some token resistance to the therapy, protecting her from the full impact of painful feelings until she is more ready to confront them. The therapist encourages the banter, often engaging in mild verbal duels with her. Her aggressiveness is a trait of the new person she is becoming, although many, including her husband, still see the more demure, reserved, and ever-agreeable Glenda of the past.

Glenda continued to take a few minutes several times a day, both at work and at home, to have fantasies. She would set a scene and populate it with male characters, not necessarily ones who attracted her. People with normal desire levels fantasize to arouse themselves, whether as a prelude to masturbatory or coital gratification or simply to provide some mental pleasure and alleviate boredom. When desire is low, fantasies can be used to put you in touch with whatever prompts or inhibits desire, even if the fantasy does not actually produce desire. The more one comes to under-

stand personal turn-ons and turn-offs, the easier it will be to generate specific fantasies that are powerful stimulants to desire.

On Your Own

You don't need a therapist to serve as a guide on your own
fantasy trips. Any person who wants to get in touch with his or her
desire level and its special trigger mechanisms can use the same
techniques that therapists employ in dealing with desire problems.
The fantasy break requires nothing but your imagination. The important thing is taking some time for it.

It does not necessarily require a *lot* of time; a fantasy break could
take twenty seconds if, for example, a person keeps a photo of a
favorite screen star in a desk drawer or purse and takes it out a few
times a day, just to look at it. You can take fantasy breaks while
driving your car, riding a bus, standing on line at the supermarket,
or waiting for the coffee to percolate.

The biggest problem with fantasy breaks is resistance. People
with no interest in sex often have little interest in getting interested.

A first fantasy can be like a first date, whose purpose is to help
you get acquainted, not get into some heavy sexual action. A
woman with low desire could fantasize making spaghetti sauce with
Paul Newman; a man could fantasize challenging Vanna White to a
game of Hangman. If you try to steer your fantasies into more
exotic channels and feel fearful, go with the fear. Ask yourself
what's the *worst* thing that could happen in the fantasy situation:
rejection, humiliation, physical harm, guilt? Try to identify the impediment, so you can get rid of it.

When it comes to fantasies, what is normal—or, at least, average? And when it comes to sharing fantasies with your partner
what, if anything, is off limits?

The New York *Times* ran an article a couple of years ago on
people's most common sexual fantasies. Sex with someone other
than one's regular partner ranked first. Our biological natures
seem to preserve a potential for attraction to many members of the
opposite sex, despite our firm commitment to one partner. When
the fantasy lover is fictitious, like Tonto, or remote, like a movie
star, spouses don't usually get jealous. When the fantasy object has
some real but fleeting contact, such as a customer who comes to

your place of business, a spouse may not be so tolerant. If the fantasy involves the neighbor next door or someone whom you see daily, spouses usually feel decidedly threatened. Affairs do happen in about half of all marriages, even though they are more apt to be motivated by interpersonal problems within the marital relationship, not by a waning of sexual desire. Melanie Griffin may be sexier than a husband's secretary and Don Johnson may be more virile than the guy next door, but Mr. and Mrs. Johnson are too remote to cause distress by their intrusions into a partner's daydreams and the extremely accessible people pose more of a threat than the extremely desirable.

According to the *Times* report, the number one fantasy—that of sex with someone other than the spouse or regular partner—provokes considerable guilt despite its popularity. The number two fantasy probably produces even more ambivalence and uneasiness, even though, according to Morton Hunt's survey of sexual behavior, it is shared by as many as one quarter of all women under the age of thirty-five who masturbate: being forced to have sex. (Fourteen percent of men under thirty-five also have that fantasy which is nearly as many as the 18 percent who fantasize being the aggressor in a "forced sex" encounter.)

Unlike a rape situation, there is no actual danger and, of course, the man in the fantasy is very attractive or, at least, exciting. That's why the fantasy appeals to so many people: it's like a thrilling ride in an amusement park, where you're hurtling toward apparent disaster but deep down you know there's no actual peril.

Other common fantasies among men and women involve group sex and homosexual encounters. The *Times* did not mention at all what we found to be the most common fantasy in our nationwide survey of men for *Beyond the Male Myth:* sexual activity with one's regular partner. This is apparently more a problem in semantics than surveying. Some investigators apparently do not consider thoughts about a real relationship to be fantasies, but it could be argued that they do qualify since they don't occur during the actual sex act and they often involve some type of sexual activity or situation that the couple is rarely or never involved in.

In 1973, Nancy Friday published a bestselling book about women's sexual fantasies, *My Secret Garden.* She carefully categorized them, and hardly any were conventional romantic fantasies about sensitive, courtly gentlemen in ardent but tasteful encounters. Common themes were sex with anonymous strangers, sex while being watched by others, rape, infliction of pain, bondage and domination, terrifying situations, sex in semipublic places where shameful discovery was a threat, being a different person during sex, sex with relatives, sex with animals, sex with men of another race, sex with young boys, and lesbian sex. The only category-type of fantasy that seemed rather tame and "acceptable" (Ms. Friday's term) involved images of the earth being fertilized.

"It's universally accepted that women, dreamers all, dream the good pure thoughts that hold us all together—especially material things connected with the home," Ms. Friday wrote. "I suggest that next time you see that pretty female face with the Mona Lisa smile you consider, just consider, that she may not be thinking of a knight on a horse, just the horse."

It is vital for men and women not to censor their fantasy breaks. Nothing is more tragic than to forgo the delights of a fantasy that will restimulate desire because the fantasy involved is rejected as sick or perverted. People who have a low level of desire are likely to be the ones who cannot readily turn on to a thought about routine sex with their regular partner in their typical bedroom. We tend to associate "kinky," far-out fantasies with high-desire, sexually active "swingers," but would be amazed and just a little shocked to discover that people who seem to have very little interest in sex can harbor thoughts about exhibitionism, sadomasochism, and love with improper strangers.

Of course, people almost never share fantasies that involve the sorts of things they would never do or even want to do in actuality. This secrecy leads us to believe such thoughts are far rarer than they are. If they appeal to you or your partner, don't hesitate to evoke them—or even experiment with an unlikely one in the privacy of your imagination; you may discover a cost-free new source of energy to power your sexual desire. Give yourself a break today —a fantasy break.

Maybe the sex researchers have proven that all orgasms originate from clitoral stimulation (or its male analogue, the penis) and invariably culminate in muscular contractions at 0.8-second intervals. But desire, fortunately, can be roused in a variety of ways. Sexual function, when it's working right, varies little from one individual to the next, but desire has more varieties than Heinz. Taste is a highly individual thing and tastes can change, once one acquires the desire to consider something new. Otherwise, we would never have had sushi bars.

ON RECORD
Keeping a Desire Diary

Fantasies are fleeting, ephemeral wisps that escape from the imagination. The desire diary captures and holds them so you can work with them.

Keeping a diary makes patients think about sex every day or *think* about thinking about it, Dr. Jerry Friedman explains. If they say, "I didn't write in my diary today, so let me think about something that has to do with sex," it brings sex to the forefront of their consciousness and, as Dr. Friedman phrases it, "primes the pump" for further thoughts and feelings. The desire diary helps patients and therapists become aware of how often sex does pop into their heads and under what circumstances they may have sexual thoughts.

While the diary may initially be limited to fantasies, with time it can include what goes on not only in the subject's head, but also in his bed. There can always be a place in the writings for fantasy fiction, and the book itself can be moved onto the nonfiction shelves.

The diary can be comprehensive enough to include not only thoughts and feelings but the physical occurrences that accompany, or result from them. The writer should record not only the date but also the time of each entry. He or she can put down whatever happened—a conversation, a fantasy, an actual sex act—followed by his feelings and cognitions. Feelings are gut responses, such as "I didn't feel very interested when my husband gave me *that* look, but after a few kisses, I started getting turned on," or "I was kind of attracted to the new girl at work." Cognitions involve a more intellectual appraisal of the situation, such as "I'd be too shy to flirt with her," or "I've really got to tell my husband that he handles my clitoris too roughly," or "Maybe there's hope for me yet!"

Women may want to keep track of their menstrual cycles in their desire diaries to see if there are any correlations between desire and specific phases in the cycles. Recording vaginal temperatures can give a more accurate estimate of just when ovulation is occurring; many women feel desire most strongly just prior to ovulation.

Women can increase their sexual awareness and improve the quality of their sex lives by engaging in and logging in their desire diaries an effortless exercise that tones up the vaginal muscles. Since the floor of the bladder is the roof of the vagina, tightening the urinary sphincter as if trying to control the flow of urine also flexes the vaginal muscles. Obviously, this exercise can be done *anywhere:* while standing on line at the bank, waiting in your car for a traffic light to change, or even during intercourse—which has been known to delight partners.

Rebecca Liswood, M.D., a pioneer in sex therapy, wrote in 1961: "If you know how to use this sphincter muscle, you can constrict and relax on the erect penis during intercourse. This will afford you a very, very pleasurable sensation and delight your husband as well. I remember lecturing on this subject to a group of people in a resort hotel. I told the women to exercise this sphincter muscle and I explained how. The next morning one of the husbands came up to me and said, 'Dr. Liswood, I blessed you all night long.' "

How important are such exercises to improving *desire?* Like keeping track of menstrual cycle days and vaginal temperature, they are valuable because they make a woman more *aware* of the sexual aspects of her body and personality. They prevent her from letting sex slip completely out of consciousness.

Men may want to note erections or sensations in the penis in their desire diaries. Depending on the individual, he may also want to note such things as how many drinks he had, how much sleep he got, how many hours of work he put in. This kind of data connects his sex life, mentally, with the rest of his daily activities.

Keeping a desire diary reminds the writer that "I am always a sexual person. I may not be calling that aspect of myself into play at any given moment, but the potential is always there. My sexuality is not something I put in storage and just bring out on Saturday night."

PUT IT IN WRITING
Using the Desire Diary in Therapy

The next step in Glenda's therapy was the desire diary. This involved keeping a notebook in which she was told to record anything that she perceived as sexual, including random thoughts, and reactions to them. She included material from her fantasy breaks, as well as information about circumstances that prompted sexual thoughts.

"Just what I needed in my life—more paperwork!" Glenda sighs, flipping open her notebook. "These entries are kind of sketchy, Doc, so I'll have to fill in the details. Shall we start with yesterday? Nothing to write home about in my celibate life, but I did have a couple of random fantasies, or at least, thoughts about sex.

"March 18. Menstrual cycle day 11. Flexed love muscle 28 times during coffee break, during phone calls, and while waiting to use copy machine—all on company time. '10:27 A.M.—Robot fantasy. Desire, plus one; men, minus three.' "

"I only gave myself a plus-one rating on that one," Glenda explains, "because I was in a down mood when I started the fantasy. I was thinking how hopeless I was, how no man seemed able to turn me on. I figured I would need some kind of technological miracle, like a super robot. Well, why not? It wouldn't have to be entirely made of metal; I'm sure they could do something with plastics and computer circuits to approximate a human male, with none of his shortcomings. Anyway, I started to work out designs while I was standing there, flexing my love muscle, waiting for Sylvia to finish using the copy machine. Then, Sylvia started cursing and I realized the copy machine must be broken again and that kind of ruined my fantasy. I thought, 'Good grief, if they can't make a copier that doesn't break down every two weeks, like the one at our office, why would a supersex robot work any better?'

"At 11:15 A.M., I had the technician fantasy. Rate that two-plus for desire, one-plus for men in general. It occurred to me that a machine is only as good as the person who designs it and not as durable. If it were possible to design a robot able to give a woman ultimate sexual satisfaction, there would have to be a guy knowledgeable and sensitive to build it, right? At first, I pictured him as a dome-headed, goggle-eyed megabrain, but then I thought that maybe he could be an average-looking guy, maybe a tall, sandy-haired type with horn-rimmed glasses and an intense expression. And you know, Doc, I think at that point the fantasy stopped being just a mental exercise and really started to be a bit of a turn-on for me."

"I hope you made a note of *that* in your diary," the therapist says.

She nods. "I did. Just before the 2 P.M. entry."

"Another entry?" he says, his interest perking. "Another fantasy?"

She smiles. "Well, kind of a warm feeling that came over me when the repairman stuck his head into my office and said the copier was working again."

"The one who comes in every two weeks to fix the machine?"

"Uh-huh!" she affirms. "Tall, sandy-haired young fellow, horn-rimmed glasses, always has this intense expression." Glenda's impassive mouth suddenly explodes into a grin. "Not all that much to look at, but with all his copier experience, he must know *something* about the reproductive system!"

On Your Own

When lighting your own fire, imagination provides the best source of high-octane fuel. The only obstacle that stands between people and their fantasies is time. Anyone *can* fantasize, but a fantasy takes time, even if it's only a matter of seconds.

If you're going to use fantasy breaks and a desire diary as self-help techniques, make sure to spend time with them every day. Someone who is seeing a therapist has to confront him with empty pages, but when you're on your own, there's no one to account to but yourself. If you've got a blank page, write *something* on it about why you think it's blank; were you too busy, too depressed, too uninspired, too disgusted—whatever! Knowing what the obstacles are may help you to overcome them.

The desire diary involves a daily account of sexual feelings. Again, the feelings do not have to be positive ones. A blank page will mean, to the resistant person, "not a single sexy feeling today." A more in-touch person would write on that blank page: "On the go since 5:30 A.M. today. Had to redo whole damn Williams file. Boss is snotty bastard. Husband expects to have dinner at 6:00 and I got home at 6:50. You expect me to feel SEXY??" Or, "Temporary receptionist—think she's single (no ring). Prominent teeth, small chin. Thin, not curvy. Long legs. Two years ago—maybe. Always liked long legs. Now? NAAAH!"

That's desire? Sure, it's negative desire. In math, negative numbers count as much as positive ones. Getting from −5 to 10 takes a little longer than going from 1 to 10, because you have to come up through those negatives before you can even get to zero. If you're overdrawn $100 on your checking account, you don't have *nothing* in the bank, you've got a debt to make up. Zero desire is not as low as you can go.

Material from fantasy breaks should be incorporated into the desire diary. You can write out some of your fantasies in detail, making the diary a type of creative arts therapy, but having the fantasy is more important than recording it and you can condense it into a sentence or two.

The point is that you took the time to have the fantasy, and even if you didn't feel much desire, you've taken a step toward recovering it. The diary can include people you meet (go ahead and be a male or female chauvinist: give them a 1-to-10 rating as prospective partners, even if you have to base your standards on the way you *used* to feel), items you read, or just ideas that pop into your head. If you felt something physical, record it, but desire doesn't have to be perceived in the body. Men who invariably had erections accompanying the first inkling of desire when they were young may have to get accustomed to feeling desire without that instant validation. Women often fail to perceive consciously the physical evidence of arousal that can be measured by lab instruments, so they are likely to have even less success than men in correlating desire with physical sensations.

Do you wish that you could have responded to a person or a situation with that old feeling? That counts. The *desire* to have desire will propel you gradually through those subzero readings on the sexual thermometer into the torrid zone.

Once you have your desire diary, where do you go from there? You go back to it. You look for patterns. You should record negative events as well as positive, such as telling your spouse you're too tired for sex or feeling anxious when a co-worker tells a dirty joke. Are your fantasies better than your realities? Does a co-worker seem more attractive to you than your spouse? What's your prevalent feeling on a given day: boredom, fatigue, revulsion, nervousness? Are things getting better or worse?

As desire improves, the diary will reflect more actual sexual activity, although not necessarily at the expense of fantasies, which don't replace reality but help us reach it. Once there are some experiences to work with, you can chart frequency of relations, who took the initiative, time of day, and most important, what you liked and disliked about the encounter. If your fantasies are getting better but your love life isn't, the problem most likely lies with your relationships, not your desire level.

How long should you continue to keep a diary? There is really no reason to stop at any point, since desire, like any other growing thing, needs care and maintenance, even after it has reached full bloom. But be sure to keep writing until you've reached the point where your sex life is so full and fulfilling that you hate to take time away for it, even for something as worthwhile as the diary.

Remember that the desire diary shouldn't be exclusively about sex. It should include brief bits of information about your physical health, your mood, stresses, successes, changes in your partner's situation, and anything else that could have a bearing on desire. The time and place where your best fantasies occur can be as informative as the fantasy content. You can set up your diary as a log, with columns to record reactions, thoughts, physical sensations, and health data, or keep it free-flowing and unstructured. The diary will confirm that—satisfactory or not—desire is an integral part of your daily life, not something that appears from time to time and can disappear for long periods.

When working to increase desire, you can't always go by the book, but your chances of success increase if *you* wrote the book on it.

STRICTLY BETWEEN YOU AND YOU
Self-dialogue

Talking to yourself is generally regarded by most people as a sign of emotional upset, if not frank mental illness. Sometimes, however, a dialogue with oneself can contribute to the understanding of what inhibits sexual desire and what will improve it.

Dr. Daniel Araoz employs internal dialogue in a technique he calls *educating the inner child,* which involves a type of mental time travel. When a patient is able to recall actual childhood situations in which guilt was associated with sex, the therapist helps him, under hypnosis, to see himself as a child again, reliving the scene and feeling all the emotions he then experienced. When this has been accomplished, the patient then mentally introduces himself into the picture and uses his present wisdom and understanding to educate his "inner child" with regard to healthy attitudes about the body, sexual pleasure, and what is right and wrong. Sometimes this technique is repeated, with the patient imagining the child at different ages in situations where various negative, guilt-producing messages were given, correcting them each time through supportive conversation. This technique is similar to that used by Dr. Araoz in the "negative processing" situation described earlier, only the patient uses his adult self as the authority figure rather than fantasizing some outside expert as the instructor.

One female patient in her early forties remembered that her father had said to her when she was twelve, "Don't ever do anything with a boy that you wouldn't do in front of me." Dr. Araoz pointed out to the patient that such advice was wonderful for a twelve-year-old, but the father never thought or had the chance to modify that counsel as she matured into a young woman. Dr. Araoz then had her "step into her picture as a mature woman" and say to herself, "Now I am a woman. I have to make my own decisions and trust my own judgment; I can do what *I* think is right and I don't need my father's presence to monitor what I am doing."

Dr. Lazarus has used similar techniques, having a patient talk to his younger self in order to overcome a sexual desire problem. In one unusual case, a patient had the problem of mentally visualizing sickly-looking men and drunkards during sex, usually when he was about to begin coitus. He couldn't understand what these strange, disturbing images meant. In the course of therapy, what emerged was that he had been told when he was young that whenever a man ejaculated it was like losing a quart of blood. This fear, coupled with the postcoital lassitude he had been experiencing, made him subconsciously imagine that he would ultimately wind up dissipated and sickly, like a derelict.

Once Dr. Lazarus had helped the patient to identify the source of the disturbing images, he used the "time machine" method employed by Dr. Araoz. The patient imagined going back in time and talking to himself when he was a young adolescent, with his adult self explaining that sex was not harmful and would not weaken him. In future sexual situations, the patient was instructed to replace the unhealthy images as they appeared with an alternative positive image, that of a respected authority figure, such as his family doctor, telling him to go ahead and not let his false fears inhibit him. The negative images grew progressively weaker and ultimately disappeared.

In a two-part dialogue with oneself, the two "participants" do not have to be of different ages. More often, as practiced under the direction of psychotherapists, a debate takes place between two different aspects of the self, usually a sexual and a nonsexual one.

Having a self-dialogue can be a bit tricky because we don't think of ourselves as having more than one identity. We do tend to segregate out our sexual elements in work situations or in casual social interactions; there are many people, particularly authority figures, whom it seems impossible to picture in the bedroom because they distill off any traces of sexuality in their public roles. On the other hand, we encounter men who relate with a nonstop series of leers, obscene innuendos, and furtive pawing gestures, or women whose every movement is a provocative wriggle and who exhale their words instead of speaking them; we wonder if there is anything *non*sexual about such people. For most of us, however, there are somewhat discrete sexual and nonsexual selves.

A person with a complaint of low desire can probably locate his sexual self, the one with a respectable level of desire, somewhere back in time. Then it's simply a matter of setting up a conversation between himself as he is now and himself as he was two, five, or fifteen years ago. We always argue with ourselves, even if we're not aware of it. The decision to buy a new car, the choice of which project to attack first, or even which movie to see will involve more than one internal point of view. We may not think of a separate self championing each argument for or against—but we could easily imagine it.

A STEREO HEADSET
Using Self-dialogue in Therapy

"It's time for a serious talk," the therapist says solemnly.

Glenda clears her throat and growls, "You don't consider the weeks of heart-wrenching, gut-spilling self-revelation that I've gone through *serious* communication?"

"I mean that it's time for you to have a serious talk with . . . you!" he announces.

She looks at him warily. "If you want me to do this, I will, but I always thought that talking to yourself was something you did in padded cells, not upholstered offices."

"All right then, Glenda, I just want you to take turns talking with . . ."

"Glenda?" she says helpfully.

"No," he declares. "There are two different Glendas here. I want one of them to be the person who used to have desire. The one that lived with Vic and loved him and looked forward to sex."

"The Golden Girl," she says softly.

"Yes. The other Glenda is the one that went to your office this morning. Do any of your co-workers have a special name for her, other than Glenda?"

"The new people usually call me by my last name, or Mrs. D., for short."

"That'll do fine," he says. "Mrs. D. and the Golden Girl."

"I can't call myself 'Golden Girl,' " she protests. "It was okay for Vic to say that, but *I* wouldn't say it to a woman, not even me."

"Then give her a name. Use her initials, maybe. 'G.G.' "

"Gigi!" Glenda exclaims with delight and hums the title song of the Lerner and Loewe film musical. "Yes, that would suit her. Young, naive, and madly in love with love."

"Talk to her, then," the therapist urges. "Tell her how naive she is."

Glenda, not knowing whom to look at, stares at the therapist's certificate-speckled wall. "You *are* naive, you know, Gigi. You really thought you had it all, with a husband, a daughter, a few dollars of your own. You never gave a thought to tomorrow. You never realized you might grow up and one day be bored silly with your life, doing trivial office tasks by day, housework by night. How old were you when you died, Gigi? Was it this year, or did you die slowly over many years?"

"Answer her, Gigi," the therapist commands.

Glenda's expression changes abruptly. The mocking smile fades and she turns her toes inward, like a shy girl sitting on the periphery of a dance floor. "Are you so sure I'm dead?" Her voice is soft and reedy at first, but gets louder and distinctly angry. "Are you sure you *want* me dead? Mrs. D., in some ways I was more alive as a child than you are now. I enjoyed life, the way you haven't been able to."

Gigi, in spite of her anger, has a softness to her features that the therapist had never seen in Glenda, and he realizes that, in spite of her exceptional beauty, Glenda had always set her jaw and her mouth with a defensive firmness that totally changed her appearance. "I'm the part of you that you lost, and that you came back looking for. Pray I'm not dead, Mrs. D., because if I'm gone forever, you're going to lose everything that I got for us, first Vic, sooner or later our daughter, Diana, and finally even what's left of you."

The therapist sees her turn her gaze toward him. He nods, and the jaw hardens again. Mrs. D. is back.

"Cool it, Gigi!" she says sharply. "You're such a hopeless romantic that you see everything in tragic terms. You're scared, but you don't scare me. I'm a survivor. If I came back for you, it's not necessarily because I needed you, but maybe now I've got enough confidence in myself to carry the both of us."

Gigi senses an opening and jumps back in. She spreads her feet a bit, her knees no longer locked together, but she still looks uncomfortable. "I'm not afraid. Were those early years so easy for me? Were you around, Mrs. D., when I was trying to get people to see a mind that was seriously trying to learn something about the world, and all they saw was a young girl? Was it easy wanting so much to be loved by someone, but being able to say 'not yet,' when you knew the guy couldn't see beyond your hairdo and your Maidenform? Who gave you Vic? He was growing up, just as I was. He wasn't complete, just as I wasn't. But we had some damn good years, didn't we? When did you become too good for him, so good that you didn't even want him to touch you?"

Gigi waits for an answer. Mrs. D. rouses herself into a slow reply. "This is stupid. You're talking as if I hate Vic and, so help me, you know I like him. You're accusing me of thinking I'm too good and you *must* know that I don't feel I've accomplished all that much. My God, it's not as if I'm on the verge of discovering how to cure cancer or even amassing fortunes for a top corporation. I enjoy what I'm doing and maybe I'm on my way to something even better, but that doesn't make me some kind of man-hating, frigid fanatic. I'm not a feminist."

"You're not even feminine!" Gigi adds. She's back, although the turnover was instantaneous this time. "Mrs. D., was it so bad being a woman . . . even being a *girl?* Okay, so I never got to say, 'I'm an executive,' but I liked myself. I felt pretty and I felt loved. Was I selling out by going to bed with my husband and enjoying it?

Watching him get excited, getting excited myself, hearing him say, 'You're beautiful, Glenda,' and knowing he meant it? Why don't you want this anymore?"

Mrs. D. shakes her head vigorously, clearing Gigi's thoughts out of her brain. "Because it's changed. Vic and Glenda aren't the same people. They belong to the past, like you do."

"Come off it!" Gigi explodes. "Vic hasn't changed one iota since I met him. The guy's not perfect, but inconsistency is not one of his vices."

"Then, damn it, maybe consistency is a worse vice!" Mrs. D. retorts. "If *I* was changing, then he should have made an attempt to change along with me, or at least keep up with me. I had a thousand ideas buzzing around in my brain, a hundred goals twinkling at me, all from different directions, and he expected me to be the same old Glenda, his pretty, sexy little 'Golden Girl.' "

Gigi sighs, her anger dissipating, and she settles into an unfamiliar take-charge role. "Mrs. D.," she says, "face it: for a long time, and maybe even now, you didn't know who the hell you were. You couldn't have bombarded Vic with all those ideas and conflicting goals, because they would have come out as the mixed-up garble they were. Okay, maybe we got a late start and maybe I held you back because I was having too much fun being sexy and secure and loving and loved, and not really wanting to think about personal growth and independence. Gee, if even *I* wanted to stay back there, maybe we shouldn't blame Vic for not keeping up with you. You're angry at him. You're the brainy one, so you can rationalize your way out of it, but I can *feel* that anger. Maybe it's me you're mad at, and because I want Vic, you don't want him."

"Anger!" Mrs. D. snorts. "You're talking emotions and I'm trying to talk *sense*. You said something about how, even way back, you knew enough not to get involved with somebody who wasn't right for you. You knew what desire was, but even then it wasn't strong enough to override good sense. Just because it's Vic we're talking about doesn't mean I can turn on desire when my head is saying, 'Who's this stranger?' I *want* to feel that desire. The doctor here said to me that the desire to desire was maybe the most important thing, but so far it hasn't been enough."

"You think you want it," Gigi answers, "or you say you do, but why don't you level with the doctor? You're afraid that if you get desire back, you're going to turn back into me. If Vic gets his sexy 'Golden Girl' back, you're going to disappear. It's as though just going to bed with Vic again is going to turn back the clock and you'll be taking phone messages and making coffee, instead of masterminding PR campaigns. You won't be clever or gutsy or funny, because 'Golden Girl' never acted that way. You're right, maybe she wasn't all that much, but Vic loved her for what she was and maybe he could love you, too, if you gave him the chance."

Mrs. D. says wearily, "I don't think I have the energy to try. You don't realize what it's like, thinking on your feet all day, your brain trying to set things up for the following day as you're helping Diana with her homework. Don't ask me to cut back. I've come too far to turn around. If sex is the price of not retreating, I'll have to pay it."

"Try falling into his arms," Gigi suggests. "That's effortless enough."

"It's also simple-minded," Mrs. D. counters. "It's not that easy."

"Then, again, who says it has to be easy?" The therapist hears Gigi say it, but for the first time Glenda's face and body haven't switched character. The dialogue is changing into a monologue. Glenda is pulling Gigi and Mrs. D. back together.

"I told the doc when I first came in that maybe I'd outgrown desire. It sounded really stupid then, but maybe I wasn't too far off. I read somewhere that sometimes one part of a kid's body grows faster than another, so she may have enormous feet for a while, and then the rest of her catches up. So, maybe when the job came along and I got so wrapped up in it, my brain raced ahead and wouldn't wait for the rest of me to catch up. I just didn't want *anything* to interfere. How could Vic genuinely like the new me if he didn't know me? Maybe he'll hate the new me if I give him the chance . . . but I guess I should give him that chance."

Glenda turns her gaze from the wall to the therapist. "Hey, where did everybody go? Wow, that must be a little bit like what hypnosis is like. It was weird talking to myself."

"You've been doing it inside for quite a while now," the therapist speculates. "You were a little too adept at self-dialoguing for a first attempt."

"So, what do you think of the old me?" Glenda asks timidly. "A little awkward, isn't she?"

"It seems to me you've been bringing her along gradually without realizing it," the therapist says. "There were times when I could hardly tell you apart."

Self-dialoguing doesn't require a hypnotherapist or even a therapist. All it takes is two viewpoints. And one person.

On Your Own

If you're ready to try a self-dialogue on your own, pull up a chair. Or two chairs, if you prefer.

In a self-dialogue, it's easy to have your dominant personality complain vocally (or in your head if you lack privacy) about how little you are feeling and all the reasons why you might have gotten to that sorry state. You might be more hard-pressed to muster an opposing point of view, but just as in all fair trials there must be an attorney for each side, you can force a "public defender" into service, to play devil's advocate. "I don't feel any sexier than you do," he might say to your "nonsexual" self, "but I've got to make a case. Maybe I'll start by saying what desire should be like. No, maybe I don't even know that much, so I'll talk about how *some* people think it should be."

Who is this alter ego of yours? It might be a more desirous you, as you were years ago or as you hope to be in the future. It might be the more romantic side of you, the more childish side, the more creative side. It might be the angry you or the frightened you, the part you never reveal to anyone. Get that alter ego to speak up, as he or she would if you could put words into that mouth.

You can switch back and forth between two chairs, if it helps, although when the interchange gets heated and arguments fly, your body might not be able to move as quickly as your tongue. Turning your head from one side to the other, as though watching Steffi play Martina, can help you keep your two personalities separate, or you might try alternating a small object between your hands.

Why is the dialogue important? We all have different aspects of personality. For the average person, the sexual self gets submerged in day-to-day interactions with the world because most of our relationships are *not* sexual. The nonsexual person tends to take over the personality and become the spokesperson. Problems of sexual desire invariably develop for nonsexual reasons: work pressures, fights with one's partner over money or relatives, physical fatigue. Now, the nonsexual person takes over the sexual realm as well, because sexual experience is reduced to saying no. On many occasions, saying no is the only reasonable option, but with time we may lose the person who might have wanted to say yes. The dialogue puts us back in touch with the sexual person who has been disenfranchised from casting an affirmative vote to make love.

We once met a young married woman who confided that she was an identical twin. It did not surprise us to learn that she and her sister had developed their own language as toddlers, since this is not unusual in infants of identical age raised together. It did amaze us when she told us that, when she started nursery school, she had to be taught English, because she had never spoken to her parents. Her more dominant sister had usurped the role of communicator with the outside and no one seemed to realize that the silent twin was not mute by choice.

In the self-dialogue, we give speech back to our silent twin. In a realm as complex as sex, we can use all the self-help we can get.

ON STAGE AND OFF LIMITS
Acting Out Your Fantasies

When working with couples, Dr. Jerry Friedman asks his patients not only to share some of their fantasies with one another, but also sometimes to act them out. He uses the acting-out technique when he wants them to "loosen up" and make sex more playful. "If she has a fantasy about being seduced by a tall, dark stranger at a cocktail party, I'll have him dress up in a nice suit and play-act that out," Dr. Friedman gives as an example. "That's a way of teaching them to be more playful and of letting sex be more fun."

Many of us play-act in our sex lives. Couples often use baby talk and cuddling behavior with one another that they would never employ elsewhere.

The "naughty lady" is another popular role. A woman may put on sexy lingerie that is unquestionably provocative and very different in style from the rest of her conservative wardrobe. She may not say, "Let's pretend I'm a hooker," but she adopts a whole new sexy personality. That's really playing out a fantasy.

As we indicated before, many people would feel threatened if a partner confessed to having desire for a neighbor or co-worker. If a couple decides to act out "another person" fantasy, the character portrayed is usually anonymous: for example, the husband might play a TV repairman and the wife's role would be to seduce him or let him seduce her. The identities assumed by one or both partners are those of characters who exhibit aspects of personality and behavior rarely shown by the actor (or actress), but the fantasy figures do not have real-life counterparts, at least not any who would be readily accessible to step into the role.

We will talk about other situations where a therapist might use some form of role playing, such as role reversal. Reversing behaviors can help one partner understand the effect of his or her behavior on the other's desire. An example of this would be the wife who is sexually pursued by her husband while she is trying to complete some household chore acting the same way toward him while he pretends to be balancing his budget.

Acting out fantasies requires a certain amount of daring and a lot of intimate sharing, both of which add to the excitement and warmth of sex.

ACTING OUT
Using Role Playing in Therapy

The woman is wearing dark glasses and one of those floppy, large-brimmed hats like the one Ingrid Bergman wears in *Casablanca*. Her hair is tucked up and hidden by the hat and her body is encased in a beige trenchcoat. Her head darts from side to side in nervous, scanning movements as she enters the room, and she presses her back against the closed door for a moment. "Vee cahn't go on meeting like ziss," she gasps.

She is Glenda's height, and from the contour of the coat, she has Glenda's shape, and this is Glenda's scheduled appointment time, so, the therapist reasons, one might logically assume this is Glenda, even if she looks like something out of a screen test that Zsa Zsa Gabor flunked. She gets to the chair in two quick strides, eases into it, and lights a cigarette. Glenda doesn't smoke.

She puffs on the cigarette without inhaling, removing it from her still-puckered lips with an elaborate flourish. "My husband zinks zat it is *you* who haff made me into vat I am, und I am afraid he iss about to do somezing very rash." She pulls off the glasses and the familiar blue eyes crinkle at the corners. "So help me, Doc, the man threatened to buy you a Mercedes."

"Would you like to supply a few subtitles for this, so I can follow what's going on?" the therapist requests. "For a minute, I was afraid the self-dialoguing had thrown you into a full-blown multiple personality syndrome."

"Remember how we were talking about acting out your fantasies?" Glenda says. "First fantasy breaks, then fantasy diaries—I figured I was ready for the next step. Vic and I have been having sex for . . . hmmm, three weeks now. It's been so good, I decided to push my luck. So, I told him on the phone to meet me on Platform 18 at Penn Station Wednesday evening instead of coming over to the house. I said it in a playful, sexy tone, so he knew I had some kind of surprise for him, maybe dinner somewhere on the Island and then checking into a motel. He asked if he should pack anything, but I told him to leave everything to me."

"So," Glenda continues, "at 7:15 P.M., when the rush hour is over, but there are still plenty of people around and trains pulling in and out, Vic is dutifully standing on Platform 18, looking around for me. He sees me coming down the stairs, but I'm sure he doesn't recognize me, between the hat, the glasses, and my hair up. I walk near the track that's farther away from where he's standing, one hand in my pocket, the other dragging the cigarette from my mouth. I walk beyond where Vic is, then start crossing toward his side of the platform, doubling back. This guy sees me stop and gives me a timid smile, like he wants to pick me up, but I hiss, 'Dolt! I am on a vital security mission.' He gets out of my way fast.

"I stalk behind Vic, blow smoke over his shoulder, and whisper, 'Pretend you don't see me.' He whirls around and stares into my shades. 'Zere iss great danger here,' I snap, and turn my back on him, still talking. 'I vill valk to ze far exit stairway. Follow at a discreet distance. Vee vill zpeak zair.' " Glenda giggles. "I've got on these really high spiked heels, so walking quickly isn't easy for me, and in spite of the noise of the trains, you can hear those heels clicking throughout the station. People's heads turn as I walk by, my right hand in the trenchcoat bulging forward, like I'm packing a gun.

"I know Vic isn't far behind, but I don't look back. When I get to the staircase, I wait for him at the foot. I put my finger to my lips. Nobody's on the staircase, so . . ." Glenda unfastens the bottom button of her trenchcoat and extends a bare leg, exposed to midthigh. "I put my leg on the second step of the staircase and say, 'I zid not haff time to dress,' and I pull a scrap of paper from a garter."

Glenda grins with mischievous delight. "You should have seen Vic's eyes bug out." She retracts her leg back under the coat and rebuttons it. "I was wearing a teddy underneath," she confided, "but he must have thought I was stark naked. Not that it would have really mattered, because the coat did cover me, but men have these *wild* imaginations."

"*Men* do?" he mutters under his breath. "Lone Ranger. Super-sex robots. Orient Express to Manhasset."

"By the way, Doc, I *do* have a skirt on under this today," she reassures him. "Just to put your mind at ease."

He says, "What was on the scrap of paper?"

"Oh, our address, of course," she answers. "Well, *my* address, but it used to be ours. And the way things are going, who knows? Hey, do you know what Vic did? He wadded up the scrap of paper and put it in his mouth. He might have even swallowed it, like they do in the movies; I'm not sure. Can you imagine someone doing a wacky thing like that!"

"Right in the middle of Penn Station!" the therapist exclaims, in mock disbelief.

"Without looking at him again," Glenda continues, "I say, 'I vill go on ahead. Vee rendezvous at zixteen-hundred.'"

"Then," she reports, "Vic spoke for the first time. He said, very distinctly, 'The wallaby and the marmoset desynchronize their ca-rafes.' I replied, 'Zere's no need to zay ze obfious,' and climbed slowly up the stairs. I grabbed a taxi, but he must have been right behind me, because I barely got home and had time to light the incense sticks before he got there. Still wearing the trenchcoat, I poured out some wine for us. He started to say something, but I said, 'Vee must vait for ze word.'

" 'This room might be bugged,' he said. 'Maybe we should go into one of your other rooms—the conservatory, the billiard room, the bedroom?'

" 'Vee must vait for ze word,' I said again. I took off my hat and glasses and unbuttoned the top of my coat.

" 'I've probably sealed my doom by coming here,' he said, 'but you're the most irresistible woman that ever drew breath and I want you, *now!*'

" 'Zat's ze word!' I yelled. Doc, we were like happy little animals. We never made it to the bedroom. And Vic is usually such a fussbudget in the bedroom, too, turning down the sheets, fluffing the pillows. Nutsy, isn't it?"

"It was good," the therapist understates.

"More than good, Doc," she affirms. "It was fun! Next stop, Chinatown!"

"Going to dinner?" he asks.

"No, I mean the next rendezvous," Glenda says. "I've got to pick up some of those Oriental combs and one of those silky dresses with a slit. Hey, don't look at me in that tone of voice!"

"No, no," the therapist protests. "I think it's fine. Really."

"You've got some doubts, though," she insists. "I did, too. Know why? First, I asked myself if this wasn't just a cheap trick, a kids' game, not what sex and love and *intimacy* should be. That word, 'intimacy,' was the key, though; it set me straight. Think about it: me and Vic, in our own little world, right there in the middle of Penn Station. Crowds of strangers all around us and they could have been miles away. They were unpaid extras in our own film epic. And when Vic said that thing about the wallaby and the marmoset, I don't think I ever felt so close to him in my whole life."

The therapist understood then why Glenda hadn't shared the Penn Station adventure with him before acting out the fantasy, even though she had previously discussed everything before and after each meeting with Vic. The spy fantasy was a new high in intimacy, and although she didn't realize it at the time, she feared that including the therapist in the planning might spoil that intimacy.

The pathway back to renewed sexual desire had been, as usual, a convoluted one, with occasional sidetracks. One thing the therapist had warned Glenda about at the start was that business pressures and the strain of deadlines do take their toll on sexual desire. He realized that obvious impediments can be easily underestimated or overlooked while a therapist delves for deep conflicts within the patient's self or between the spouses.

Glenda's new career did play some role in the problem, but there was nothing intrinsically harmful about her work. She was employed with a small, but highly successful all-female staff. Her two supervisors were sympathetic to the demands of homemaking and child care and were flexible in letting Glenda set her own schedule. Buoyed up by their support and enjoying the female camaraderie, Glenda relaxed enough to let her previously suppressed wit and creativity be released. Her innovative contributions launched her on an upward spiral of increased responsibility at the job.

Glenda began to feel like a new person, and in a way, she was. She wanted to share her new identity with Vic, but somehow she didn't seem to be able to do it. If she tried to share a work project, he would look uncomfortable and say he didn't know anything about fashions or "women's stuff," and she couldn't seem to explain that fashions were only the product, and her job really entailed the type of salesmanship that could have just as easily been applied to power tools or sports cars.

Turning to other men was unacceptable to Glenda, so she short-circuited her libido, telling herself she was far too preoccupied with more important matters to worry about sex. Becoming an asexual being solved the problem only temporarily; Vic refused to continue with the deteriorating situation, which led to the trial separation.

As therapy progressed, Glenda realized she had not become as asexual as she thought. She and Vic had decided not to attempt to resume sexual relations until she truly felt a desire to do so, and they adhered to that agreement. Glenda vetoed the therapist's suggestion that they be treated as a couple, feeling she had too many of her own personal issues to deal with. Through the experiential therapies of fantasy breaks, desire diary, self-dialogue, and role playing, she was able to get back in touch with herself as a sexual person and keep her desire from getting entangled in nonsexual conflicts. Glenda agreed to reconsider marital therapy with her husband if her desire did not improve.

The therapist never did get to meet Vic.

On Your Own

If you and your partner have never been into acting out fantasies, start by just sharing your favorite fantasies. The process is not much different from theater. You begin by talking about plots and characters, then move into reading from scripts, progress from that into rehearsing scenes on a bare stage without props, and finally do a full-scale production with costumes and props. If your fantasy is a very elaborate one, imagining it may be more stimulating than trying to stage it—except for the big bedroom scene at the end, of course.

Let's say, for example, the man enjoys an occasional fantasy about Oriental women. The woman might be more turned on by Latin types. Just simply sharing with one another what their exotic dream-mates might look like and how they might act might be stimulating in itself. Taking the next step might involve a bit of unconventional ambience. The wife could provide the scent of jasmine or incense in the room, some Oriental music on the turntable, and the substitution of sake or plum wine for the usual chablis. For teetotalers, a steaming pot of Chinese tea and some appetizers from the local take-out counter would serve as well. The man could, in turn, provide his mate with an authentic flamenco album, a pitcher of sangria, some hastily mastered Spanish love phrases, and a few fajitas sizzling along with the libido.

As they get accustomed to boudoir travel, the couple might even try on new personalities to go with their costumes. You don't need a new wardrobe or a costume rental service. An Oriental-style housecoat or robe should be easy to find, or decorate an old one with a few Chinese words or an appliquéd dragon. Wooden sandals, geisha-style makeup, or just putting up her hair in a Japanese-style bun can turn a woman out of her cocoon and into a Butterfly. The associated personality can range from the subservient and demure geisha to the wonton Susie Wong. A sombrero, a cape, or a pair of boots can help transform an all-business junior executive into a suave aristocrat or a bawdy bandito. It's probably best not to try to fulfill one another's fantasies simultaneously, although a liaison between a hot-blooded gaucho and a mysterious lotus blossom just might spark some unusual fireworks.

When you want the bedroom to be the climax, not the beginning and end of a memorable evening, set the stage outside your doors. Start your rendezvous in a lounge, restaurant, theater, or park that provides the right atmosphere for the fantasy. Don't worry whether your choice of places might clash with your fantasy. In fact, the secret of intimacy lies in sharing the fantasy just between the two of you, shutting out all the people around you. It is far more exciting for Don Carlo de Lupe to be seducing the virtuous Señorita Margarita de Guapa at a corner table in McDonald's than for

Mr. and Mrs. John Q. Mundane to spend a few unimaginative hours and half a paycheck at a four-star exotic gourmet palace like La Fonda de la Bolsa.

When it comes to acting out your fantasies with your partner, what, if anything, is off limits? Asking your partner to pretend to be a specific other person is generally not a good idea, although someone unlikely to intrude on your relationship, such as Madonna or Sylvester Stallone, might be fun to try.

We have acknowledged that many people are turned on by fantasies of domination and "forced sex." Is S-M O-K? According to Morton Hunt's survey, about 5 percent of men and women have experienced sexual pleasure through inflicting or receiving pain. These acts undoubtedly included a lot of love bites, pinches, squeezes, and spanks of a playful and innocuous nature, with a minuscule amount of disciplinary rituals, fetishistic accoutrements, and real distress. Even in the more extreme cases, the "masochist" controls things. *Control* is invariably the key as to what's healthy and what isn't, whether it's in fantasy or actuality. You can try anything you both want to, as long as it's agreed that either partner can blow the whistle at any time to stop play.

Anything goes in Fantasyland, *provided* both partners are agreeable. That's the best guideline for play-acting and *all* sexual activity. Tastes can be acquired or changed; however, taste is a highly individual thing, and if a man or woman is frankly opposed to a certain practice, it doesn't matter if 99 percent of the people are doing it and a clergyman gives written permission.

In trying to improve the desire of a reluctant spouse, you might fall back on the oldest type of behavioral therapy, which associates a reward with a specific behavior, so that the pleasure attached to the reward becomes transferred to the behavior. One woman telephoned a TV talk show to say that since her husband started paying her fifty to a hundred dollars "spending money" for performing sexual acts she would "usually rather not do," she has found their sex life very enjoyable. Similarly, a wife who lures her husband away from the TV football game in the living room with X-rated rented video cassettes for the VCR in the bedroom may find that in a short time he is more interested in live action than in television replays or video cassette foreplays.

Are there fantasies that should not be shared with a partner? Often, the problem is not with the fantasy's content but its timing. In the opening chapter of *My Secret Garden,* author Nancy Friday tells of a personal fantasy of her own during sex with her partner. She is at a Baltimore Colts–Minnesota Vikings football game with several other people, all huddled under a blanket. They all rise with excitement, still covered by the blanket, as quarterback Johnny Unitas breaks for the goal line. As they scream encouragement, one of the men, whose face she does not see, manages to have inter- course with her from behind, with the aid of a rip in her tights. Her orgasm coincides with Unitas making it over the goal line for the winning touchdown.

Ms. Friday made the colossal mistake of relating her fantasy to her lover when he asked, in the midst of their actual lovemaking, what she was thinking about. When she answered truthfully, he got out of bed, silently put on his pants, and went home. Ms. Friday concluded that her lover could not tolerate her fantasy because it involved another man and because it was unconventional ("What would you have thought of the one about my Great Uncle Henry's Dalmatian?"). Probably the only thing he could not tolerate was that she was using the fantasy to help herself climax during actual lovemaking, meaning that he, in the heated flesh, was inadequate and certainly inferior to the wisps of imagination that could so excite her.

If only her lover had asked about her fantasy at a less impas- sioned moment! Can you imagine the joyous surprise of discover- ing a woman who not only had some degree of tolerance for profes- sional football, but could actually become sexually excited by it? Think of the millions of husbands who, every autumnal Sunday, must listen to female voices shrilly berating the time they spend watching a spectacle that their wives deem moronic, savage, and just plain boring—they would kill for a woman who climaxed over touchdowns and possibly had multiple orgasms with instant re- plays.

Nevertheless, it is a wonderful fantasy, including not only foot- ball but kinky, frequently encountered fantasy elements such as the anonymous lover, exhibitionism, fear of discovery, and a bit of the ever-popular forced sex. Yes, she *should* have shared it with her man, only not at that climactic moment. Maybe women should never fake orgasms during intercourse, but they should sometimes fake fantasies.

Sharing fantasies with a partner can accomplish three different things. It can help the partners learn more about one another's sexual preferences and turn-ons, creating a more intimate relationship. It can guide the listener in how to increase desire in the partner. It can increase desire in the listener who finds the partner's fantasy exciting.

Hearing a partner fantasize about experiences with someone else can be very threatening to some and difficult to tolerate, unless the fantasy lover is fictitious, anonymous, or remote. There are a few people, nearly all male, who actually get excited by the thought of their partner's being with another man. This proclivity might stem from the wish to be a voyeur on whom no performance demands are placed or a latent wish for homosexual experience. Other men may be too possessive and insecure to endure even the thought of their women with outside partners. Even though sex with an outside partner is probably the most common sexual fantasy, caution should be used in sharing it, based on past experience with one's regular lover.

The stimulus for novelty in a relationship need not come from infidelity; don't be afraid to take on the role of someone new and invite your partner to do the same. Chances are that your characters won't really be "new," just a part of yourself that you've kept buried inside. Nothing adds spice to marital sex like an intramarital affair.

❧ 12 ❧

The Best-Case Scenario

A Cognitive Approach

Nature seems above all to avoid the painful and aim at the pleasant.

—ARISTOTLE

Okay, okay, that may not sound particularly profound, but Sigmund Freud got a lot of mileage out of his "discovery" of the "pleasure principle," which says essentially the same thing as the old philosopher's pronouncement two thousand years earlier:

People like to do what is pleasant and try to avoid what is unpleasant.

Why dignify such a self-evident statement with special mention? Because the truth is so basic that we often disregard it in the course of trying to analyze a desire problem. While there is a subgroup of people with desire disorder who avoid sex because it is a distinctly unpleasant experience for them (sexual aversion disorder)—usually because sex reminds them of past traumatic experiences or overwhelms them with shame, guilt, or revulsion—most people with low desire find sex pleasurable, or at least not unpleasant, and have no difficulty functioning, including experiencing orgasm.

So, we have an apparent paradox here. Why would a person risk a relationship and suffer conflict with a partner instead of willingly and eagerly doing something that is pleasurable? In most cases, there is no paradox because, while physical gratification may be present, there are too many unpleasant components to the experience to make it worthwhile. We avoid the pleasant to escape a situation whose unpleasant aspects outweigh the pleasure. We endure the unpleasant to avoid something even more unpleasant.

If sex were unmitigated enjoyment, people would never develop desire disorder. Ask yourself what you *don't* like about sex or your partner or the relationship. If your sex life is enjoyable but David Letterman is more so, your sex life isn't enjoyable enough.

Even a sexual experience with no strongly negative components can leave you disappointed. Why?

> *Satisfaction depends not on what you get, but on what you expected.*

You can think of any number of examples. If your boss gave you a 300-dollar Christmas bonus, you would be unequivocally delighted if you never expected a bonus, but if you expected at least 1,000 dollars, you would be furious. If you ordered a "regular" container of soda, ten ounces would satisfy you, but it would anger you if you ordered a "large" one somewhere else, even if the two establishments charged the same price for that amount. You might be pleased when an average-looking blind date showed up if the person had been described previously as "nice," but crushed if the date had been touted as "gorgeous."

In cases of low sexual desire, partners should always ask: (1) What would I expect from a good sexual experience? (2) Am I getting it in *my* sex life? (3) Are my expectations reasonable?

Note that we said "from a *good* sexual experience," not their typical ones. Sex *should* be good. Getting exactly what you expected from your own experiences is not going to encourage you to repeat them if what you felt does not coincide with your ideas about "good sex." Finally, question how reasonable your expectations are, so you can modify them if they are unreasonable. Dissatisfaction has nothing to do with how appropriate the expectations were, as long as the person really thought they could be met.

Expectation in sex is a two-way street. People question not only what they get from it in relation to their expectations, but also what the partner got, in terms of perceived expectations. A sense of having failed as a lover can be more lethal to desire than the keenest disappointment in personal satisfaction.

One way to analyze—and perhaps even attain—your expectations is to write a scenario describing the very best sexual experience you could imagine. A scenario of this type should be different from a fantasy in the sense that it's something that could plausibly happen and that you would want to happen. If you can get your spouse to write up a scenario of his or her own, the two of you might just be able to collaborate on a producible script that brings you both a lot closer to your fondest expectations than you ever thought possible.

Most couples are dealing with a secondary decrease in desire, not something that's been stuck at zero from the beginning. If you can't seem to visualize a scenario set in the near future, throw your thinking gear into reverse. Think about the best sexual experiences you ever had and try to recapture some of the atmosphere that made them that way. If you can't see or imagine yourself feeling desire in *any* situation, it's going to be nearly impossible to make it happen, so capture or build an image you can believe in before you put yourself into the picture.

As an example, let's consider Natalie and George. Natalie's "best case" scenario might be described by her as follows:

"At 3 P.M., a florist delivers a dozen roses, with a card that reads, 'Counting the minutes till I can be with you. Passionately, George.' (The last time George brought home any sort of plant life was two years ago when he bought some mint sprigs so he could make juleps while watching the Kentucky Derby. And the only time he counts the minutes is in the last quarter of a football game.) George comes home half an hour early, looking guilty, confessing he sneaked out of the office early because he was so eager to see me. He kisses me with such fervor that I'm glad the kids have been left overnight with my mother. (The last time he left Billy anywhere overnight was when he had a free ticket to a Knicks game and I was in the hospital with Jessica, who was two days old.) George has brought a bottle of my favorite rosé wine, already chilled. (He always says alcohol should be clear or amber, and that pink is the color for Kool-Aid.) George says, 'Natalie, you look so lovely! I just want to sit and talk to you for a few minutes and simply look at you.' (He usually wants to sit and eat in a few minutes, after he's looked in the microwave oven and the pots on the stove.) He doesn't just talk, though. While he asks me how my day has been, he's stroking my cheek and looking into my eyes as though he can't tear his glance away. (The last time George stroked my cheek, he said, 'You've got some kind of chocolate crap on your face.')"

You get the idea. Natalie's scenario would proceed into the bedroom and include the type of foreplay she likes, how intercourse would go, and what would happen afterward. Based on George's recent attitudes, she might think that the chances of that happening would be remote. And her thinking would be correct; nothing like that is going to happen, but not because it *can't* happen. It won't happen because George isn't a mind reader. She has to share that scenario with him.

If Natalie is trying to reawaken her desire, hopefully she and George will have discussed their mutual dissatisfaction with their sex life and agreed to do something about it. Natalie should be sure to invite George to come up with his own "best case" scenario.

What's in it for George and how can Natalie be sure he's going to cooperate with her scenario? The answer to the first question is good sex, or at least a way out of boredom and mediocre sex. The answer to the second question is Natalie *can't* be sure. George may be too embarrassed and dismiss the whole idea as ridiculous, but at least he will have been exposed to her scenario and encouraged to think about his own, even if he won't share it.

Now, the first thing that may strike George about Natalie's scenario is that a lot of it, such as the roses and the wine, doesn't seem to have much to do with sex at all. Apparently, though, to Natalie such things are as much a part of sex as foreplay. So, maybe he can spring for a few flowers and a bottle of that terrible pink stuff.

As for leaving the kids with somebody just so they can have sex in complete privacy, he would have been mortified to suggest such a thing to maternal Natalie. How about *her* coming up with that! Maybe she's got more desire left in her than he realized.

George's own scenario might include that peek-a-boo black bra Natalie never wears anymore and a videotape from the "adult" shelf of the rental shop. With the kids safely gone and a few glasses of wine, Natalie might really get into it.

It might be a little awkward to present your spouse with an unexpected script in which he or she will play one of the two leading roles. You might want to open with something less provocative, such as "Hi, honey! How was your day?"

THE INEVITABLE COME-DOWN
Confronting the Effects of Time

By identifying a misconception or a false expectation, we can often achieve a marked improvement in desire. A realistic appraisal of a situation makes it easier for someone to work toward a logical, plausible goal rather than endlessly pursuing an impossible dream.

Sometimes, expectations are so firmly entrenched in our minds and so connected to other values and beliefs that we find it difficult to give them up in favor of more realistic ones. The toughest truth to confront is probably this one:

> *For nearly all couples, sexual desire tends to decrease with time.*

Nearly all sex therapists admit this is true, but it is a highly disturbing fact for many people. It seems to strike at the core of our society's values, which center on monogamous marriage and a stable family life. We want to believe that sexual desire is directed exclusively toward another person and the more we love that person, the stronger will be our sexual desire. Love should increase with time, and desire should increase along with it.

When sexual desire decreases, the person who expected it to be otherwise reacts in one or more of the following ways: (1) I don't really love my partner anymore or my partner doesn't love me, (2) I am getting old, (3) there is something wrong with me (or my partner), or (4) there is something wrong with the relationship.

Diminishing desire is not associated exclusively with aging. Couples who marry in their teens may find a marked decrease in desire before age twenty-five, scarcely qualifying them for senior-citizen status. Aging actually plays a minimal role in most complaints of diminished desire in couples who have been together for several years. Likelier causes are additional work pressures, the demands of children, and chronic emotional conflicts.

George Bernard Shaw said that marriage was the most licentious of institutions because it combines the maximum of temptation with the maximum of opportunity. Shaw was wrong in this because temptation decreases as opportunity increases. It is the people who live in New York City all year long who rarely go to Broadway shows or visit the Statue of Liberty. They reason that they can go any time they please; the result is that they never go. A security guard assigned to protect some valuables for one night is far more likely to succumb to temptation than one who has the same assignment night after night with plenty of time to wrestle with his conscience.

Finally, and probably of greatest importance, is Nature's lack of cooperation, at least in comparison to her efforts in the initial stages of a relationship. In Shaw's *Man and Superman,* Don Juan observed, "The sex relation is not a personal or friendly relation at all. . . . The pair may be utter strangers to one another, speaking different languages, differing in race and color, in age and disposition, with no bond between them but a possibility of that fecundity for the sake of which the Life Force throws them together into one another's arms at the exchange of a glance."

One cannot dispute that many sexual relationships occur between the most incongruous of pairs, and intellectual or emotional compatability has little to do with desire. People will use their common sense in putting the brakes on desire when it points to a partner who promises nothing more than fleeting gratification, but this is a matter of intellect overriding desire, not partaking of it. Nature has a great need for couples of every species to mate, but no vested interest in having the same couple mate repeatedly.

Some sociobiologists have advocated the theory that the human female, by becoming free of the estrus cycle that dictates sexual responsiveness in lower mammals, provides a strong incentive for a male to remain with her and care for a family because of her ability to have sex at any time. The problem with the theory is that most couples do not consider the opportunity for regular sex to be their primary motive for staying together.

The biggest single difficulty with marital sex, and one that is rather easily remedied, is that couples do not disregard sex completely, but give it such a low priority on their list of scheduled activities that, like the New Yorker who never visits the Statue of Liberty, they never get around to it, rationalizing that there's always tomorrow.

The remedy, of course, is to move sex up on the priority list and treat it not as something you can always get around to, but something that *must* be done, like typing a report or picking up a child after school. Some will object that scheduling sex ruins all spontaneity and could even result in a couple's being together when neither happens to want sex. Fine, then use the time to talk, play together, or read to one another. Regular sex may not be absolutely essential for a healthy marriage, but emotional intimacy is. Intellectual stimulation or nonsexual physical closeness are human needs as much as sexual gratification, and desire can encompass these needs as much as the strictly sexual ones. If you think about the origins of your desire for a special partner, they probably began *not* as a purely physical reaction to a body, but as a response to the partner as a total person.

We are already drifting from the problem of low desire stemming from false expectations into the realm of interpersonal relationships, but that is inevitable. Sex is a two-party activity and is best when the efforts of both are involved, even if the lack of desire is perceived as unilateral. Sexual desire requires work; if both partners contribute to the effort, so much the better.

We live in a generation where our appliances give the illusion of work without effort. Nearly all television sets today instantly produce a picture when you turn the On knob and younger people probably have never experienced having to wait a few seconds for the set to "warm up." Most people fail to realize that even when the set is "off," it is "on," drawing enough current from the wall socket to keep itself in a state of readiness to flash the picture immediately. The point is that everything requires energy, and the expenditure of energy is work. Nature contributes some cosmic energy of her own from time to time and desire may temporarily flow as effortlessly as an automobile rolls downhill without our pushing the gas pedal. But just as we can't expect an automobile to run on nothing but gravity, we should not expect Nature to keep our desire at a consistently high level without some energy and work on our part.

Are there couples who don't experience a waning of sexual desire with time? Absolutely. Some of these may be high-desire pairs. More likely, these are couples who benefit from a healthy habit pattern; the time they spend together engaged in sexual activity increases their emotional intimacy and their regard for one another, leading to further positive sexual experiences. In other words, these couples are not the passive beneficiaries of a spontaneously high desire level, but are continually working at their relationship.

A ROUSING DISCUSSION
Separating Arousal from Desire

Since we are discussing desire problems related to unrealistic expectations, this is a good point at which to discuss arousal and its relationship to desire disorder. Its effect on men is a strong and common one:

> *Men tend to equate arousal with desire and over-estimate its influence on desire. Women tend to under-estimate arousal or ignore it completely.*

Earlier in the book, we talked about how arousal and desire are two different stages of sexual response, but since in young men arousal occurs so readily, many men equate the two stages and view arousal as a confirmation of sexual desire. Problems develop because the erections that appear in response to visual and mental stimuli when men are younger later occur only if there is tactile stimulation of the penis. This may happen quite early in life, even prior to age forty.

A man in his sixties may accept the fact that his erections are not as firm or that it takes him longer to have another erection after completion of a sex act, but a man in his forties or fifties tends to become anxious when the spontaneous erections to which he is accustomed fail to materialize.

Some men continue to have erections without tactile stimulation late into life, but even they may find that the familiar sight of a partner's naked body no longer evokes an automatic erection, even though a more novel experience or fantasy might. It is important that spouses do not fall into the error of equating lack of erection with lack of desire and be willing to form new patterns of lovemaking to accommodate the man's changing needs.

There are many similarities between arousal in men and arousal in women. Masters and Johnson point out that the chief feature of both is the filling of the genital tissues with blood. The increased size and firmness of the penis is caused by the filling of the spongy tissues with blood, which keeps the penis hard until orgasm. In women, the lubrication of the vagina that occurs in arousal is the result of the tissues becoming engorged with blood, just as in the penis; the fluid is not a glandular secretion, but simply plasma extruded under pressure from the swollen capillaries in the vaginal walls.

Physiologically, male and female arousal are similar, but how they are perceived in the mind of the aroused subjects may differ considerably. Julia Heiman, Ph.D., director of the University of Washington Medical School's Interpersonal Psychotherapy Clinic, did research involving arousal responses in men and women as a result of fantasizing or listening to erotic audio tapes. Male arousal was measured by a mercury-filled rubber strain gauge that fit around the shaft of the penis. Female volunteers used a somewhat more complicated device, a vaginal photoplethysmograph, which is a clear acrylic hollow cylinder, nearly two inches in length and one-half inch in diameter, containing a small lamp, photocell, and connecting wires. When inserted in the vagina, the amount of light reflected back to the photocell from the vaginal walls is affected by the degree of vascular congestion, which increases with arousal.

In one such study, Dr. Heiman found that every one of the men reported physical arousal correlating with the recorded genital response, but more than two thirds of the women claimed to experience no physical arousal despite physical responses similar to the men's. Women, according to other studies done by Dr. Heiman, vary in their consciousness of how physically "aroused" they are. Women who have difficulty attaining orgasm got just as aroused in response to erotic material, but they *reported* much lower levels of arousal than women who were sexually functional.

Ten years ago, Dr. Peter Hoon, co-director of the Sexual Dysfunction Clinic at the University of Tennessee College of Medicine, researched women who complained of low sexual arousal. Dr. Hoon and his associates gave them a course of short-term sex therapy employing Masters and Johnson's techniques plus biofeedback therapy. While none of the women showed an improvement in sexual arousal as measured by vaginal blood flow, almost all of them enthusiastically reported improvement in response to the treatments.

These studies seem to indicate that women's subjective desire, unlike men's, bears little relationship to the physiological changes of arousal; therefore, while physically stimulating a man to arousal may turn on his desire in retrograde fashion, physical stimulation of a woman may not increase her desire at all, regardless of how "excited" her organs get.

Classical sex therapy focuses on promoting arousal in an atmosphere of relaxation and absence of performance pressure. As far as treatment of desire disorder is concerned, it would seem that putting women in the right mental frame is more important than promoting physical arousal, while men might profit more from being able to attain arousal because of the closer mental association between desire and body response.

On Your Own

"The problem ain't so much what people don't know, but that they know so many things that just ain't so," an American humorist once observed.

Education is supplying information that was not previously there. Cognitive therapy is the replacing of false ideas with correct ones. It is obviously more difficult than education.

How do you know if you're a victim of faulty thinking? One good indication is that you think you're doing everything right, but the result keeps coming out wrong. If you find yourself protesting, "But I'm trying so hard," you're probably trying the wrong things.

When it comes to satisfying a sexual partner, there are two common mistakes: (1) if it worked with him (her) before, it will work again, and (2) it's worked with other partners, so it will work with this one.

When your own desire for sex has been on the wane, do not say that everything is fine because you enjoy sex once you "get into it." The fact that you're rarely getting into it means there's something in it that's unpleasant for you. Even if there is nothing frankly distasteful or distressing about sex, you will avoid it if it's not as exciting as it used to be, or if you feel it could be so much better; disappointment can be as big a deterrent as distress.

That's why the "best case" scenario, where you plot out an ideal sexual experience in detail, is important. It puts you in touch with what you *really* want from sex. Some of the elements might be very accessible and some might be unattainable; sort them out and see if you can modify some of the impossible ones into plausible ones.

Once you've thought about what you want, share it with your

partner. Don't expect your partner to read your mind. Even professional "mind readers" rely not on true clairvoyance but on their ability to pick up information without the audience's detection. You do not have to tell a partner, "Read my script," but you will have to say, "Read my lips," and let your mate know what you like.

The bedroom is not a good place for altruism. Many people, particularly women, when asked what they enjoy in bed, will say, "Whatever you want to do is fine." They feel that at least one of them is sure to be pleased, but they don't realize that much of a partner's satisfaction in sex lies in the knowledge that he has been a good lover and made his mate happy.

Dr. David Reuben once wrote about a woman who criticized her boyfriend as an insensitive, inept lover. When asked why she felt this way, she replied, "He doesn't even know enough to stroke my earlobes the way my father did when I was a little girl!" Not only do we often make the grave error of assuming that all members of the *opposite* sex like the same things when it comes to sex, but we sometimes assume that all members of *our* sex like what we enjoy. Then, if a partner does not satisfy us, we conclude that he or she is a lousy lover, lacking the most rudimentary knowledge and lovemaking skill.

A frustrating—but very common—situation is a partner who simply will not communicate. If you have a partner who has little desire for sex, how can you try to make sex more pleasurable if he or she does not seem motivated and rebuffs your attempts to explore things by saying that everything is fine?

Since your sex life is definitely far from ideal, don't be afraid to try new approaches. It would be so easy if all men or women were turned on by the same thing, but they are not, and the only way you'll know what your mate *really* likes, short of being told, is to experiment. Perhaps there are turn-ons they haven't discovered yet. We all know *the* erogenous zones, but there are trigger points beyond the penis, clitoris, and female breast. Some men find that having their nipples touched excites them, while others may experience it as ticklish and annoying. Comedian Dick Martin made a popular phrase out of "Blow in my ear and I'll follow you anywhere"; not everyone is into aural eroticism but many would be delighted to give you a receptive ear. Anal stimulation will be perceived as repulsive by some and intensely arousing by others. Some women like direct touching of the clitoris even during the act of intercourse, while others prefer indirect stimulation by traction on the labia or mons and find direct touch actually painful. The only infallible guide to what your partner likes is your partner.

Preferences are not limited to the physical. Some men love to hear four-letter expletives from women in the heat of passion, even though they would be appalled to hear those words spoken in casual conversation. There are liberated women who would adore being treated roughly once in a while, even if they selected a man because of his sensitivity and gentleness. A man who undresses his partner but does his own disrobing might enjoy having his partner remove his clothes for a change.

Not only should women read an occasional men's magazine to appreciate some of the common male fantasies, but men should peruse women's publications to get a woman's viewpoint of sex. The articles and letters may not reflect the sentiments of one's particular mate, but such information can put you more in tune with an opposite-sex perspective.

Everyone warns you not to criticize, but nobody reminds you to praise. The feeling that you've done something well makes you eager to do it again. Nobody wants to repeat a failure. And when it comes to sex, success is more often defined as the pleasure you have given, not what you have received.

Do not ask for a grade. Never say, "You were wonderful! How was I?" Even honest praise will sound insincere under those circumstances and it will shut off future improvement if you fall back into the "everything is great" rationalization.

If you *really* don't feel like having sex on a particular night, be honest about it. Don't feign a mood you're not in. Partners are nearly as hurt by faked desire as by faked orgasms and feel that your relationship should be intimate enough to share the truth. It's okay to accommodate your partner after confessing your low level of interest, but don't make him or her feel guilty by acting aggravated, abused, or impatient. Next time, it will be your partner who is not in the mood.

While ideal scenarios take preparation and time, don't attempt to make every sexual encounter a painstaking production. If you always save sex for a time when you can spend an hour or more together with no possible danger of interruption under the best of circumstances, you're not going to have sex very often. Some sex is better than none, even if it means an occasional unscheduled "quickie" to keep tension down and awareness up. But *do* leave a place for sex on your schedule and don't expect to fit it in when the opportunity comes, because "opportunity" never seems to knock at bedroom doors.

Do not compare your partner with others, even if you feel he or she is honestly the best lover you ever had. Reminding your partner during your most intimate moments that you have been intimate with others usually elicits jealousy and anger, followed by guilt over feeling that way. And if asking for a grade is taboo, never ask how your partner has rated past lovers; when it comes to lovemaking, consider that you're in a class by yourself.

Don't be obsessed about your partner's orgasms—and that includes *men's* orgasms. An orgasm is a 3.5-second culmination of many pleasurable minutes. Foreplay, arousal, intercourse, and afterplay are extremely enjoyable activities, not a means to or afterlude to orgasm. If your partner says he or she enjoys sex even without orgasm, believe it! Modern men have learned to delay orgasm and in doing so may short-circuit the sexual response cycle and "miss" the orgasm once in a while. If the lost pleasure of orgasm results in the prolonged pleasure of erection and intercourse, the exchange of a few seconds for many minutes may be deemed more than worth the exchange.

Summing up the cognitive approach to desire loss, it is important to remember that people who have good relationships with a partner and who are free of any significant emotional hang-ups can get into trouble simply because they have false ideas and expectations about sex. The most common and deadliest error is the assumption that sexual desire should always be present and effortless, and should never diminish in intensity. Many people fall victim to this misconception because our society bombards us with images of people who are obsessed with and consistently gratified by sexual activity, leading people who have other things on their mind to conclude they must be abnormal. Also, self-help experts tend to imply that if a relationship is good, sex will automatically be good and desire will be high, whereas a loving, compatible couple might be no more enthusiastic about sex than about playing tennis together.

Everyone knows there are countless definitions of love, but few acknowledge that sex means something different to different people. *Do* think about what good sex means to you and figure out what you don't like about the sex you've been having; then, take the time to detail a plausible scenario that would typify your concept of a good sexual experience. *Don't* aggravate the problem by assuming you have a bad relationship because desire has fallen off, by expecting desire to take care of itself, or by confusing a lack of ready arousal with a lack of desire or, worse, a lack of love.

Desire is mental. It requires mental work—i.e., thought.

Think about it.

✿ 13 ✿

A Different Focus

Sensate Focus Exercises

Can you imagine going to a tennis clinic and being told *not* to pick up a racket or going to a golf pro who instructed you *not* to swing a club? It might seem strange to some patients when sex therapists tell them not to have intercourse.

The interdiction against intercourse is temporary, of course, and scarcely revolutionary. Dr. John Hunter, the renowned eighteenth-century surgeon, advised an impotent patient to avoid intercourse with his partner for six nights "let his inclinations and powers be what they would." The man's fear of inability was soon replaced by apprehension that he would be possessed with too much desire, and thereafter, "the mind and powers went on together."

Sensate-focus exercises are at the heart of the new sex therapy, and have been used with great success in the treatment of arousal problems. They consist of one partner's touching and massaging the body of the other, avoiding the genital areas and breasts in the early stages. The partner receiving the stimulation concentrates only on the sensations he or she is feeling, letting his or her partner know what feels good and how to provide maximum pleasure through touching. The partner on the receiving end is freed of all pressure to perform, and the prohibition of intercourse ensures against a fear of failure. The sensate focus exercises promote a new awareness of one's own body; both men and women often devote most of their thoughts during sexual relations to the partner's response and lose touch with their own sensations. Touching of erogenous zones is gradually included in the assignments, with steady progression to stress-free intercourse.

Bearing in mind that most people with desire disorder have no difficulty with sexual functioning once they engage themselves in activity, are sensate focus exercises of value? They usually are, although the emphasis is more on what is going on in the subject's mind during the exercises, rather than the physical sensations being experienced.

Dr. Friedman of Stony Brook knows that patients with desire disorder are going to be more anxious in a sexual situation free of performance demands than those with functional problems. He says, "I use the Masters and Johnson sensate focus not only to desensitize them in sexual activities but to make them aware of whatever they are feeling. I fully expect that they are going to be anxious and I want them to be aware of their anxieties because once they are, then they can start to deal with them. So, I use sensate focus slightly differently—to help put them in sexual situations that will make them aware of whatever negative or anxious feelings they have about sex."

Dr. Sheila Jackman frequently uses sensate focus exercises for people with low sexual desire. "The aim," she explains, "is to get them out of their own heads, to teach them how to quiet down the conversations going on in their heads that have them wandering all over the place; then, teach them how to pay attention to body sensations—how to lie back and be touched, how to sit up and touch, so that it is effective."

Dr. Jackman uses the exercises to bring awareness of physical sensation back to the brain, because many of these patients are suffering from what she terms "pelvic anesthesia." She says, "What happens from the neck down is *nothing*, because people are saying in their heads, 'This is boring. What am I doing this for? I feel guilty when I don't, but when I do it's just out of duty, because I'm expected to.' So, they don't *feel* because where they are in their heads is negative. They are having a conversation about 'I'd rather be someplace else,' and so, as I often put it, 'The blood is in their head, and not in their pelvis where it belongs.' "

Dr. Jackman is very direct in prescribing the sensate focus exercises: "I tell them, straight out of Masters and Johnson, 'No breast touching, no genital touching.' One partner lies down, the other partner touches him or her, and then they switch, really taking their time, using all kinds of touches."

Communication with the partner is very important. Dr. Jackman tells her patients they can let the partner know what they are experiencing by using code words that they make up, words without any other connotation, so that nothing gets in the way of specific communication.

For example, a man enjoying his partner's caresses and touches during a sensate-focus pleasuring session might choose to adopt some airplane pilot lingo for his code words. "Throttle back" might mean "use a softer touch." "Climbing" could mean "that's feeling better and better." "Rudder right" could mean "massage a bit to the right," "That's a Rodge" would indicate "you're doing great," "rev it up" would be a request for a firmer touch, and "on automatic" would convey, "I'm totally relaxed."

Why not simply say, "That feels good" or "Not so hard, dear"? Dr. Jackman advises against this direct approach because such communications were probably a part of past sexual interaction, which might have posed problems leading to desire loss. Just as the nongenital pleasuring is a new form of physical experience, the new words provide a vocabulary to go with it, free of any past negative connotations.

The new method makes it impossible for couples to fall into old patterns of sexual behavior. People may have to learn how to be comfortable in just lying back and being touched. The same person who is indifferent to being touched by his partner might pay forty dollars for a massage and love every minute of it, because in the latter situation there are no demands. Dr. Jackman says of people who cannot find pleasure with their partner, "Either they don't have the desire, or the desire is covered over by performance anxiety. There may be desire and they don't even know it."

Dr. Evalyn S. Gendel, director of the Human Sexuality Program at the San Francisco School of Medicine, University of California, gives couples specific assignments, which include physical as well as mental remedies. "I will give them a regular nongenital pleasuring assignment," she says. "It may not be the whole body, it may just start out with the face and shoulders. It depends upon the couple and where *they* are. Usually you have to go by the barometer of what people bring back. If any of this has created more of a positive ambience and you find that they are talking, you almost don't have to make the suggestion about going further. They feel more comfortable and are beginning to perk up. They'll find their *own* way—and I tell them that from the beginning."

Prescribing sensate focus exercises for people who don't seem to have a problem with getting aroused, having intercourse, and achieving orgasm may seem like putting training wheels on a bicycle for someone who has no trouble riding the thing but lacks the desire and motivation to get on it. The sensate focus exercises do, however, let a couple get "in touch" with one another, both literally and mentally, and this may be precisely what the couple needs.

The sensate focus exercises are a perfect example of *behavioral* therapy; they involve specific assigned tasks designed to promote relaxation, the antithesis of anxiety. In treating desire disorder with this method, the therapist usually adds a *cognitive* component to the therapy; if disturbing thoughts arise during the experience (e.g., "This is a waste of time" or "I feel I should be doing more") the patient is asked to analyze and correct them rather than just clear his mind. There is usually a lot more mental discomfort during sexual activity in desire disorder patients than they are willing to admit. The patient who complies with a partner's wish for intercourse may be making the partner happy, but isn't doing much for his or her own satisfaction. By being able to accept the role of receiving physical stimulation, a low-desire person can focus on his or her *own* sexual wishes—and that, after all, is the essence of sexual desire.

On Your Own

If you hate exercise, then sensate focus exercises are perfect for you—half the time you do absolutely nothing!

You and your partner should take turns touching and rubbing each other's bodies, deliberately avoiding the erogenous zones. Where do you touch, how hard, how long, and with what movements? You guide each other by explaining what feels best and what you'd like more of—when you're on the receiving end, you're in charge. You can use lotions or oils if you like. Set a time and stick to it, whether it's twenty minutes, thirty minutes, or an hour, before switching roles. When you're on the receiving end, concentrate on your own enjoyment and don't be hesitant about indicating to your partner what feels good and what doesn't.

But don't get upset if somehow you don't find this activity very enjoyable. Does being passive make you feel childish, helpless, inadequate? Do you feel that stimulation without sexual release is pointless and frustrating? Does your partner seem to be incapable of following instructions? Does spending so much time in such an unproductive activity make you feel guilty?

If negative thoughts are intruding on what should be a positive experience, you can seize those cognitive bugbears, inspect them, and figure out what they're doing where they don't belong. Is it your partner who's lost his or her touch? Is there something about your makeup that won't let you relax? Are there things about the situation that violate your convictions about the way things *should* be? Remember, sensate focus exercises are *not* sexual, and if they make you uncomfortable, maybe your desire problem has roots in other than sexual soil.

Either way you win, whether by finding a quick improvement in desire or by understanding what's getting in the way. Ay, there's the rub—and it's invariably worth the effort in improving desire.

IN THE MOOD
Confusing Mood with Desire

Another advantage of sensate focus exercises is that they give a couple some experience with noncoital physical intimacy, something that may have been missing from their relationship since early courtship. Many people confuse "being in the mood for sex" with desire.

Dr. Constance Avery-Clark of the Masters and Johnson Institute frequently treats career women who have developed desire disorder. She describes how her tired patients get trapped in faulty thinking: "Usually the woman thinks, 'I'm exhausted. I've had a really busy day. If I begin to touch or if I respond to my partner's touching, I'm going to have to go ahead and have intercourse for which I am not ready, because I'm so tired. I can't say yes to just touching or to cuddling and caressing, because he's going to want to go ahead and have intercourse; therefore, I won't say yes to *anything.* I'll stop even before things get going and, therefore, I will set down any interest I might be able to develop if I were able to get involved."

Many people who claim they have no desire are confusing desire with arousal. Sexual response is an accelerating process, progressing from intention to orgasm. Some people, particularly young men, proceed almost immediately from the first inklings of desire to the early arousal stage, but for others the progression is more leisurely. A person who claims to be "in the mood" for sex may be already in an early arousal phase; that is, the nervous system has already begun sending an increased flow of blood into the pelvis to ready the genitals for action. Women, as we have pointed out, may not be consciously aware that this is happening, but they know a certain erotic "feeling" is coming over them. If this occurs, fine, but it is not essential to genuine desire, which is basically a *mental* process.

Just as an erratic erection or an orgasm that fails to come as expected can ruin the functional aspects of intercourse, so can a faulty mental process block desire and anything physical that would have followed it down the path. One of the worst cognitive errors is the notion that desire involves not only a conscious wish but a certain mood or feeling without which there is no sense in continuing.

> *Desire is a mental process, not a mood or state of*
> *arousal. Desire that begins without strong "feelings"*
> *is just as valid as the more passionate type.*

Cognitive therapy for this problem centers on getting the patient to realize that she thinks she must do something (i.e., get aroused) in a limited period of time and that she feels she cannot later say no. Her thinking about the future interferes with her perception of the present. While she might be quite amenable to cuddling and nonsexual activity that might revive her interest in sex, she stops herself from even this limited interaction because of her conviction that she will not be able to disengage herself if she wishes.

Her relationship with her partner, of course, plays an important part. If any physical contact or show of affection has always led to intercourse, the husband might, indeed, expect this pattern to continue and view any attempt to stop short of intercourse as a rejection. If she communicates her feelings, the wife may find that her husband would prefer physical closeness (even if it did not lead to sex) to being turned away. Something is nearly always better than nothing.

SMELLING THE ROSES
Developing Sensual Awareness

Sensate-focus exercises are designed to increase sensual awareness in a situation which, if not really sexual, does involve a partner and some tactile stimulation. Sometimes we need to tune up our senses so that they can appreciate the most basic stimuli, the everyday sights, sounds, and smells to which we have become nearly oblivious.

In order to feel good, you have to be able to feel.

We spend a lot of time thinking and not much time feeling, even in the midst of sexual activity. A man may say his last sexual encounter was "good." He will tell you how many minutes were spent in foreplay, how many minutes were spent in intercourse between the moment of penetration and that of orgasm, and how intense an orgasm his partner had. His mental notes are so complete that you wonder how he was able to detach his intellectual machinations long enough to enjoy himself. Enjoyment for this type of person has come to mean justifiable pride in a job well done.

People who experience events with their conscious minds and not their senses are like the man who went to a concert by one of the world's greatest violinists and reported that he had spent two hours watching a man drawing a horsehair strand back and forth across four strings of animal gut. The description was flawless from the point of objective reporting, but very deficient in terms of conveying sensory awareness.

Dr. Gendel, director of the Human Sexuality Program at the San Francisco School of Medicine, finds that when people are "in a blue point about their sex lives," it helps to raise their sensual awareness about everything, even how good the air smells. Just as sensate focus exercises make people aware of pleasurable body sensations that are not specifically sexual, sensual awareness can be increased through appreciation of nonsexual aesthetic experiences. As an example, Dr. Gendel notes, "Many people get into the water and swim as though they are competing with themselves to set a better record. But others will say that the feeling of the water over their body is just marvelous, the most relaxing part of it." Such enjoyment is not sexual, but it's sensuous. Listening to music or even reading can be sensuous, if the persons let themselves *feel* the sensations.

Dr. Gendel has found that it helps to teach people to get in touch with their bodily sensations while alone before they move into a situation with a partner, even if the exercises with a partner are based on nonsexual touching. "We try simple exercises," she explains, "so they can feel what concentrating on a particular part of the body is like. We ask them to think about anything that gets them in touch with a particular body process. I use as much of whatever prior experiences people can identify with to move them into the current situation."

Even something as elementary as breathing can be used. "During these breathing exercises," Dr. Gendel says, "I am trying to get them to understand that they are going to use a physiological process to learn concentration. I use breathing because anybody can do that." She has her patients listen to their own breath as they slowly inhale and exhale. "I ask them to go home and really do that, and tell me about it," she said. "You can't do it if you are thinking about sixty million other things."

Many people have difficulty relaxing and concentrating at the same time. Having gotten accustomed to focusing their attention on breathing or some other physical sensation, people can more easily carry this technique of relaxed awareness into the sensate focus exercises or other forms of physical touching.

It may seem very strange to think about something as automatic as breathing, but there are many voluntary things that we come to do automatically once we lose awareness, and sex, unfortunately, is one of them. Once we stop concentrating on our physical sensations, all sorts of extraneous thoughts flood in to fill the mental void, ranging from performance monitoring to ruminations about matters that have nothing to do with the pleasure at hand.

You *can* have sex without paying attention to it, but it's not likely to be very memorable.

On Your Own

When people detach themselves from pleasurable physical sensations during sex, they lose pleasure. When something is not pleasurable, you lose the desire to repeat it. So, often the desire for sex disappears for the most obvious of reasons: the typical sexual experience for that person has become *undesirable.*

How do you heighten sensory awareness? You can deliberately focus on each of your five senses. Instead of simply tossing on that jacket you carefully selected months ago, look at the color and pattern that once attracted you. Make yourself stop and actually listen to the music that blares unheeded from your kitchen radio. Smell the morning air as you emerge from the house. Taste each ingredient in the lunch that you usually bolt down. Run your fingers over things: the lining of your glove, the surface of your desk, the petal of a flower.

Dig into your purse or pocket, and pull out a penny. What aspect of it grasped your imagination? The portrait on the "head," the building on the back, the motto, its color, its shine, its circular shape, its cheapness, its status as money? It does not take a great work of art to expand our awareness, only the brief effort to look directly at things we usually disregard.

You can try blending the senses in unconventional ways, so that sounds have color and smells have shapes, a process the scientists call synesthesia. Walt Disney's *Fantasia* matched original images to familiar classical music. One of the simplest exercises is to close your eyes while listening to music and conjure up pictures that the music suggests.

For something a bit more challenging, think of a favorite city of yours and ask what color it is. New Orleans might suggest the red of band uniforms, boiled crayfish, and festive cocktails, or the gold of jazz trumpets and the blazing sun glinting on the Mississippi. San Francisco might suggest green for its bay waters and Chinatown dragons, while New York might be mostly metallic gray like its skyscrapers. What color are *you?*

When you move your imagination to sex, try to recapture the

appearance of that special person, the sound of a voice or the music in the background, the feel of a sheet or soft flesh against your body, even if you really weren't paying that much attention to them at the time. You will pay more attention to them the next time.

❦ 14 ❦

Tandem Treatment

Overcoming Desire Discrepancy

"We have met the enemy and they is us!" Walt Kelly's "Pogo" declared decades ago.

In sexual desire disorder, the adversary is often the couple, a habitual interaction that contributes to the perpetuation of decreased desire, even if the problem originated with the misconceptions, false expectations, or hang-ups of only one partner.

There is an old joke that defines an alcoholic as "anybody who drinks more than I do." Low desire is always defined in relation to some higher level, usually that of the other partner. It is rare for two people to come into treatment because neither wants sex; far more often, they come into treatment because one partner's desire level is considerably higher, leaving that partner dissatisfied. Given this situation, it is hard to treat only one member of the pair. Sex therapy has always been based on shared responsibility, even if the problem being treated seems exclusively male, such as erectile dysfunction, or exclusively female, such as lack of orgasm.

It is usually erroneous to designate one partner as solely responsible for the problem, because the low-desire person could become involved a short time later with someone even less interested in sex and thus become the dissatisfied "high-desire" partner.

Sexual desire levels are high or low only relative to someone else's level.

True, someone who never had desire for sex would be at zero level and could never be high relative to any living object. Beyond such rare cases of primary global desire disorder, it's almost impossible to classify anyone as unequivocally low, since there are many cases of single women who go for years without any appreciable desire for heterosexual or masturbatory gratification, but quickly revert to average or high desire levels when they met a suitable partner. Desire disorder can be evaluated accurately only in the context of an available partner, which necessarily draws the partner into the equation.

Every couple experiences some degree of desire discrepancy. Even if a couple could agree on the exact frequency with which they desired sex, they might be in disagreement about the particular day or time at which they wanted it. If they were in perfect agreement about that, they might not concur on the type of sexual activity or the ambience. They might not be in accord about the amount of time to spend, how to initiate foreplay, how to end their lovemaking. And nearly everyone, male or female, says at some point, "Not tonight, dear."

When the discrepancy becomes too wide, we have a union that is in disequilibrium. The therapist's task involves working with both partners not to eliminate the gap, but to narrow it or bridge it. Whatever remedies are invoked, there are two principles that govern the interaction and should never be overlooked. The first of them is:

> *The partner with the lower level of sexual desire*
> *controls the frequency of sex.*

We discussed this principle earlier, but it bears repeating because it is one of those paradoxical concepts that runs counter to popular impressions. Since the higher-level partner is usually the initiator, we might assume that he or she is in control. Consider, though, that the frequency of sex is always what the low-desire partner wants or acquiesces to. Even in rare cases where the high-desire partner gets as much sex as he or she wants, it is only because the other has agreed. In most relationships, neither partner gets exactly what he or she wants, because some sort of compromise is reached, but it is the low-desire partner who determines the level of compromise.

The next principle has also been previously discussed, but it, too, bears repeating since it relates to desire discrepancy:

> *The initiator in a sexual interaction is in a higher*
> *state of arousal than the partner and tends to remain*
> *at a higher level as the sex act progresses.*

In most relationships, the partner with the higher desire level usually assumes the role of initiator. The natural progression of sexual response puts the low-desire partner at a double disadvantage, first because he or she starts at a minimal desire/arousal level, and second, because he or she, even if accelerating at the same rate as the initiator, will lag behind in the race to the plateau stage of maximum arousal, the launch point for orgasm.

We can think of a compatible couple as a team in harness pulling toward the same goal. But they are not hitched side by side—they are always in tandem, one ahead of the other. The aim in treatment of desire disorder is not to align their desire levels in perfect parallel, but to keep the gap between them at a minimum and keep them headed in the same direction.

DON'T JUST SAY NO
How to Refuse a Partner

No relationship founders simply because of a low frequency of sexual relations. Career obligations or illness often necessitate periods of abstinence and physical separation, which most unions survive rather well. When it comes to the slow destruction of a relationship because of desire conflicts, the nays have it; saying no to a partner not only withholds a pleasurable experience, but adds the pain of rejection.

While much professional effort has been focused on the art of having sex, very little has been said about the art of *not* having it. A rebuffed initiative is not a zero that adds nothing to a good relationship; it is a negative quantity that takes something away. With sensitivity and skill, a person can say no and still add something— perhaps not as much as a yes would have added, but a small increase nonetheless.

Dr. Peter Kilmann of the University of South Carolina shows his patients different ways to refuse sex. He feels it is important to give a reason why they are not interested at that particular moment, while suggesting an alternate time or making it their responsibility to initiate next. "A person doesn't want to feel he or she is always being set up for potential rejection," he says.

In his chapter in *Principles and Practices of Sex Therapy,* Dr. Bernie Zilbergeld describes a case in which a low-desire husband was actually encouraged to decline his wife's sexual advances at times. The couple, who were in their late twenties, came into therapy when the husband discontinued sexual activity after two years of marriage. The wife had a considerably higher sex drive, whereas the husband was obsessed with his work and felt guilty about the time sex took away from his projects. He brought the same perfectionistic preoccupation with achievement into their sexual activities, so that foreplay was always lengthy and mutual orgasms were always reached. He began to see his wife as too demanding and he became so angry at time lost from his work that he finally refused to have sex altogether.

The wife, who was a nurse, was getting little emotional satisfaction from her job, so she depended on sex, which she felt she was "good at," to bolster her self-esteem. The therapists in this case imposed a moratorium on sex until the husband felt better about it. Fifteen-minute limits were placed on the couple's pleasuring activities, which initially took the form of nonsexual touching, talking, or just being together. The time limit reassured the husband that marital interactions did not necessarily have to be lengthy. When sexual activity was resumed, the husband, who had been eager to resume it sooner than the therapists advised, was instructed to decline his wife's advances occasionally, so that both could learn this was not necessarily disastrous. When the husband did decline sex, he invariably spent some time with the wife, talking or cuddling, which, to her surprise, she found to be nearly as satisfying emotionally.

The husband's range of sexual cues was expanded by helping him to regard thoughts of touching or just being with his wife as potentially sexual. Such fantasies, even if not frankly arousing, helped him relax and unwind during the course of a workday. When they were out together, the husband found that touching his wife's thighs or buttocks proved exciting for both of them and helped him by giving sexual cues in a situation that obviously would not require intercourse. The husband came to regard his wife's sexual eagerness not as a threat, but an advantage. "She's always ready," Dr. Zilbergeld quotes him as saying. "I used to see that as a problem but I'm learning it's just the opposite—a real treasure."

Meanwhile, the wife was encouraged to change jobs and to put in extra hours on a research project that interested her, which boosted her self-esteem. She was asked to explore new ways of dealing with low moods, such as discussing her feelings with her husband or asking him to "mother" her. When she found that nonsexual interactions often served her needs as well as intercourse, she was asked to compare carefully the distinctions between those cues, moods, and sensations that could be satisfied by nonsexual contact and those that were more specifically sexual.

The therapy was very successful and was accomplished with seventeen sessions over a twelve-week period. Dr. Zilbergeld ponits out that the strength of the marital relationship was vital, since the couple was committed to their relationship, loved one another, and made a good attempt to work through the problems despite initial frustrations. The husband's obsession with work posed a tricky dilemma, and was dealt with by encouraging him to look upon sex as an aid to doing work better, rather than attacking his commitment to work, which might have evoked strong resistance.

Dr. Zilbergeld's case provides an excellent illustration of the different facets of treatment for desire disorder. Most people would have assumed that the problem lay entirely with the husband and, therefore, any valid treatment would be directed solely at him. Instead, the therapy focused on the couple.

While efforts were successfully made in increasing the husband's sexual interest, the therapists were also able to identify an overvaluation of sex on the part of the wife. By getting her to recognize that not all of her cravings were specifically for sex, her desire level was diminished. This does not imply that the therapists inhibited a healthy sexual appetite, but rather that she was taught to distinguish between true sexual desire and other needs that were vicariously, and probably inadequately, met by sex.

Note that the therapists temporarily prohibited sex to reinforce the idea that desire does not have to equate with intercourse. Expanding the husband's range of sexual cues further weakened the association between feelings of desire and pressure to perform.

Both partners in this case harbored faulty cognitions about sex:

in the wife, "nothing does it like sex," and for the husband, "work must always come before pleasure." The wife's overdependence on sex and the husband's avoidance of it could be overcome only by altering the ideas that motivated their respective behaviors.

On Your Own

We have already discussed many ways in which a person can increase sexual desire, but the gap in desire-discrepancy relationships can be narrowed from either end. Helping the high-desire partner to become less dependent on sex for all-purpose gratification may be as important as raising the desire of the low-level partner.

Suppose there's a woman who, after a slack period, has found some effective ways to increase her desire and who now looks forward to sex a couple of times a week. And suppose her partner is *still* at a higher desire level than she is. Maybe he wants sex five times a week, and although she enjoys sex, she just doesn't want it *that* often.

The high-desire husband will probably press his wife to get a little *more* motivated and put an increased effort into having sex more frequently. A more appropriate, and possibly easier, approach would be for the couple to explore why he couldn't be happy with sex a little less frequently.

A woman whose husband wants sex more often than she does will often make the generalization that men want frequent sex because (1) they're horny and (2) it's there. Men don't make a strong attempt to contradict the mythology of male ever-readiness, because a high desire level is considered "masculine," a term that in our culture also connotes all manner of admirable traits, such as courage, strength, stoicism, and sex appeal. High desire is not, of course, a particularly masculine attribute since there seem to be as many men as women today with low sexual desire.

If the woman were to ask her husband why he wanted sex so often, the best answer he could probably muster would be that he *needs* sex physiologically. It's as senseless, of course, to say that a man needs sex four or six times a week as it is to say he needs three meals a day or eight hours' sleep every night. We all need some food and some sleep, but not necessarily that amount. What he likes is one thing and what he needs is quite another.

How do people get partners (male or female) to tell them why they want sex more often than their mates? How do you get them to tell you what they themselves profess not to understand intellectually? See if you can get them to fill the blank in this question: "The only time we (or I) _____ is when we have sex."

There are many possible answers: "we're really alone together"; "we talk to each other"; "we say, 'I love you' "; "we hold one another"; "I feel relaxed"; "I feel needed"; et cetera. People always assume that women are having sex when they really want something else, such as emotional intimacy or a little physical closeness. Men aren't all that different. The prevalent myth is that nothing is more important to a man than sex—which is disturbing to those men who feel inadequate because sex is far from their highest priority. Seriously, how many wives could seduce their husbands away from the TV during a championship sports event? Or persuade them to cancel their golf games and spend the day having sex?

Maybe men seem to want sex so often because they don't know how to ask for anything else, like the immigrant who ate ham and eggs at every meal because he didn't know any other words in English. Men don't often say, "Come here and cuddle with me" or "Hey, I need somebody to talk to" or "Do you love me?" because they think those are women's lines. So, they say, "How about going to bed, honey?" After a while, it becomes apparent to the man that going to bed was not what he really wanted to do, so he stops asking for something that is more often unsatisfying than satisfying and his high desire becomes a sexual desire disorder.

Women may not feel the pressure to preserve an image by making sexual advances, but they may ask for sex because they feel it's all they can get, even if they would rather have some nonsexual contact. They may be right, but the couple may have simply fallen into a pattern where the husband feels obligated to "complete" any experience of emotional or physical closeness by having intercourse.

Maybe you can't say to an amorous mate, "You don't want to go to bed, you want to have a nice conversation," but you can say, "Gee, I'm not really up to it tonight, but why don't I pop a frozen pizza in the oven and we'll relax a little together," or "I'm too tense right now, but let's play some Scrabble and if you beat me, I'll give you a rain check."

Partners are not going to be delighted with a "no, thank you," but insult shouldn't be added to injury by insinuating, even silently, that the fault lies with them. Offering them a substitute pleasure and a rain check may help. Many husbands and wives really don't share any activities other than sex. The more things they're able to share, from tennis to balancing the checkbook, the less they'll have to depend on sex for the sheer satisfaction of being together.

Besides "fill in the blank," another helpful query is "Says who?" That phrase may be fighting words in a tavern dispute, but can help put things in perspective where a couple is concerned.

Many men and women get uneasy because they have an internalized timetable. They feel they should have sex three times a week or once a week or certainly at least twice a month. So, a "no, thank you" after a previous night of sexual activity might be shrugged off gracefully, while a four-day period without sex, no matter how valid the interfering circumstances, might precipitate a marital crisis. Try to learn whether there is such a time standard and, if so, say, "Says who?" Most people don't even know how they came by their personal criteria, but you'd think someone would foreclose on the mortgage or repossess their libidos if they go past that magic number. Once they realize that they are enslaving themselves to some meaningless number, the pressure can be reduced.

Nothing succeeds like communication. If a couple understands what their mutual goal is, instead of carrying out secret plans to improve things and mystifying the partner in the process, adjustments *can* be made, as they must be made under the nearly universal conditions of desire discrepancy. Any man or woman is bound to prefer good sex twice a week to bad sex every night. (Of course, if bad sex is all they ever get, they can't appreciate the difference.)

THE TURN-ON SWITCH
Switching Roles in Desire Discrepancy

There is a Native American prayer that says: "O Great Spirit, let me not judge my brother until I have walked a mile in his moccasins." Switching roles long enough to view the situation from the mate's perspective may be far more effective than exchanging view-points verbally.

Dr. Peter Kilmann uses role-playing as a means of giving his patients insight into what the other partner may be feeling. "For example," he illustrates, "in one case a guy would always turn off his partner because he would come in from work and start patting and grabbing her while she was doing something else. And she kept saying, 'I'm not really interested in doing that,' but he kept doing it anyway, laughing. She was, in a way, giving him two messages, because she wasn't saying no adamantly or explaining how it bothered her.

"So, we role-played him doing some work on the job, him working at his desk or doing something at home, and she would come up and try to seduce him while he was really interested in something else. That would be an example of how role-playing helps people see it from the other side."

The most practical role reversal of all would be to delegate the role of initiator to the partner with the lower level of desire. Of course, partners with low desire may sometimes initiate, but in many relationships they settle into a strictly passive role.

The initiator is not necessarily the one who extends a verbal invitation. By nonverbal behavior, such as wearing certain garments, embracing her mate more warmly than usual, or announcing pointedly that she is on her way to bed, a woman may make it clear that she is in the mood for sex and receptive to an advance, leaving it to her spouse to make the perfunctory suggestion. A man may, similarly, make an indirect overture simply by forsaking his customary seat in front of the living room TV set or changing into a pair of silk pajamas and a robe before bedtime. Defensive maneuvers can be equally indirect, such as tuning in a late movie, burrowing into a pile of paperwork, or falling asleep on the sofa.

If the low-desire partner assumed the major responsibility for initiating, this would tend to ensure a maximum level of satisfaction for each encounter, since pleasurable experiences foster a desire for more of the same. Initiating when truly desirous would give that partner the advantage in the arousal spiral, although a high-desire partner would be able to close the gap more easily. Indeed, some therapists are able to improve couples' sex lives precisely by this strategem of putting the low-desire partner in the initiator role.

Letting the low-desire partner initiate when he or she is most receptive to sex alleviates the fear of being pressured by the high-desire mate. This pattern ensures that any sexual encounters that do occur will be more mutually satisfying than when one partner participates under protest.

On Your Own

If it's apparent that in your own relationship one partner clearly wants sex more often than the other and is dissatisfied with the prevailing frequency, try the role switch and agree that the low-desire partner will make all the advances for a while. If all goes smoothly, the low-desire person will feel less harried and more relaxed. Often, a spouse will unconsciously act in an aloof or even hostile manner simply out of fear that any warmth will lead to an unwelcome sexual advance. In such cases, the relationship becomes strained and there is an atmosphere of discontent that pervades the bedroom even when the low-desire partner is amenable to sex.

But suppose things don't go according to plan and the partner who agreed to try the new role of initiator somehow never gets around to initiating? Don't scrap the program; try to analyze the problem.

One explanation may be that the low-desire partner was better off under the old system, as the pursued. He or she was only acquiescing when experiencing a relatively good desire level anyway, and initiating may incur an obligation for more frequent sexual activity, since sooner or later the high-desire partner will directly or indirectly express some desire, regardless of the terms of the pact.

Another possible reason is that the initiator may be held responsible for the quality and degree of satisfaction experienced by both partners and risk being reproached with, "After all, it was *your* idea!" Accustomed to the role of follower, where acceptance is the line of least resistance, the low-desire partner may not be sure how *much* desire warrants an advance. Does a person initiate sex in an attempt to maintain a decent showing on the statistical frequency chart, or does a person wait one more night in hopes of feeling a higher level of desire? Despite professions of a sincere, though sporadic, desire for sexual interaction, does the person really have an aversion to it?

A less obvious problem may be that the partner with the higher desire level does not want to give up the initiator role. Because of the inevitability of desire discrepancy, we can nearly always label one partner as having "higher" desire. This does not mean, however, that the partner is someone who is always eager and ready for sex, or even a person with a higher-than-average level of desire. People tend to settle down with partners of somewhat similar temperament; that means someone whose low desire level would frustrate the needs of an average partner often winds up paired with a mate whose even lower desire makes that someone seem like an insatiable satyr or nymph, a not-unflattering self-image for many.

A high-desire partner will not be happy to have his or her overture turned down, but a rejection is not without some value. The partner who said "no" is now in the position of having to offer the unsuccessful initiator some sort of compensation, either sexual or nonsexual. The high-desire partner might feel that having the spouse constantly in the position of having to make amends because of guilt is more valuable than more frequent sexual relations; therefore, the high-desire partner may be just as reluctant to switch roles as the partner with low desire. Consider also that the customary initiator may resist switching roles out of fear that his or her libido will not be high enough to accept every overture from the low-desire partner whose inclinations would become the new basis for having sex.

Change the cognitive errors that are getting in the way. Note that the stumbling blocks often involve power and control, rather than sexual pleasure, which should be the mutual aim. The goal is to enjoy sex, not to get a perfect score. Delaying an initiative until that elusive perfect moment when desire and circumstances are optimal usually results in no initiative at all.

Being a high-desire person does not make you mentally healthier, more masculine or feminine, or give you more sex appeal than a low-desire person. Don't "one-up" your partner by preserving your image as the sexy one.

Don't try to trade in a sexual turn-down for compensation in some nonsexual area. While it's okay to accept a "rain check" for sex in the near future, don't expect to use a rejection to obtain gifts, services, or exemptions from obligations, or to induce guilt or subservience in your partner. If your husband wasn't in the mood for sex last night, don't suggest going out to dinner at breakfast the next morning. His guilt may lead him to say yes and make you feel the rejection wasn't a total loss, but you're complicating your love life when you use it for nonsexual advantage. If your wife said, "Not tonight, dear," don't forgo your usual cooperation in doing the dinner dishes the next evening to punish her.

You don't have to play-act or designate one partner to initiate sex if you want to experiment with role switching. If you simply try to identify recurring patterns in your sexual interaction and do anything at all to vary them, you will disrupt an established system that isn't functioning very well and perhaps give yourself a glimpse of the situation from your partner's perspective.

READ ANY GOOD MINDS LATELY?
Improving Desire Through Verbalization

Marlene Dietrich, while entertaining several hundred GIs during World War II, suddenly announced she could read minds. Kneeling at the foot of the stage, she peered intently into the eyes of one rapt young soldier, then shook her head and said, "No, sonny, don't think that; think something else, or I can't say it aloud."

The only time, of course, that we can "read minds" is when the subject's response is entirely predictable, as when Costello would say to Abbott, "I can read your mind right now. . . . You're thinking I can't do it." In the early, exciting stages of a relationship, sex is probably on everyone's mind and this transient predictability may give people the illusion that where sex is concerned the mind is an open book to anyone who hopes to curl up between the covers. At least where books are concerned, their content doesn't change, whereas people do change with regard to their sexual preferences and wishes. Communication must be an ongoing process, not an occasional exercise.

On one "Saturday Night Live", there was a skit in which a sex therapist encouraged a couple to play a game of waitress-and-customer. The man was instructed to refuse to tell his wife what food he wanted to order, until she finally exploded in frustration, exclaiming that she was not a mind reader. One of the most common cognitive errors we harbor is the semiconscious conviction that others know what we are thinking.

Evalyn S. Gendel, M.D., works with couples on acquiring a more realistic perspective with regard to "mind reading." She says of her patients, "I tell them that I may not be taking them step by step back to a more sexy life, that a lot of it is going to have to come out of an understanding of themselves. We do a lot of concentrating on that aspect of the relationship, on getting to know each other. People live together for a long time and they don't talk about anything personal in a real sense. We concentrate on their own feelings and particularly on what I call 'mind reading,' figuring out what they think is going on in the other person's mind."

Sex, rather strangely, is sometimes a thing that's easier to do than to talk about. Most therapists have had the experience of treating patients who seem to have no qualms about getting involved in the kinkiest sexual adventures with virtual strangers, yet blush and stammer when recounting them.

Most people have a bilingual sexual vocabulary. There are the obscene words they learned from friends and from publications read behind locked doors as adolescents, and the clinical words they learned in textbooks and classes. (Many have a third vocabulary, the euphemistic words they were taught as children to describe body parts and functions, or the private slang terms that some couples adopt.) The obscene words seem to cheapen the emotional attachments in sex; the clinical words rob the activities of their eroticism. The result is that people rarely talk about sex at all with their partners, relying on a minimum of inarticulate phrases and sounds during the act itself.

Occasionally a therapist will encounter a couple who are bored with the relationship and long to add some variety to their lovemaking; but they're convinced that the other is far too conservative and reserved to be open to such suggestions. They fear they will be thought perverted or weird and might even be rejected if they verbalized their thoughts. One great advantage of working with a therapist is that people will confide things to the therapist that they would not dare to say to one another and the therapist finds that there is more concordance than dissonance between the couple's respective wishes.

While some of the "homework" assignments Dr. Gendel gives her patients may involve physical activity, like the sensate focus procedures, she also uses assignments that involve verbal communication and the recollection of happy memories. "I ask them to go home," she said "and really talk about when things were the very best, what was going on, what the circumstances were then." The couple is asked to develop scenarios for the sort of sexual experience they would find most satisfying. This usually works best when the two look at instances in their own lives then and review what was happening when things were better in their sexual relationship.

The therapy does not focus strictly on sexual experience. Dr. Gendel has found that when she asks couples what they do together that they *like* to do, as opposed to tasks they have to share, they often answer in the past tense: "Well, we used to do this and we used to do that." When Dr. Gendel asks them why they don't do such things any longer, such as going for a walk or on a picnic, they say they haven't thought about it or there's no time or they just don't know.

Even things that people do alone for sheer enjoyment are rare or nonexistent. People exercise or get involved in projects because they feel "it's good for me," not because they enjoy it. If you lose the knack for enjoying yourself by yourself, you can anticipate problems in finding enjoyment with your partner as well.

On Your Own

Three wives were complaining about their miserable sex lives, each trying to outdo the other in the misfortune department. The first complained that her husband was "50 percent impotent." The second sneered unsympathetically and said her man was "100 percent impotent." The third told them to be grateful, because her spouse was "200 percent impotent." When this statement was challenged, she explained, "Last night, the jerk bit his tongue."

Animals use their tongues a great deal in sexual preliminaries and humans use them even more, especially since one of the most effective ways to improve sexual desire and satisfaction is through the power of speech. Lack of communication is deadly to sexual desire, but poor communication can be almost as lethal. Foot-in-mouth disease can inflict as much sexual distress as a blistering case of herpes genitalis.

Consider that when you want some exercise, you and Ms. Fonda don't immediately launch into thirty minutes of exhausting, excruciating, vigorous physical activity, do you? No, first you launch into ten minutes of an exhausting, excruciating, vigorous physical warm-up.

The importance of warming up holds for communication as well. Sometimes people think that communication is an unequivo-cally positive thing from which only good can come. Well, declara-tions of war are communications, too. If you just sail into your partner with "I've been totally turned off and I know the sex has been lousy, but I might get more into it if you would do the things I've written on this list," your partner's desire level will drop below yours. Of course, if you don't talk about things at all, nothing is likely to change.

The admission that there's a problem you want to work on is intrinsically positive, especially if the problem is one of sexual desire. Saying "I want to desire you more" is a type of desire in itself. The desire to desire means you *do* care. No husband or wife could be offended by hearing the partner say, "I want to make our sex life better."

Before you start talking to partners about the things you want to change, tell them some of the things you like about them. Since most people have enough psychological "smarts" to see through flattery, you don't try to con them. Play the cards open. You both agree at the start that you're going to share what you *like* about one another, even if it's only something unrelated to sex, such as their know-how around car engines or their pasta primavera recipe. *Then,* you talk about what you might change.

You don't blame your partners or ridicule them with remarks such as, "You're great in the kitchen, but with what you serve up in the bedroom, I'd rather order out." Why attack someone whom you are about to trust with your orgasm?

You say, "I would like it if . . . ." You don't say, "You're too rough" or "You should do . . . ." Accusations lead to denials and commands lead to resistance. Nobody, however, can give you an argument about what *you* would like. They don't have to accommo-date you, but they can't fault you for expressing your wishes.

Do you have to warm up verbally before every sex act? Some-times, after all, actions speak louder than interpersonal circumlocu-tions. You don't have to warm up if you're both already hot, but bear in mind that a warm-up doesn't have to be immediately prior to physical involvement. You might talk about how things are going before dinner or over coffee, hours before you go to bed. We've been talking about some pretty specific communication, but just getting to know and appreciate one another can do a lot for desire.

BED AND BORED
Avoiding Predictability

Did you hear about the husband who found that sex was most enjoyable if he lay on his right side? It was the only position in which he could really see the television screen. Or about the yuppie wife who always kept her eyes closed while having sex so she could fantasize that she was shopping?

Why are marital jokes about sexual apathy funny? Because they contain a grain of truth. But the disinterest of the people involved is grossly exaggerated; husbands and wives *do* have sex together and *want* to have sex. If they truly always avoided sex, we would have subject matter for tragedy, not comedy. The humor lies in the listeners' reluctant acknowledgment that married couples (and for that matter, unmarried couples who have been together for a time) do let boredom and outside distractions get in the way of enjoying one of life's greatest pleasures.

While we are on the subject of humor, perhaps we can indulge ourselves by telling an old story with a pertinent point.

There was a group of hardworking peasant farmers in France, simple men devoted to their families. As they approached middle age, they were plagued by the gnawing feeling that they would never experience some of the great sensual pleasures offered the more fortunate. So, they decided to pool their meager savings and choose one of their group, by lot, to travel to Paris and visit one of the famed houses of pleasure. He would then report back to them so that they could at least experience vicariously something of the great world beyond.

When the lucky winner returned from Paris, they eagerly pressed around him to hear of his experiences. "Ah, my friends," he said, his face enraptured, "I went to the address I was given and found what was truly a palace. There were thick red carpets on the floor, magnificent paintings on the walls, enormous chandeliers of crystal, and a great staircase that was carved of the finest marble. We have nothing like that here at home!

"Then, trembling with excitement and fear, I was taken upstairs to a bedroom. The bed was the size of three of our beds, the headboard and posters carved with figures, silk sheets the color of ivory, and pillows as white and soft as great clouds. There was music, as though an orchestra was in the very room. I was served iced champagne from a glass that sparkled and twinkled like a diamond. Oh, my friends, we have nothing like that here at home!"

"The woman!" they pressed eagerly. "What was the woman like?"

The farmer sighed. "Her perfume filled the air with the scent of a rose garden. Her hair was piled half-a-foot high, in a thousand golden curls. Her lips were redder than the ripest tomatoes and her cheeks were the color of summer peaches. She wore a nightgown of black lace, her white skin peeking through scores of tiny windows. Over her gown, she wore a robe as thin as a spider's web, and her slippers appeared to be made of pure gold. Ah, my friends, we have nothing like that here at home!"

"And then? And then?" they urged, gasping with excitement.

The narrator shrugged. "Oh, after that, it was just like at home."

The French have a word for it: *ennui.* It means boredom, yet it is a boredom that is chronic, that penetrates to the core. We can feel boredom while waiting on a slow-moving line at the bank, but *ennui* is a state of being so bored that you don't even complain about it, because you've forgotten you could feel otherwise. "Apathy" is probably a better English synonym, a state where the person is too numb even to complain about boredom.

The joke about the French peasant is particularly funny because it is really a joke played on the listener. Just as the narrator gets to the juiciest part, where the listener expects to hear a titillating account of some exotic, possibly shocking sexual escapade, he is abruptly cut off and told, "There is nothing you don't already know. Sex is what it is and you can't expect more." Yet, there is another, more positive aspect to the story. The peasant is not angry; he does not feel cheated. He did not make the trip to Paris for a few minutes of physical contact, but for a total sensual experience, and he was not disappointed, because there *were* things that he could not have at home. And the happiest part of the story is that the finest physical experience money can buy is, after all, no different from what you can get at home; only the ambience and the preliminaries may be different.

Is the moral, then, to be content with what you have and not aspire to anything better? Of course not! The moral is:

> *Familiarity does not breed contempt. It breeds in-difference.*

This statement may provoke a wail of frustration from those in well-established relationships. How can you *not* be familiar with someone with whom you've spent years? Paradoxically, the longer we are around someone, the less effort we make to be in touch with them. Extramarital affairs usually start with meeting an "interesting" person, with intimate conversations and shared confidences. Soon the straying spouse knows twice as much about the lover as about the person he or she is married to. In fact, this intimacy helps to justify the affair. "My wife (or husband) doesn't understand me" is a line that's used more than 911, because it has a ring of truth. Spouses don't understand one another because they stop talking to one another.

One of Shaw's characters in *Getting Married* says that a man is like a phonograph with half-a-dozen records. The wife soon gets tired of them all, yet has to listen while he plays them for each new visitor. The phonograph analogy may have been appropriate in 1908, but people today constantly buy new records. We age, our ideas change, and our spouses often mistakingly think they have heard every song in our collection when the last thing they listened to had John Lennon singing lead.

The paradox detectors are about to raise another objection. If we *do* get to know our partners better, we will become more familiar with them. Familiarity breeds indifference. Isn't that moving in the wrong direction?

Objection overruled! The familiarity that kills desire is the utter predictability of an unvarying routine. People could have a different conversation each night, with no two interactions ever the same, but the sound of silence is monotonous and unchanging. What can transpire between two people is infinite; what can occur between two bodies is very limited.

"I get a lot of giggles from people when I ask them, 'What are the things you used to do when your sex life was best?' " Dr. Gendel confided. "They talk about going away for the weekend or about locking up a part of the house and telling the kids to go somewhere else. You ask them when they last did that and they can't remember."

Note that people tend to discuss their best sexual experiences in nonsexual terms. The excitement generally lies in a setting or a set of circumstances, rather than in a particular physical technique or act. One erection or orgasm is pretty much like another; the chief distinguishing feature that sets one sexual act apart from another in terms of satisfaction is the mental component. Desire is the stage of sexual response that relates to mental components and desire is headquartered at the start of the act, so it's not that surprising that so much will depend on the preliminary aspects of an encounter.

Emily Hoon, Ph.D., a Florida psychologist, conducted a series of studies to measure the effect of anxiety on sexual arousal in women. Vaginal probes were used to measure vaginal blood volume, as an objective test of arousal. The female subjects were shown three different brief videotapes, in different sequences: an anxiety-provoking film about tragic automobile accidents, a neutral travelogue about Nova Scotia, and an erotic film involving a nude couple engaged in noncoital "foreplay." Predictably, when the women in a state of arousal from the erotic film were shown the anxiety-provoking film, their arousal state was more quickly terminated than in those shown the travelogue.

Contrary to expectations, however, when the women were shown the erotic film after having previously viewed the anxiety-provoking film, *higher* levels of sexual arousal occurred. Classical behavior therapists had always believed that anxiety and erotic arousal states are reciprocally inhibitory regardless of the order in which they occur. The Hoon study suggested that the *context* in which subjects perceive the stimuli is the important determinant of how these respective arousal states will interact.

Note that anxiety and sexual desire both lead to *arousal* states, with increased pulse rate and respiration and heightened mental awareness. Since Dr. Hoon's subjects were in no real danger, their responses would not be comparable to those in a sexual situation where there was a real threat, such as having an extramarital affair in your own home. While arousability might be hindered in the presence of real danger, a mild threat of discovery, such as having sex outdoors or in the back seat of a parked automobile, evidently does turn some people on. The *context* in which subjects perceive the circumstances is more important than the presence of an anxiety-provoking stimulus.

If circumstances get our pulses racing and our hot blood flowing in a nonsexual situation and the situation suddenly changes into an erotic one (the sort of thing that always happens to James Bond), the body has a head start in the arousal process. And even though desire is supposed to come first, a lot of positive feedback from the body can fan the first glimmer of desire into a flame. Now, if excitement, regardless of the source, can aid desire, what would we expect boredom, the opposite of excitement, to do?

Yes, it does, doesn't it?

Dr. Hoon was surprised to find that the more sexual experience a man had, the less he said he would be aroused by specific fantasized situations. Women, on the contrary, were more aroused by fantasy as they became more experienced. This difference might be explained by men's more facile perception of their physical arousal, since they are acutely aware of penile erections in adolescence, when fantasy is the major component of their sex lives. Women often are unaware of physical arousal until they grow older and have actual sexual experience, which leads them to fantasize more than in adolescence.

It would seem that men were most easily aroused when everything was new and when fantasy held greatest promise. Is it possible, then, that experience is more a minus than a plus, a concept that seems to violate our hallowed belief that experience is the best teacher and a prerequisite for any responsible job? Experience is best when it encompasses a wide variety of adventures and worst when it involves repetition of an unvarying routine. Sexual experience is no different from work experience, where you would not want to repeat the same activity in the same way, no matter how efficient it proved to be. After a time, you would start setting other goals or developing innovations to escape the stagnation of monotony.

You would probably even sacrifice some measure of efficacy to evade the horrors of boredom, like the laborer who was apprehended by his boss while pulling a loaded wheelbarrow behind him. "I thought you told me you've had thirty years' experience!" the boss fumed. "You don't even know that you're supposed to push a wheelbarrow, not pull it!"

"Sure, I know!" retorted the laborer. "It's just that after thirty years of pushing one, I can't stand the sight of the damned thing!"

On Your Own

When novelty and innovation are mentioned regarding sexual encounters, people tend to think in terms of unconventional sex acts, bordering on the kinky or perverted (kinky is using a feather, perverted is using the whole chicken). When it comes to the treatment of desire disorder, the innovations that most therapists recommend have little to do with physical sex acts. You can best work on intimacy by spending more time with your partner in nonsexual activities, getting to know and like one another again.

Except in those rare cases of primary desire disorder, where a partner has *never* had any interest in sex, most people can remember a time when desire *was* good. If you recall those times in your own relationship and compare them with the present, you'll probably find that the difference lies not in the physical acts you performed, but in the things you did before having sex, the conversations, walks, and quiet dinners together. You may be trying to make time in your busy schedules for sex, but alloting *minimal* time by skipping the preliminaries and moving directly into the physical action. Desire is supposed to precede arousal. By starting the sexual response cycle in midstream, you can just about predict what you'll get: arousal and maybe orgasm without desire, which is *sexual desire disorder* in a hard-to-crack nutshell.

It is curious that at least two modern writers have depicted hell not as a place of pain, but of boredom. Jean-Paul Sartre's *No Exit* trapped three people in a fashionable sitting room for eternity, and Shaw's Don Juan told the Devil, "Rather would I be dragged through all the circles of the foolish Italian's Inferno than through the pleasures of Europe. That is what has made this place of eternal pleasures so deadly to me. . . . Your friends are all the dullest dogs I know."

If you and your partner want to revitalize desire by doing something new, think back to a time when things were good. It may well be that the new thing you need is something old.

PARTIAL CREDIT
Failure Management in the Bedroom

"Failure management" is not the reason your company's profits were so low last season. It's one of the most important aspects of patient assessment used by Thomas Stewart, M.D., assistant professor of psychiatry at Harvard Medical School. It refers to what the patient does when he "misfunctions" in an attempted sexual encounter. Dr. Stewart calls this, "for want of better words, failure management or damage control."

He said "I get such stories as 'Well, she gets up out of bed and is crying in the bathroom. I run downstairs and get a can of beer.'" Many of Dr. Stewart's patients are surprised when he tells them that if they are in bed with a woman to make love to her and lose their erection, they can continue to offer affection and pleasure without it.

Dr. Stewart does much of this therapy with men who have erectile dysfunction. The impotent man will say that he *wanted* to have sex, or he wouldn't have been in the bedroom to begin with. Assuming there is no physiological impediment to erection, one could always question whether the man truly wanted to have sex or if he was making the attempt to reassure himself of his virility or to try to satisfy his partner.

Dr. Stewart's advice to men with erectile problems is to "stay in the flow," continue to express affection, and maintain physical contact with the partner even without intercourse rather than terminate the encounter. This makes good sense for desire patients as well. Failure management—what to do if there's a physical malfunction—is generally overlooked, yet the threat of failure aggravates the distancing maneuvers that are practiced by people with low desire. They may say to themselves, "I don't feel like it, but if we start I might get into it," only to ask themselves immediately, "But suppose I *don't?*" Some back off at this point because they feel they could not cope with "failure"; others are able to see that nothing is guaranteed to run smoothly, including sex, and that complications *can* be managed when and if they occur.

On Your Own

Even if the bodily parts tend to function satisfactorily, people worry, "If my partner sees that I still really don't want sex after I've made an effort to work up some feelings, isn't that even worse than just saying at the beginning, 'I'm not in the mood. Let's leave it for a better time'?"

If you agree with that logic, you're making the error that sex is an all-or-nothing prospect; either it goes great from desire to afterplay, or it's a total washout. If you must think of sex as some kind of a *test,* then remind yourself:

> *Sex is not a matter of doing it right or wrong. You*
> *can always pick up some partial credit.*

Remember how you would walk into an exam feeling you were reasonably well prepared and get hit with something like: "Discuss the influences and/or effects of the industrial revolution, the Boxer Rebellion, and the Gadsden Purchase on the Smoot-Hawley Act. Compare, contrast, elucidate, expatiate, and regurgitate." What did you do after you cried? Did you hand in a blank piece of paper? No, you went for *partial credit!* You filled sheets of paper with anything remotely related to the question. Maybe you'd get extra credit for neatness or for knowing today's date or spelling your name right. Maybe the teacher didn't really expect you to do that well, so *anything* you wrote would come as a pleasant surprise.

Did you feel like a phony? Not really, because what you were doing was saying, "Listen, teacher, I'm sorry I can't give you what you want at this moment, but I'm not a total moron and I did try to prepare (though obviously not the right thing), so let me give you the best I can, even if it's not exactly what you're asking for. Maybe next time your expectations and my contributions will match up a little better." Teachers (most of them) being human, will usually give you more partial credit than you expected, certainly more than the kid with the blank page.

The desire to be with someone, to be close, to touch, to love, may not be the same as the desire to have sex with him or her, but is, nevertheless, usually welcomed by the partner and preferred to physical distancing and communication shutdown. Even if your partner says, "I want to make love tonight," this doesn't have to mean, "I expect to have an orgasm through intercourse with you." Orgasms, after all, are relatively easy to come by, virtually at one's fingertips. Desire is for a person, not an activity or a sensation. A sincere wish for noncoital closeness with your partner may be a better approximation of sexual desire than a compliant but detached coital act.

Partial credit stays on your record. Partners, like teachers, usually surprise you by giving you credit. Maybe that's because, like teachers, partners (most of them) are human.

Infuriating Obstacles

Fair-Fight Techniques

---

*"Do I look very pale?" said Tweedledum, coming
up to have his helmet tied on. (He called it a helmet,
though it certainly looked much more like a saucepan.)
"Well—yes—a little," Alice replied gently.
"I'm very brave, generally," he went on in a low
voice: "only today I happen to have a headache."*
—LEWIS CARROLL, *Through the Looking-Glass*

Some people get aggressive when angry and engage in fights.
Others, when angry, get headaches and don't engage in anything.

Even when a desire problem is rooted in a couple's relationship,
there may be very little detectable conflict. Desire often wanes
because poor communication has led to an inability to bridge a
desire discrepancy between the partners; the pair has no quarrel
with one another, but simply can't get it together.

There are cases where the apparent conflicts are so severe that
the therapist marvels that there is any sexual interaction going on,
much less some decrease in desire. Often the anger that seems so
clear to an outside evaluator has been repressed or denied by the
partners, who only perceive the desire loss.

A man encountered a drunk one evening, diligently searching
and re-searching a stretch of pavement. The drunk morosely explained he had lost his wallet and the samaritan was moved by

compassion to assist in the search. After many minutes of painstaking scrutiny, the man asked the drunk if he was sure he had lost the wallet on that street. No, the drunk answered, he had, as a matter of fact, lost it on a street about six blocks away. "Then, why," exploded the man, "are you looking for it here?"

"Because the light's a lot better here," the drunk replied.

There are many couples who are searching for solutions in the wrong areas. They misidentify their differences as problems with sexual compatibility, when they are angry at each other over non-sexual issues.

The opposite type of situation also occurs—namely, one or both of the partners develop a desire disorder and the couple soon begins quarreling about a completely extraneous issue. The most common detour is "You don't love me anymore." Once this giant misstep is taken, it's a quick hop to *why* one is no longer loved: e.g., she thinks I'm a lousy provider, he's competitive and jealous of my career, she hates my mother, he thinks I'm too old. Sometimes it's easier to refight an old battle on familiar grounds than to tackle the mysterious and embarrassing problem of lost desire.

You wouldn't try to play Ping-Pong on a pool table or chess on a backgammon board, yet you might find yourself waging a battle with a partner on completely inappropriate grounds. This can happen because sex is a difficult subject to fight about. How do you argue with someone who says, "I just don't feel like it"? You can't say, "You never feel like it"—your partner might just nod. You can't say, "You do *so* feel like it"—the partner probably doesn't.

So, you say something like, "If you didn't spend so much time watching stupid TV shows, you just might get interested in something healthy adults do," in which case you can have an excellent battle even if you've lost track of the main issue.

On the other hand, one can have an equally heated battle in the dark about sexual desire when one wishes to avoid discussing the conflict that caused the sexual avoidance. Take, for example, the case of a man married to a woman who is overly dependent on her mother. The wife talks to her mother at least an hour a day on the telephone, consults her mother on every decision and follows mother's advice, and spends leisure time running errands with her mother. The husband either has tried with no avail to curb this or he instinctively knows that he cannot possibly come between wife and mother-in-law. So, he gets angrier and angrier, until he stops having sex with his wife. Finally, desire overrides anger and he tries to initiate sex, but now the wife rebuffs him to avenge his rejection of her.

This couple can now have a rousing donnybrook without ever having to bring up the troublesome, irreconcilable mother-in-law situation. They may make some sort of compromise about sex, effecting the illusion of a solution. The wife may use the fight as an excuse to spend even more time with her mother and the husband may use it as an excuse for avoiding both women. Whatever the outcome, difficulties will arise again because the main issue has not been addressed:

> *Many fights about sex aren't really about sex. And many fights about nonsexual issues are really fights about sex.*

This is readily explained by the simple fact that nobody wants to fight a battle he or she feels cannot be won. Battles are deemed hopeless for several reasons. One is the conviction that the partner will not be able to change his or her behavior even if a sincere attempt is made (for example, alcoholism or philandering). Another is fear of the partner's reaction (violence or abandonment) or fear of one's own anger (I can fight about sex without losing control, but I'll go berserk if we get started on money). Still another is guilt (how can I be so angry about her spending so much time with the kids and neglecting me when, after all, the kids really do need her attention?).

Why do people fight at all if they're not going to fight about what is relevant? They get to express anger and hostility, which does relieve tension, if only temporarily. Perhaps they will realize, if not acknowledge, the real issue of contention and take steps on their own toward resolving it. Or if they're mostly at fault on the real issue, they can put their partners on the defensive by dealing with the secondary issues, taking some of the heat off themselves.

The sex therapist gets to intervene in only a fraction of these battles in search of a battlefield, those that meander into the therapist's territory because of a lack of desire in one or both partners. When anger is identified, the therapist will direct the couple to fight constructively, along the lines of fair fight techniques. In essence, the combatants are moved off the sexual field and led to a more appropriate arena, where the fight is scheduled and tailored to conform to rules that limit the battle's scope and keep damage down to a minimum:

(1) A discussion is scheduled for a time when the partners' attention will not be diverted and adequate time will be allotted.

(2) The discussion is limited to the one issue that prompted its scheduling.

(3) The partner with a complaint is urged to speak from a first-person perspective (*"I* feel"), rather than in terms of second-person accusations (*"you* do this"). The fair fight attacks an issue, not a person, and pejorative name-calling is forbidden.

(4) The person with a grievance is asked to make constructive suggestions about what the partner could do to improve the situation.

Just as pugilists are permitted to throw punches, but not kicks, stools or water buckets, so are fair-fighting couples restricted from throwing anything they can dredge up during the course of the discussion. When combatants are not specifically prohibited, they often use sex as a weapon in nonsexual disputes; when fighters go for the groin, the injuries can be severe. Sexual criticism makes the person attacked feel inadequate and kills any desire to risk further criticism; at the same time, it promotes hostility toward the critic, making that person less desirable as a sex partner, completing the two-pronged thrust.

BALANCE OF POWER
Withholding Sex to Gain Control

There are many situations where power is gained as desire is "lost," whether having less interest than the partner is genuine or feigned. Lysistrata's band of holdouts classically exemplifies this principle: the Greek women would *never* have sex with the men until the men fully capitulated to their demands. Zero desire meant infinite power.

If, for example, a husband and wife have a whale of a fight, neither may be in the mood for sex that night. By the next night, the husband is feeling some desire, but the wife remains totally aloof. One night later, the husband's desire rises even further and by now he begins to think that their disagreement wasn't that serious after all. If the wife responds to his smiles and cordial approaches, the mutual reward is sex. If the wife holds out a little longer, she can also get an apology and an admission of guilt. If she can keep her desire down, her power rises.

This sort of tactic is prohibited by fair fight rules. The quarrel should be settled independently of any sexual interaction. If the discussion cannot be immediately scheduled, the partners know there will be a fair fight in the near future and they can carry out lovemaking as usual.

Often post-nuptial declines in desire are due to the couple's rearrangement of priorities. During courtship, both partners are very wary about rejecting any show of sexual interest by the other, not wishing to jeopardize the relationship. Once the relationship has been solidified by marriage, more attention is paid to the business of keeping the union running, to careers, money, and household management. Partners who approach sex with ulterior motives will usually have lower desire and more control than the ones who initiate or comply sexually in simple accordance with current libido.

Fertility rites often breed fertility fights, because a decision to have a child may abruptly shift the balance of control. Where the husband was always the initiator previously, the wife's eagerness to conceive may give intercourse a new urgency. The wife may try to time intercourse to coincide with ovulation or seek to have intercourse as often as possible. The husband might then come to view sex as a series of command performances detached from his own inclinations. A husband's loss of desire under these circumstances would not necessarily mean a resistance to the responsibilities of fatherhood. The loss of control and the performance demands alone could account for his desire loss.

On the other hand, when the only change in a couple's usual routine is the discarding of contraception and one or both partners are continually begging off, second thoughts about pregnancy might well be the cause of desire disorder.

UP IN ARMS
When Fighting Increases Desire

The best part about a marital fight is making up afterward.

Usually. If the ball game ain't over till it's over, a fight between sexual partners isn't really over until they have sex again. Sometimes getting to that last step can generate more trouble than the main event itself did.

For many couples fighting kills desire (no surprise). For many couples fighting increases desire (surprise!). And for battling couples where one opponent's desire is rising while the other's is falling, you can get the kind of stormy result that occurs when a high-pressure weather front meets a low-pressure front head-on.

Why would fighting increase sexual desire in some? There are occasional sadistic or masochistic types who are sexually turned on by a partner's or their own distress, but these are rare and, like all paraphilics (psychiatry's modern euphemism for those formerly called sexual deviates), their sexual gratification and desire are *dependent* on inflicting and/or suffering distress. In other words, no pain, no gain in desire.

You can, however, experience increased sexual desire as the result of a fight without being some sort of sadistic pervert. How many times have you seen a movie or play where a man says to a woman, "Gee, you're beautiful when you're angry!"

Just as reasonable amounts of anxiety and fear may contribute to, rather than inhibit, sexual desire by increasing the same physical responses of heart rate and respiration that accelerate in sexual arousal, so can anger put the body in a generalized state of excitement, awakening it from its customary torpor. Thus, sex after a fight is often experienced as more exciting and interesting than sex in a quiet, congenial atmosphere.

Once again, we will point out that desire and arousal are different stages of sexual response and that arousal is usually viewed as something that follows and depends on desire. There is, however, a feedback process that occurs between arousal and desire; the reaction does not travel exclusively in one direction. Consider, for example, a situation where you feel hungry (i.e., you desire food). If when you duck into the nearest fast-food restaurant, you like what you see and smell, your stomach will increase its secretion of digestive juices (physical arousal) and your appetite will escalate. But if you are greeted by noxious odors and the sight of unappetizing charcoal patties simmering on a film of liquified suet, the physical arousal process will slam into reverse. Your stomach will shut down production and execute a 180-degree backflip. Your desire will, likewise, shift into reverse, as you decide you're not as hungry as you thought.

Feedback to the brain is the rule in almost all bodily processes. We put meters, gauges, and dials on all our machines so that we can monitor them, and the human brain adheres to this principle—it does not give directions and take it for granted that the peripheral body parts will execute the commands flawlessly. Even with your eyes closed you know where your hands and feet are at all times; you may not be conscious of what your thyroid or adrenal glands are doing, but your brain *does* know and will adjust hormonal output according to the feedback it receives. The brain monitors sexual arousal so that it can say, "Yes, this feels good, I want more of it," or "No, this is not exciting me, I don't desire to continue."

During the hostile stages of a fight, of course, sexual desire may be nil and so might sexual arousal, with respect to physical changes in the genital areas. However, some of the extragenital components of arousal, such as the skin flushing, pulse acceleration, and adrenaline flow, are in gear. When the storm calms and friendlier feelings reemerge, the first glimmers of sexual desire are reinforced by an awareness of physical excitement that would not, in more peaceful times, have been present at the starting point. This signals the brain that the body does seem to be proceeding, even more efficiently than usual, along the route to sexual gratification.

With men, especially, sexual desire can occur coincidentally with anger. Testosterone promotes not only sexual desire but aggressive behavior. Even though calm, rational discourse would be the best solution in the battle of the sexes, the body will usually respond to hostile feelings with the primitive reaction of pouring testosterone into the bloodstream, so that the man can use his muscles to subdue his foe. It's not well understood how much of this goes on in women—female adrenal glands do produce androgenic hormones and maybe some of these are mobilized in battle situations, though the level will be much lower than in men. When the fighting is over, the testosterone can devote its full efforts to libido.

This link between male aggression and sexual desire is very practical in certain species, those in which males fight for one or a herd of females. Having vanquished the rival, the male does not take a well-deserved rest, but proceeds immediately to the sexual activity that was the whole rationale for the fight.

The biological difference between men and women, based on testosterone production, can lead to severe hostilities after the initial bout. The man is highly desirous of sexual activity and the woman, still recuperating from the conflict, is totally turned off. She views this intense desire on his part as totally inappropriate to the situation—and unnatural. Either he is sadistic and enjoys making her suffer, or he wants to assert his ultimate power in the relationship by getting her to acquiesce when she's so obviously turned off, or he wasn't as genuinely upset during the fight as he seemed to be. This gives her new ammunition to hurl—she can accuse him of being phony, sick, sadistic, and exploitative, leading to a battle worse than the first. If she understands that his high libido is very natural, even though it doesn't coincide with hers at the moment, the woman will feel reassured rather than hostile and her own sexual desire can return, unobstructed.

For most couples, routine spats do not usually cause prolonged suppression of sexual desire. A wish to restore an atmosphere of caring and love will motivate both sexes to return to lovemaking as soon as possible to cement reconciliation. Some women may actually welcome a show of aggression in their mates, particularly if the men are passive types who rarely display emotion and if this aggression carries over into sexual activity.

George R. Bach, Ph.D., who has developed and refined techniques of fair fighting in love and marriage, says in *The Intimate Enemy* that couples have difficulty in assessing the amount of aggressive behavior preferred by their partners in lovemaking. Dr. Bach uses a seven-level scale, ranging from "Gentle Throughout: I never like to be handled aggressively" to "Violent Aggressive: I like to be physically hurt in sex: bitten or pinched or pinned down or hurtfully slapped, squeezed, etc. This turns me on and makes me more passionate." He asks people to rate not only their own preferences but also to guess the way their partners would answer. Women, he has observed, usually think a man prefers higher amounts of aggression in lovemaking than he actually does. During the uncertain period of courtship, women will accommodate to what they expect to be the males' preferred aggression level. They keep secret their own desires for more or less tenderness. Dr. Bach coined the word "sextacks" to designate the aggression brought to a sexual encounter, even the level-one approaches, which involve *no* aggressive behavior.

Two decades ago, Eric Berne, in *Games People Play,* described the intimate maneuvers used by some couples whereby they initiate fights to avoid sex; for example, if a movie date is invariably followed by lovemaking, a nondesirious partner will start a fight about which movie to see or about check bouncing so that they never go to the movies. The partner has nothing against movies, just against sex that particular night. Just as people may start fights, so as to avoid sex (often unconscious of their motivation), they may start fights to increase their desire. If a woman really wants her man to be more forceful and active in sex and comes to realize that he acts this way only after a fight, one can predict that her behavior will produce an increase in marital squalls.

Bedroom pillow fights and wrestling matches can be staged to promote desire, through the physical arousal feedback mechanisms. One sex therapist gave a pair of her sex therapy clients two buckets of Ping-Pong balls and instructions to stage a fight with them, in the nude. (Paddles were *not* supplied.) The battle predictably ended in a sexual encounter.

Couples should be able to recognize the possibility of a connection between aggression and libido and the potential to harness destructive energy for sexual enhancement. They should also be aware of how dangerous it is to rely on fighting as a main source of putting excitement into an otherwise dull relationship.

Chaucer's Wife of Bath said that she belonged to Venus in her feelings, though she brought the heart of Mars to all her dealings. The love goddess, who carried on a torrid affair with the war god, is not as gentle as her soft, usually naked body leads one to believe. She harbors as much aggression as her more patently armed Olympian sisters. Minerva has her spear, Diana carries her bow and arrows, but Venus always goes for the groin.

On Your Own

Good sex requires communication and some couples, unfortunately, communicate only when they fight. The only time they say anything meaningful to one another is when it's mean. Even if what they say is cruel or critical, the partner is at least getting some attention. Some people are raised in families where parents would scold and holler, then add, "I'm doing this for your own good, because I love you." That's the only time the parents said, "I love you," so anger, in a perverse way, gets equated with caring.

You can see how bedroom conflicts can develop when one partner puts a different interpretation on anger. The one who subconsciously associates anger with caring says, "Okay, we've said our piece, we love one another, let's make love." The other says, "Are you crazy? Do you expect me to forget all the terrible things you said just a minute ago? Well, forget about sex!"

Except for those rare instances where the only way a sadistic partner can turn on is by abusing the mate, aggression between couples can, in moderation, heighten sexual desire, as well as leading to resolution of conflicts that should be confronted. Instead of harsh words, you can stage mock physical battles with bodies (preferably unclad) and use pillows (standard bedroom equipment) or raid the kids' rooms for water pistols, Whiffle balls, rag dolls, or any of the wonderful harmless devices children use to release *their* aggression. From there, the warfare may escalate to hand-to-hand grappling, which doesn't hurt libido any.

Sex, even good sex, won't solve everything. It doesn't solve what made you angry at one another in the first place, if there was a conflict to begin with. The issue may have nothing to do with sex; maybe he's using money as a weapon or he feels she's holding him back at his career because she demands he leave the office at 5 P.M. sharp. "Make-up" sex after a spat is not a reliable indication that anything was resolved, because one combatant may acquiesce out of fear of abandonment, not out of a sense of reconciliation.

When people fail to recognize the real issue in a fight, they attack one another's ego: "You're a selfish slob," or "You're a neurotic bitch," which deflates the partner's self-esteem and extinguishes desire.

Remember that fair-fight techniques schedule a fight to be held in an unheated atmosphere, limit the quarrel to one issue at a time, and forbid nonspecific character assassination. Fair fights are never sexy, because either the issue is not a sexual one or, if it is, the way to resolve it is in a calm, cognitive way, not a heated, emotional one. Of the two, the heated style of fighting is more conducive to increasing desire, but fighting is not the best way to ignite desire and alternative methods of kindling should be sought.

If bad feelings kill off desire, why would fighting be an aphrodisiac for some people? It depends on the couple's style of battle and their "peacetime" characteristics. The spouse who sulks or cries and retreats is not going to feel sexy or be perceived as desirable. But someone defending himself or herself, eyes flashing, muscles tensed, spitting fire, may be viewed by both partner and self as quite exciting, especially if that person has tended to become listless and apathetic around the house.

Fair fighting helps to resolve problems in a sensible, unemotional way and its positive effect on desire results from the alleviation of hostility between the partners. Commitment to fair fighting does not mean a couple has to deny themselves the stimulation of an occasional physical pseudo-brawl. Just as sexual behavior can alternate between encounters that are quiet and sensitive and those that are lusty and bawdy, so can an afternoon of cerebral discourse be capped by releasing some of the past annoyance and frustration through playful grappling. Reliance on fair-fight negotiating provides the reassurance that the couple can keep their more emotionally and physically heated encounters controlled and exciting.

Whether you're excited because you're angry or because you're doing something you enjoy, you might be able to connect that excitement with sex, even if it wasn't originally associated with sex. If you have a stereo unit at home, you don't need one plug for the phonograph, one for the radio, and one for the tape recorder. Once the power is flowing, you can just flick the dial and switch from one instrument to the other.

Desire plays an important role, of course. That entertainment system is never going to switch, on its own, from a radio broadcast of a heavyweight-title bout to a romantic instrumental on the phonograph. The human who owns it has to want to make the switch. But you don't have to start the electricity flowing; you're already turned on.

TENNIS SERVES TO NET ADVANTAGE
Converting Nonsexual Enthusiasm to Sexual Desire

To a tennis player, love means nothing, but just because tennis players use the term "love" for zero, it does not follow that they are a heartless bunch. Dr. Bernie Zilbergeld treated one woman with a passion for tennis and not much else with a unique and very successful approach.

Betty, as Dr. Zilbergeld called his patient, was a woman in her late thirties, who had been married for fourteen years to a man about the same age. The couple's complaint was decreased frequency of sex for several months, with a corresponding increase in frequency of arguments about sexual and nonsexual matters.

Betty had never experienced an orgasm, but when a girlfriend in sex therapy talked about her first orgasm in such enthusiastic terms, Betty decided she would like some of the same. Betty achieved her own initial orgasm through masturbation and sought similar satisfaction in her marital relations. The problem was that reaching orgasm was a long and arduous process for Betty, requiring twenty-five to fifty minutes of careful manipulation with complete absence of distraction. Her husband, Tom, was understandably frustrated by having to stimulate her manually for such a long period without being able to talk, change positions, or rest for fear of "distracting" her.

Sex became a task and they both withdrew from it, to the point where they stopped touching for fear it would lead to sex. Dr. Zilbergeld thought that the main problem was Betty's low arousal potential, which accounted for her complex needs. Asked what things excited her, Betty said her husband's orgasms gave her "a rush of warmth and relaxation." The only other thing that excited her was tennis; she found a good set "absolutely exhilarating."

Dr. Zilbergeld asked Betty to make comparisons between her movements and feelings on the tennis court and in the bedroom. She was instructed to move at home the way she did on the tennis court, alternately tensing and relaxing certain muscles, and to recall a particularly strong orgasm of her husband's as she was moving about and fantasizing. She was then to introduce sexual thoughts about what she wanted Tom to do to her that would give her pleasure.

Figuring that tennis already had Betty "halfway there" in terms of arousal, Dr. Zilbergeld advised her to engage in sensual activity with her husband immediately after a game whenever possible, instead of showering and cooling down. Also, when she had not been playing tennis, she should take a few minutes to swing her racket in the bedroom while her husband observed and commented from the "sidelines."

"Teasing" and nondemanding pleasurable exercises were incorporated into lovemaking, without any emphasis on achieving the orgasms that had taken on the status of a chore. Betty had become almost phobic about clitoral stimulation, so contrary to the course of most similar cases, she achieved orgasm first through vaginal penetration, later obtaining orgasms through manual stimulation of the clitoris as well. After the tenth therapy session, Betty no longer felt the need to swing her racket in the bedroom, although she hung it on the wall there in case she ever needed a reminder.

Given the success of this fascinating case, one would think Dr. Zilbergeld would be exploring the possibility of merchandising tennis rackets in sex shops, to be displayed beside the vibrators, edible panties, and two-headed dildos, whereas he is actually rather cautious in his enthusiasm. He sees the "tennis lady's" problem primarily as one of arousal, although loss of desire was certainly a component. Still, he would not be adverse to trying the approach in cases of low desire, if it seemed promising. He was considering its use in the husband of a female patient whose complaint was an absence of passion on her husband's part. When she said that he was not really a lover, not "into that," Dr. Zilbergeld asked what he *was* "into." The wife replied, "When he skis and when he plays racquetball, he sort of gets all glazed over, as if he were in a trance."

Almost everybody gets excited about *something.* Many never feel any real emotional excitement about sex, regarding it as an obligation or something they do to have an orgasm. They enjoy orgasms, but don't experience the mental desire leading to the arousal that propels them toward release. The therapist tries to associate a feeling of excitement in one area of their lives with their sexual activity. While the technique draws on the principles of behavioral conditioning, transferring an emotional response evoked by one stimulus to a different stimulus (e.g., from a sport to a sexual situation), the treatment is primarily experiential since it depends on an individual's unique areas of mental fascination.

"There's this one guy I had," Dr. Zilbergeld recalls, "whose greatest excitement in his whole life was World War II. He was a gunner on a B-17 and he used to bomb Germany. Since that was his greatest excitement, I tried to get him to associate that with sex. There was this incredible power of firing those machine guns and the great feeling of elation when a gunner sometimes shot down a German plane. There was overwhelming anticipation, expecting flak and enemy fighters, mixed with fear—but it was a good kind of fear, because that kind of fear can improve your performance." The patient had little desire for sex, so Dr. Zilbergeld asked him to relive those thrilling war experiences in his memory prior to any sexual encounter. The excitement and mental arousal produced by the fantasies carried over to the sexual situation when the patient turned his thoughts from making war to making love.

On Your Own

It's difficult enough to reactivate desire in someone who once had an adequate level and then lost it, but what can you do if you or your partner never had much interest in sex from the beginning?

One approach is for such a person to ask, "What turns me on?" We don't mean in a sexual sense—just anything that can get you really interested and excited. It can be a sport or a hobby or even something connected with your work. Suppose a woman who complains that she has no sexual desire (even though she loves her partner) is into running and really enjoys it. She isn't running merely because it helps keep her weight down or because she feels it makes her healthier, she actually gets a sense of exhilaration as her heart rate and breathing accelerate. This woman might try running into the bedroom when she gets home, instead of into the shower.

Even though there is a movie called *Some Came, Running,* you might object that a "runner's high" is not a state of *sexual* excitement. Objection sustained, to the extent that in the mind there is no thought of sex. Yet, rapid heartbeat, faster breathing, higher blood pressure, and muscular tension are all associated with physical arousal during sexual activity. The body of this girl-on-the-run has a head start on her head and her genitals, so if she can just bring these components into play, those first twinges of sexual desire won't be cold cognitions.

Another factor to consider is that when you're physically "up," for whatever reason, and the adrenaline is flowing, your entire body is more alert. That same adrenaline that sharpens all your senses to warn you about danger can make your body more receptive to pleasurable sensations of touch, sight, sound, and smell.

Speaking of smell, if his own adrenaline is not flowing and sharpening his sense of olfaction, the runner's partner might not appreciate a boudoir that reeks of essence of gym locker. The lady can hose down, as long as she doesn't cool down. She could invite her partner to share her shower, even if he won't join her on her runs. She shouldn't, however, follow the typical routine of getting all relaxed and wound-down, so that she has to rev up from ground zero again.

What about the couch potatoes, the nonjocks? Is there hope for them?

Of course. Suppose a man's home computer mesmerizes him for hours. He turns on the screen and *he* turns on. Adrenaline is adrenaline, whether you get it from physical or mental stimulation. So, instead of his saying, "Darn, I'll have to put this on the floppy disk and get ready for bed," he should move directly from his keyboard into the bedroom, without winding down in the bathroom or in front of the eleven o'clock news. We read somewhere that an Apple can lead to all sorts of temptation.

Or suppose a wife gets really dreamy after watching "Dallas." She never misses watching all those rich, powerful, sexy women and their handsome, dynamic lovers. Normally, putting a TV in the bedroom makes as much sense as hiring Count Dracula as a blood-bank technician, but in this case the TV might provide perfect foreplay for a ten o'clock Friday-night tryst. On the other nights, thank God for syndicated reruns and the VCR.

❧ 16 ❧

Out of Your System

Family Systems Therapy

———————————————————

"I saw a case where a couple hadn't been sexual in a long time," Dr. Jerry Friedman recounts. "She was ready to divorce him and he didn't want that to happen.

"The wife was short, very dark, and a very, very heavy woman. One of the things that I tried to deal with in his therapy was whether he found her unattractive. Was it the weight? He said, 'No, no, it wasn't the weight.' Sex just never occurred to him; he never thought of it. In the course of treatment, it became clear that she tried to look nicer and would go on diets, and every time she would lose a little weight, he would try to sabotage it and bring home ice cream cakes, which she loved.

"It turned out, in getting his history, that he had had a very close relationship with his mother. He was the youngest of eight kids and there was about twelve years' difference between him and the next oldest, so he was like an only child. His mother was very protective and didn't want him to go out with girls, and she would sit at the window till he came home from a date. He had a lot of anger and resentment toward his mother. And his mother was a very short, very dark, very obese woman. It was so clear what was going on."

It was clear that Dr. Friedman was dealing not with two people, but three. The mother might even have been deceased, but she was nevertheless an important part of the *system* in which this couple operated. If the therapist had tried to deal with the desire problem by using conventional sex therapy methods, such as having the husband relax with nonsexual pleasuring techniques, the therapist would undoubtedly have failed because the husband could not desire to desire until he first resolved the pathological identification between his wife and mother.

The therapist initially assumed that the wife's obesity was contributing to the problem. He was probably skeptical when the patient denied that the weight was a turn-off and perplexed when it became obvious that the husband was interfering with the wife's attempts to lose weight. It didn't make sense, and whenever things do not make sense, there is a basic rule to fall back on:

> *If things just don't add up, you're probably miss-*
> *ing one or more pieces of information.*

Given the information about the husband's mother and his childhood, the system makes infinitely more sense. The husband chose a wife who reminded him of his mother and he really wanted her to be more a mother than a wife. Since Mother was sexually prohibitive, any normal tendency to suppress sexual feelings toward a mother figure would be even more intensified.

Note that whenever the wife made an attempt to change her physical image, the husband would sabotage her efforts by bringing home high-calorie desserts. Even though their system was causing distress to both, he was taking steps to preserve it and keep it from changing. This is the rule, not the exception.

> *In any system, the participants direct their energies*
> *toward preserving that system and opposing change in*
> *it.*

You've heard the expression, "You can't beat the system!" What exactly does that mean and what is a system? A system is an aggregate of all the components that influence actions and behavior—the whole conglomeration of people, agencies, and events that have an effect. A recent innovation in family and couples therapy is the systems approach by therapists, where, instead of focusing on one individual who is identified as having "the problem," they address the interaction of all parties, realizing that you cannot change any one aspect without altering the whole system.

For example, a therapist may encounter a situation where a teenager continually misbehaves. It might be useless to work individually with the adolescent because the whole family depends on his misconduct for its stability. Mother and Father may have considered separating, but rationalize their remaining together by saying that the disturbed child needs them. An insecure sister may enhance her self-esteem by taking on the role of "good child," superior to her brother. Another child may blame his own aggressive behavior on the "disturbed" brother's provocative actions. The family may be able to avoid social obligations on the grounds that they cannot leave the "patient" alone.

In a case such as this one, you cannot change the behavior of the adolescent without throwing the whole family into confusion and turmoil. The systems therapist is able to see through the family's emotional involvement in preserving the status quo and analyze their contributions to what appears to be the child's problem.

To some extent, we cannot avoid being part of a system. We have a strong emotional need for togetherness and a wish for love, sharing, and validation. On the other hand, we also have a human need to establish a sense of independence and autonomy, free from emotional ties and demands. The quest for personal independence stirs in us as soon as we are old enough to toddle away from our mothers; it rapidly escalates in adolescence, and remains active throughout our lives. Independence is the antithesis of togetherness and we have a need for both.

In any system (and even a childless couple constitutes a system), any attempt by one party to assert independence may be met with resistance by others who are more interested in preserving dependency. The person who is pulling away may be accused of not caring about or loving the partner or other family members. Sexual desire is augmented by a wish for emotional closeness and inhibited by an atmosphere of hostility.

Systems therapy focuses not only on pairs, but on triangles. A triangle is a three-person relationship (such as parents and a child) in which, at any given time, two of the parties draw closer while one moves apart. As the need for togetherness waxes and wanes, the equilibrium shifts. A four-member family has four possible triangles (parents and one child, parents and other child, children and father, children and mother). A five-member family has ten potential triangles.

Generally, when the situation is calm, people prefer togetherness, but in anxiety states people tend to pull apart. Therapy focuses on the most important triangle in the family system, usually the parents and the child who is acting out a conflict. Movements that affect equilibrium are made automatically and without awareness. Therapy is aimed at helping a person gain conscious control of movements while being able to maintain emotional closeness to the others despite his newly enhanced independence.

A family provides a practically perfect model of a system in operation. Each member has his or her assigned role and knows what part to play in relation to the others. The system has been functioning on a daily basis for years, so that everything moves automatically. When a person is able to modify his role consciously, he can observe the changes in other members that result from altering the situation. In time, other members of the system will make their own moves, either to change the interaction in their favor or to return everything to the system that originally prevailed. Without conscious effort and persistence, the system tends to drift back to its original state.

A couple is enough to constitute a system; the addition of a therapist forms a triangle, which allows for shifting in the togetherness/autonomy movement. In classical marital therapy, the therapist encouraged the couple to talk with each other in his presence, while he observed and interpreted their emotional interaction. General systems therapists use a different approach, asking each partner to talk about his or her views and feelings to the therapist in the other's presence. If the partner is relatively uncommunicative, the therapist will continue to draw out that person with questions. The spouse who has been listening is then asked to tell the therapist about the reactions he or she experienced while listening.

This innovative approach replaces emotionally charged communication between partners with a more detached and intellectual account of mental perceptions. Couples find that they really understand for the first time how a partner thinks as they listen in a way they can never manage to do when talking to one another. This better understanding of a partner leads to the development of intimacy in the home, where the partner's motives and reactions become less of a mystery.

Family systems therapy incorporates principles of cognitive therapy; a rational, calm attitude directs the moves in a shifting system, replacing the unconscious, automatic maneuvers that tended to preserve the system in the past. Any disruption of the system increases tension, and tension usually intensifies the need for emotional closeness. The partner may feel threatened whenever a person alters the system in the direction of personal autonomy and may react in a variety of ways to thwart change. The threatened spouse may adopt a clinging or seductive posture, to lure the changing one back into the old relationship. Or the reaction may be one of hostility, fighting, arguing, tyrannical demands, or rejection. Children may be drawn into the fray or the unhappy partner might turn to alcohol, drugs, or outside sexual partners. In a therapeutic situation, the professional can ensure that both members are involved in any changes and deal with resistance in a constructive way.

In problems of sexual desire, the system may involve only the couple, rather than an entire family, but third (and fourth and fifth) parties may also be affecting the relationship and be affected by it. For example, suppose a husband immerses himself in work and shows little desire and affection toward his wife. She turns to her mother for solace, which results in their improving their mother-daughter bond. The husband, meanwhile, has curried his boss's favor by putting in hours of labor beyond the call of duty and is being considered for a promotion. During the course of a fight over money, the wife, who is on the defensive, changes the course of battle by berating the husband for his sexual inattentiveness. Shaken by her truthful accusations, irrelevant as they were at the moment, he resolves to spend more time in sexual initiative and activity.

The wife expresses appreciation for his change of heart, but her gratitude is short-lived because by now both have become very comfortable in their system of sexual avoidance. Mother becomes more distant now that daughter no longer indulges so eagerly in criticism of the husband and of men in general. The husband fears that his closest rival at work is overtaking him in the quest for a higher rung on the corporate ladder. Without their being aware why, the couple begins to lose their newly found sexual interest and actually is fighting more. You can't beat the system—unless you change the system. In this case, career goals and in-law conflicts have to be considered, reassessed, and reprioritized. Changing an attitude may be sufficient to change the whole system.

Dr. David M. Schnarch, director of the Sex and Marital Health Clinic at Louisiana State University in New Orleans, uses a systems approach to treat a variety of couples' problems, including desire disorder. "You look at everything when you see a patient," he says, "including the system that they have been operating under. You have to change the system whether or not they are aware of it, and you have to go about changing it very carefully, because there are rules in relationships about how change is allowed to occur or not occur, and they differ for every relationship.

"These people may not even be aware that they are operating under this system. We look at their cognitions and their behavior, and we try to devise a new system of approach for them. Every relationship is different, but it turns out that people aren't that different, so you tend to see repetitive types of systems if you see a large number of couples."

Giving an example of how a therapist might intervene in a system, Dr. Schnarch cites an incident involving a couple. The wife had asked her husband to look after their eight-year-old daughter while she was making a lengthy business phone call from home. He became engrossed in some activity of his own inside the house and the child, who continued to play outdoors, fell off her bicycle and came in crying, which interrupted the wife's phone conversation.

"The wife was thinking, 'That son of a bitch, he doesn't think my work is as important as his,' " Dr. Schnarch relates. " 'He said he was going to watch her and now he's embarrassing me. What am I going to do with this guy on the other end of the line, with my kid screaming?' Maybe five years ago, she would have said, 'What the hell!' in spite of the same behavior and provocation." What the wife was thinking in response to her husband's behavior was more important than the behavior; five years ago, his behavior would have been the same, but her reaction would have been different. As her child grew older, the woman put more emphasis on her career and expected the husband to take a more active role in child care.

Dr. Schnarch points out that communication hadn't helped, because the two of them *had* talked about who was going to handle what during her phone call. According to their pattern of interaction, the wife would berate him for his failure and he would listen in a passive way. Having accepted his verbal chastisement, the husband would simply revert to his indifferent ways while his wife silently fumed.

Dr. Schnarch suggests that the next time such an incident occurs, the wife, instead of ranting at her husband, should pick up a telephone in his presence and pretend to be talking to someone. She should make some comments praising her husband for his kind and considerate nature. This uncharacteristic response by the wife would force the husband to make some new responses of his own.

He might initially try to suck her back into the old patterns, because he would not know what is going on and would become uneasy. He might try to get back into the old system, which is familiar to him and in which he knows how to operate. But if the wife refuses to get drawn back into the old patterns, his habitual responses become incongruous and unworkable.

"Part of the problem," Dr. Schnarch says "is that very often you will make responses that you don't want to make, that you will regret later on, and you have the feeling that the responses were being sucked out of you. Not only do people build systems, but once they get going, the system is self-perpetuating and it's very hard for people to break out." If you are not aware of the system, you continue to do what you have always done because it's safe and you know how it will end up before you even walk into the room. But when one person changes, the system has to change with it.

Sometimes people who are in a system can't see it, just as you cannot see what you really look like without a mirror because you are inside your body. The therapist is like a mirror, reflecting back what the patient expresses. Insight into the system is not always necessary for the patient. Because people get defensive about any tampering with their established systems, they may be less resistant to change if they don't see it coming. Often, a spontaneous event will change the system for better or worse, such as a death in the family, a major illness, or some upheaval in circumstances. A change, planned or randomly occurring, will affect an entire system if it has sufficient magnitude, but expertly guided alterations will have a better outcome than chance happenings.

Couples entering therapy will often try to focus on one aspect of their relationship that they would like to change, thinking this will make the therapeutic task easier. Of course, you can never change one thing without inducing change in many others. This is more of a blessing than a bane, because it means people do not have to attack an entire system all along its length and breadth. One effective move will trigger off a series of new responses. Disrupting patterns of hostility that interfere with sexual desire can bring about a resurgence of desire even if the couple has not worked specifically on that problem.

On Your Own

A systems viewpoint is most helpful if you happen to be in a relationship where you are acutely aware of and distressed by your situation but your partner has no motivation to change. The low-desire partner in this type of system says, "We are doing just fine." He or she refuses to enter therapy or even make any sort of effort to change anything. Your partner wants to keep things exactly as they are, not because he or she is deliriously happy with the arrangement, but because the system is predictable and, therefore, comfortable.

You will then tend to say, "What's the use? My mate is never going to change." You accept, reluctantly, the premise that the situation will never change and ensure it by not changing your own behavior one iota. But you can disrupt the workings of the system simply by refusing to continue to play the game by your partner's rules. This won't solve the problem by itself. Things won't immediately get happier; indeed, they will probably get a lot rockier for a while, but they will not continue as before, which is the important first goal.

If the high-desire partner says, "We have had sex every Saturday night and *only* every Saturday night for two years and I refuse to have sex *this* Saturday night," the other may say, "Well, then we won't have sex at all this week. Isn't that worse?" Whereupon the disrupter can answer, "Maybe, but at least it's not the *same.*"

Just as in a system of complex machinery you can't add pressure at one point, open a valve at another, heat up one end of the apparatus, or slow down some of the gears without causing changes up and down the line, one little change in a couple's habitual interaction will change the whole relationship, provided they don't fall prey to the nearly automatic attempt of one or both partners to respond to the change by reverting to the old patterns of action and response.

Let's illustrate how couples who claim a lack of sexual desire are really victims of an intricate established system in which they are enmeshed and how they can break out.

Case 1: Christine and Matt are in their mid-thirties, have been married two years and lived together for one year prior to their wedding. Christine was very eager to have a baby before too many more years elapsed, but lately she has been disturbed by Matt's "violent" behavior toward her, which not only is dampening her sexual desire toward him, but giving her qualms about bringing a child into such an atmosphere. Christine was raised in a large family where her hardworking father was rarely home and never said much. She wanted a husband who would be supportive and communicative. Matt has a domineering father, who was occasionally physically abusive and always authoritarian. Matt tends to keep his thoughts to himself, although his temper often flares when he deals with subordinates at his office. Although his father lives in a distant state, Matt has become his parent's partner in a number of business deals, which has resulted in frequent trips to be with his father, away from Christine. He telephones his father often, not only from the office but also at home.

When Matt is at home, Christine attempts to engage him in intimate conversation. He invariably retreats into a book or magazine. Christine then brings up some inflammatory topic, such as their poor sex life. Matt says he is not in the mood to talk just now. Christine insists they discuss things. He moves away. She pursues him, ultimately standing jaw to jaw ("in my face," Matt says). At this point, Matt becomes "violent"; he throws a pillow, upsets a coffee table, or knocks a pile of books to the floor. Christine withdraws in terror. The next day, she berates Matt, who expresses contrition and resumes his old silent patterns.

The system here involves not only the couple, but Matt's father. Christine would be more tolerant of Matt's silences if he did not spend so much time sharing confidences with his father. Matt avoids Christine because he is afraid she will demand he stop being so dependent on his father—which he is not psychologically ready to do. Matt's "violent" outbursts are actually carefully controlled displays of aggression just intense enough to make Christine back off. She can change the system by not insisting they "communicate" when Matt is most threatened and let him schedule the time for a quiet discussion. Her persistent pursuit blocks his withdrawal temporarily, but only results in his driving her away with sound and fury. Only by letting Matt confront the issues when he feels most in control and least vulnerable will Christine be able to establish true communication and compatibility.

Case 2: Jack is a forty-eight-year-old physical therapist and Rhoda, his wife, is a forty-six-year-old part-time librarian. It is the second marriage for both and their children are grown and living independently. They live in a small, cluttered apartment and have taken advantage of its high ceilings by building loft platforms to add a sort of second floor where they sleep. Rhoda is taking some college courses in her nonworking hours. She rarely cooks and they eat out practically every night, usually at the Leprechaun's Lair, a local restaurant more famed for its generous libations than its cuisine. Jack orders at least two cocktails while waiting for dinner, washes down his meal with a couple more, and then begins the rounds of after-dinner drinks. Rhoda used to join him until she developed a peptic ulcer, so she limits her liquid intake to seltzer. The place is full of regulars, like Jack and Rhoda, so other customers stop by their table to chat, sometimes even pulling up a chair to join them. After dinner, Rhoda gets bored and excuses herself to go home and study or relax, while Jack lingers to talk and drink with cronies. By the time Jack weaves his way home, Rhoda is up in the loft, reading, watching TV, or sleeping. Jack pours himself a stiff nightcap and turns on the second TV set, usually falling asleep in his armchair. Rhoda says that Jack is either disinterested in sex or is so drunk by the time he gets around to it that he repulses her. She feels that advanced age and alcohol abuse have just about finished him as a lover.

The system here again extends beyond a couple and their small apartment. It includes all the habitués of the Leprechaun's Lair, who provide Jack with a small bit of the intimacy Rhoda does not supply. Rhoda could break out of the system, even if she doesn't want to cook, by ordering food to be delivered at home or by suggesting restaurants that emphasize food over beverages. Rhoda used alcohol as a defense against intimacy herself in the past; when her health prohibited this, she ensured that Jack continued to use the defense mechanism. A sober analysis of the situation could lead to some constructive restructuring of this couple's sexual and marital interaction.

Case 3: Andre, a twenty-eight-year-old dentist, is furious at his twenty-five-year-old wife, Gloria. "She always gets her way," he fumes. The strange thing about Gloria is that she is *not* a domineering woman. She is passive, meek, and acquiescent. She never argues or insists; yet somehow, Andre, who considers himself a forceful person, always winds up doing what she wants. For example, they always wind up spending *every* holiday at her parents' home, even though they live a considerable distance away and Andre hates to travel, especially on holidays. Since Gloria is so passive, they have sex only when Andre wants it and as he gets angrier he wants sex less frequently. They never did have sex that frequently, because Andre always was afraid he was taking advantage of Gloria's compliant nature. If you ask Andre why he never does what he wants, he explains that he hates to hurt people; he knows what Gloria wants and her uncomplaining acceptance of his wishes makes him so guilty that he ends up dictating that they will do what *she* wants.

Andre was raised by a mother who was never happy. She would bitterly complain about the burdens she had to endure and about how unfair life had been to her. Since his mother could never be made happy, Andre ultimately realized that viewing herself as self-sacrificing and abused gave his mother a sense of self-esteem and worth that she could never achieve by merely getting what she wanted. Actually, people close to her often did go out of their way to try to please her, so she could get her way and still find something to complain about. By spending holidays with Gloria's parents instead of his own, Andre gave his mother the gift of an injustice truly worthy of grievance. Gloria never complained, so that made Andre feel unbearably guilty when he opposed her wishes.

Andre's system includes his mother and the lessons she taught him. To break out, he has to change the way he regards his wife. When he knows that he and Gloria have different wishes about an issue, he should confront her and offer to negotiate. If she says, "Whatever you want, dear," he must take her statement at face value. Gloria has learned that to get her way all she has to do is nothing. Paradoxically, being more assertive could result in getting less, but once Andre changes the rules, she will have to abandon her silence. Andre's guilt will not let him be a dictator, but his anger is interfering with his being the conciliator. Only by initiating a system of discussion and compromise will this couple achieve any sort of intimacy and restore sexual desire to their marriage.

How does your system work? How many people can affect it in a positive or negative way? Tamper with it mentally by asking yourself, "What would happen if I did it this way instead of the usual way? What would change if I behaved in this way or that way? How would my partner respond if I did this?"

Review some average events in your life, such as planning a weekend, budgeting expenses, or making love. Plot out the usual scenario. Then change the script in some way and see what other changes you would have to make in order for the script to follow a logical course. That's how a system changes: one alteration sets off a chain reaction.

You *can* work within the system and use its rechanneled momentum to your own advantage. Consider Jack Nicholson's classic and memorable maneuver in *Five Easy Pieces,* when he wanted an order of plain toast and the waitress adamantly told him the restaurant did not serve plain toast. He could have demanded that she violate the system by bringing him toast, but he "made it easy" for her by working within the system and ordering a chicken salad sandwich on toast—"hold the mayo, hold the lettuce, hold the chicken salad" (specifically, between her knees).

It doesn't necessarily take a revolution to effect change. One small adjustment is sufficient to ensure that *something* will be different, and if that doesn't work, further adjustments may prove more profitable, as long as you don't regress to the longstanding, disappointing interactions of the past. You might need the full cooperation of a partner to make a revised system work smoothly, but one person alone can divert a malfunctioning system from continuing on its poorly destined course.

If you and your partner have fallen into a pattern of desire and response that leaves one or both of you unhappy—get it out of your system!

The Paradox of Desire

A Postscript

Sexual desire is natural, yet it can be very troublesome. It leads to some of life's most exhilarating moments, but it can disrupt our concentration on important matters or influence us to do things that go against our better judgment. When we feel desire for our partners, it can increase our love; when we feel desire for someone else, it can threaten and even destroy that love. Desire can make us feel guilty, dirty, helpless, or out of control.

This psychological conflict produced by desire is nothing new. Plato stated that in desire we think and act as animals, while in love we participate as rational beings. We should, therefore, Plato argued, make every effort to eliminate the element of desire, which is so radically opposed to our human intellects that desire and pure love cannot peacefully coexist in a single consciousness. To this day, people who have never read Plato speak of platonic love, a love free of sexual desire, which, to the old philosopher, was the ideal toward which we should strive.

Sexual desire, as humans experience it, is *not* animalistic. It is directed toward another human and is a wish for union with that other person. Whether or not one believes in a soul that exists independent of the body, as long as we are on earth our bodies are inseparable from "us." We can know and possess one another only through our bodies, and our desire to join with someone can only be accomplished through our physical parts, whether we establish this contact through our eyes, mouths, or genitals. Like goldfish in adjacent tanks, our selves can never get closer than the physical barriers that allow us to glimpse one another, but contain us within.

There is, in desire, the wish to possess the other. We want them to surrender completely to us, of their own free will. This is paradoxical, because giving up your individuality to belong completely to another is the ultimate concession of freedom. The wish for exclusive possession makes jealousy an intricate component of sexual desire and love. Shaw's Cleopatra told Pothinus she was sure Caesar was not in love with her because she could not make him jealous, although she had tried. Where love exists, the price is the threat and pain of jealousy, and it is not surprising that as sexual prohibitions and monogamy have decreased in recent years, more and more people have developed an avoidance of love and a fear of commitment and intimacy.

Cannot sexual desire exist as an impersonal hunger for another's body, without becoming concerned with him or her as an individual? The paradox here is that you cannot become physically close to another without being aware of that person as an individual. Even most johns want the illusion of personal intimacy with a prostitute. And the woman, certainly if she commands a higher fee, sells not anonymity, but the fantasy of caring and self-disclosure. The pornographer and the sadist know that sexual desire can be rendered devoid of interpersonal aspects, but this is a perversion of desire, not desire's essence.

Desire is never stronger than in those first moments when a couple know their merging is inevitable, but they haven't quite gotten there. This realization led to the cult of courtly love that obsessed male and female nobility in medieval Europe: they believed that the very essence of romantic love was the difficulty, even the impossibility, of obtaining sexual gratification; therefore, romantic love could not possibly exist between husband and wife, where sex was not only an inevitability but an obligation.

"The energy released when man and woman come together is proportional to the distance that divides them when they are apart," writes philosopher Roger Scruton. When sexual union comes too easily to casual partners, this tension is understandably diminished and desire wanes. It seemed paradoxical that in the wake of the Sexual Revolution our society seems to be experiencing a loss of sexual desire rather than an increased interest in sex, but Scruton sees it as predictable: "The recent decline in the practice of modesty, and the disposition to speak openly about the sexual act, has accompanied no heightening of the sexual passion, but, on the contrary, . . . a 'decline' . . . in the sentiment of sex."

The greatest paradox in sexual desire is one with profound practical implications. Sexual desire seems to arise effortlessly when we first meet someone and it decreases in intensity the longer we stay with that person. In the most extreme cases, sexual desire diminishes to a minimum or is lost entirely, the condition we have been calling sexual desire disorder. The experts tell us that while desire decreases with time, love increases. Desire draws us together, but love cements the relationship and gives it permanency. This is scant consolation if loss of sexual pleasure is part of the trade.

Intimacy, the total union with another's being, is the very aim of human sexual desire. There are people who, after long years in a union together, continue to feel a high and continual level of sexual desire for one another, and invariably these couples have a genuine liking for and attachment to one another. Intimacy *does* increase desire; familiarity rarely does.

People confuse familiarity with intimacy. An astronomer who peers nightly at the heavens is familiar with them, but it is only the astronaut, floating in space, who is intimate with the heavens. People say they are bored, because there are no surprises, because they know everything there is to know about their partners. Then, you talk to them awhile and it turns out they haven't had a meaningful conversation with that partner in years, even though they live under the same roof.

One woman in therapy, who had been married for ten years, was strongly attracted to a male co-worker. While she did not succumb to the temptation of an extramarital affair, she agonized over how much more emotionally compatible she was with this other man. Even his favorite movie was the same as hers. Then the therapist asked what her husband's favorite movie was. She didn't know.

Even if you thoroughly knew your partner yesterday, that knowledge is obsolete today. A day doesn't go by when you don't have a slew of ideas and experiences. Keepers of desire diaries will realize how rich and varied that one corner of their lives can be in the course of a single day.

Desire is a mental phenomenon. So is intimacy. You may come as close as you can to possessing another in the physical act, but the true union is outside the act. Physical proximity alone is definitely not enough.

People say, "I feel like having sex," but they rarely bother to add mentally "with John" or "with Mary." We tend to think of desire as something rising and falling within ourselves and forget that there's a person at the other end. A quarterback can have the greatest throwing arm in the league, but when he lets go of the football, there's got to be someone to receive it. Even a single person with desire is in search of a specific receiver. The quarterback must know just where that receiver's at before he lets go or he's got an incomplete pass—no gain, you've gone nowhere.

Communication must be added to individual skills when a pastime involves more than one player. The football players have their huddle, the pitcher who is getting clobbered calls his catcher to the mound to talk over their signals, and the bridge player who has failed to make four straight contracts says, "Excuse me, partner, I think we'd better review our bidding conventions before we lose our home." You can draw analogies between sex and team sports, but as a game played by partners, it's like no other game on earth. There are no opponents except yourselves. You can be playing together one moment and against each other a moment later.

We are emerging from two decades influenced by scientists who advocated the unrestricted indulgence of those aspects of our sexuality that they could quantify (desire being thereby excluded) while ignoring the counterbalancing forces that arise from psychological elements that evaded their instruments. In this new era of sexual moderation and control, where many protest that sexual abstinence is inconceivable, others, despite their conscious wishes, are finding their sexual desire rapidly ebbing away. The retreat from all sexual intimacy may be as psychologically foolhardy as unrestrained indulgence is physically hazardous, but the victim of dying desire can no more hope for a spontaneous resurgence of libido than the libertine can expect a divine infusion of continence.

Now that the purveyors of passion have nearly all been driven from the marketplace, we seem to have learned, at last, that desire, so freely available in the beginning, can be sustained only where there is intimacy, and intimacy cannot develop where desire is indiscriminately expended. Sexual desire disorder is not the inevitable legacy of the new era. In fact, we may at last discover how to keep the flame of desire burning despite the passage of time, its eternal enemy. To learn the secret, however, we must keep our minds open to *all* the factors that breed and destroy desire: the biological, the psychological, and the philosophical.

Is it me, is it us, is it them? Any or all of the personal, interpersonal, and social forces can affect desire. It is up to us to discover which ones affect us and to direct our energy toward correcting the problem. Desire, fortunately, resides in the mind. An ailing stomach or heart cannot analyze its condition and can repair itself only in certain preordained ways, but a mind with a problem can find its way to a solution. Thought and emotion, fantasy and intellect are not inimical, they are complementary. Unless you can picture the solution in your mind, you will have great difficulty making that solution a reality.

In the preceding pages, we have reviewed the innovative techniques used by sex therapists, with great success, to reawaken sexual desire. The behavioral therapies replace bad habits we have learned with practices that enrich our awareness and bring us satisfaction in place of frustration. The cognitive therapies replace false ideas that discourage and undermine us with healthy concepts of what desire and sex should be. The experiential therapies harness and strengthen the power of our imagination, helping us to develop our own personal brand of desire, one that capitalizes on our individuality and guides us toward what we really want from our sex lives. Most of these therapies can be used as self-help techniques in the privacy of your head.

You have the knowledge and the tools to restore desire. All you need is some effort and motivation. The first step to increased sexual desire is the desire to desire.